Palgrave Studies in Educational Media

Series Editors
Eckhardt Fuchs
Georg Eckert Institute for International Textbook
Research, Braunschweig, Germany

Felicitas Macgilchrist
Georg Eckert Institute for International Textbook
Research, Braunschweig, Germany

Managing Editor
Wendy Anne Kopisch
Georg Eckert Institute, Braunschweig, Germany

Editorial Board Members
Michael Apple
University of Wisconsin–Madison, Madison, WI, USA

Tânia Maria F. Braga Garcia
Federal University of Paraná, Curitiba, Brazil

Eric Bruillard
ENS de Cachan, Cachan, France

Nigel Harwood
School of English, University of Sheffield, Sheffield, UK

Heather Mendick
Independent Scholar, London, UK

Eugenia Roldán Vera
Departamento de Investigaciones Educativas, CINVESTAV
Mexico City, Mexico

Neil Selwyn
Faculty of Education, Monash University, Clayton, VIC, Australia

Yasemin Soysal
University of Essex, Colchester, UK

There is no education without some form of media. Much contemporary writing on media and education examines best practices or individual learning processes, is fired by techno-optimism or techno-pessimism about young people's use of technology, or focuses exclusively on digital media. Relatively few studies attend – empirically or conceptually – to the embeddedness of educational media in contemporary cultural, social and political processes. The **Palgrave Studies in Educational Media** series aims to explore textbooks and other educational media as sites of cultural contestation and socio-political forces. Drawing on local and global perspectives, and attending to the digital, non-digital and post-digital, the series explores how these media are entangled with broader continuities and changes in today's society, with how media and media practices play a role in shaping identifications, subjectivations, inclusions and exclusions, economies and global political projects. Including single authored and edited volumes, it offers a dedicated space which brings together research from across the academic disciplines. The series provides a valuable and accessible resource for researchers, students, teachers, teacher trainers, textbook authors and educational media designers interested in critical and contextualising approaches to the media used in education.

More information about this series at
http://www.palgrave.com/gp/series/15151

Germán Canale

Technology, Multimodality and Learning

Analyzing Meaning across Scales

Germán Canale
Facultad de Humanidades y Ciencias de la Educación
Universidad de la República
Montevideo, Uruguay

Palgrave Studies in Educational Media
ISBN 978-3-030-21794-5   ISBN 978-3-030-21795-2 (eBook)
https://doi.org/10.1007/978-3-030-21795-2

© The Editor(s) (if applicable) and The Author(s) 2019
This work is subject to copyright. All rights are solely and exclusively licensed by the Publisher, whether the whole or part of the material is concerned, specifically the rights of translation, reprinting, reuse of illustrations, recitation, broadcasting, reproduction on microfilms or in any other physical way, and transmission or information storage and retrieval, electronic adaptation, computer software, or by similar or dissimilar methodology now known or hereafter developed.
The use of general descriptive names, registered names, trademarks, service marks, etc. in this publication does not imply, even in the absence of a specific statement, that such names are exempt from the relevant protective laws and regulations and therefore free for general use.
The publisher, the authors and the editors are safe to assume that the advice and information in this book are believed to be true and accurate at the date of publication. Neither the publisher nor the authors or the editors give a warranty, express or implied, with respect to the material contained herein or for any errors or omissions that may have been made. The publisher remains neutral with regard to jurisdictional claims in published maps and institutional affiliations.

Cover illustration: © Igor Stevanovic / Alamy

This Palgrave Macmillan imprint is published by the registered company Springer Nature Switzerland AG
The registered company address is: Gewerbestrasse 11, 6330 Cham, Switzerland

Dedicated to the memory of my mother, Lidia Fazzini de Canale

Acknowledgments

This book is a revised and extended version of my PhD dissertation in Second Language Acquisition at Carnegie Mellon University. While data collection started in 2014 and finished in 2016, it took me around a full year to write the dissertation and around another full year to turn it into a book manuscript. Moving from one stage to the next helped me focus on particular aspects of the research that hadn't caught my attention in the first place and also posed new challenges.

Many people were involved in both stages, and I am grateful to all of them. Gunther Kress has been very generous with me. He carefully read my work on several occasions. He taught me the difference between *stuff* and *data* at a time I was struggling with research design. His feedback has been invaluable and his pioneer work in social semiotics and multimodality is always inspiring. Our conversations at conferences in Uruguay, Argentina and England have been both enriching and enlightening.

Mariana Achugar was my PhD advisor. She shared with me her expertise in discourse analysis and supported my work in many ways. Now she is a colleague and a friend who continues to help me grow both professionally and personally. Dick Tucker has also taught me a lot. His Language Policy class and our many informal conversations at the dinner table with him and his wife, Rae, were crucial for me to develop an interest in Plan Ceibal policy and to find a voice to narrate this story. His support was fundamental for me to complete my PhD.

I am indebted to Barbara Johnstone for sharing her expertise in discourse analysis in her Language and Globalization class and for her generous comments and feedback on an earlier draft of Chap. 5. I am also thankful to the Georg Eckert Institut für internationale Schulbuchforschung (Leibniz Association, Germany) for granting me a fellowship in the Spring of 2016 and to the Centre for Multimodal Research, Institute of Education (University College London), for allowing me to spend some time there doing research and presenting some of the preliminary findings at the Multimodality Forum in April 2018. I am also thankful to Comisión Sectorial de Investigación Científica at Universidad de la República (Uruguay) for granting me the "Recently-earned PhD Award" in 2017 and to the Palgrave Studies in Educational Media editorial board and the anonymous reviewers for their support and their constructive feedback on my work.

Pía Gómez-Laich and Cecilia Molinari carefully read an earlier draft of the full manuscript and offered insightful comments and suggestions. Irene Madfes read an earlier draft of Chap. 6 and also offered very valuable feedback.

Last but not least, I would like to thank Plan Ceibal staff and the Fleetwood School staff, parents, teachers, students and Vera for their prolonged engagement.

Any remaining mistakes in this book are my sole responsibility.

Praise for *Technology, Multimodality and Learning*

"This book represents a remarkable achievement. It brings the calm of clear, principled discussion to the contemporary turbulence and cacophony of contesting voices and claims in sites of profound social, technological and pedagogic change. It confronts the inordinate complexity of practices, materials, technologies and policies by assembling a powerful, seamlessly integrated, coherent toolkit. It will serve practitioners, greatly advance theory and offer strategies for policy makers in equal measure."
—Professor Gunther Kress, *UCL, UK*

"Germán Canale expands Halliday's notion of 'learning how to mean', emphasizing learners' agency as meaning-makers in new school practices of communication and learning. From a multimodal socio-semiotic approach to learning, he proposes new ways to understand semiosis as a situated practice at different scales, challenging us—educators and discourse analysts—to recognize the learning that takes place in classrooms."
—Professor Dominique Manghi H., *Pontificia Universidad Católica de Valparaíso, Chile*

Contents

1 Situating Learning in the Twenty-First Century: Technology, Policy and Meaning-Making   1

2 Analyzing Meaning across Scales   19

3 Toward a Multimodal Socio-Semiotic Account of Learning   41

4 Plan Ceibal Policy and the 1:1 Model in Uruguay   83

5 Technology and EFL across Policy Scales   105

6 Laptops and Textbooks as Curriculum Artifacts: Audience, Authorization and Ideologies in the Classroom   137

7 Learners as Sign-makers: Technology, Learning and Assessment   177

| 8 | Conclusions | 235 |

Appendix: Description of All Five Units of Classroom Work (As Documented by the Researcher) 249

Index 257

Abbreviations

ANEP	Administración Nacional de Educación Pública (*National Administration of Public Education*)
CEIBAL	Comunidad Educativa de Informática Básica para el Aprendizaje en Línea (*Project of Educational Connectivity for Online Learning*)
CEFRL	Common European Framework Reference for Languages
CLE	Centro de Lenguas Extranjeras (*Foreign Languages Centre*)
CPLEP	Comisión de Políticas Lingüísticas para la Educación Pública (*Language Policy Commission for Public Education*)
CREA	Contenidos y Recursos para la Educación y el Aprendizaje (*Contents and Resources for Education and Learning*)
CT	Classroom teacher
EFL	English as a Foreign Language
MERCOSUR	Mercado Común del Sur (*Southern Common Market*)
OLPC	One Laptop Per Child
RT	Remote teacher
SFL	Systemic-Functional Linguistics
TEFL	Teaching English as a Foreign Language
TNLG	The New London Group

List of Figures

Image 3.1	S7's *"I go to high school at 7:30"* with PlayComic	59
Image 5.1	XO laptop "Coco" in Plan Ceibal's website reproduced with permission by Plan Ceibal	109
Image 5.2	XO laptops (see roofs) in "Ceibal en Inglés" local TV spot (0:07) reproduced with permission by Plan Ceibal	111
Image 6.1	Students' division of labor for laptop use (Unit 5, Day 10)	145
Image 6.2	Vera's orientation to students and to each artifact while framing their use (Unit 5, Day 4)	166
Image 7.1	Default template for *Open Office's Impress* (reads: "Click to add title" and below reads "Click to add text")	188
Image 7.2	S4's design on paper	191
Image 7.3	S4's final project (*Impress*)	192
Image 7.4	S3's text design	198
Image 7.5	S3's final animated text. Slide 2 (above) and slide 3 (below)	199
Image 7.6	Student using both XO laptop and desktop (Unit 5, Day 11)	209
Image 7.7	S5's representation of cupola	214
Image 7.8	Stills from S5's *YouTube* tutorial	217

1

Situating Learning in the Twenty-First Century: Technology, Policy and Meaning-Making

By the early 1990s I was completing my primary education in Uruguay. Unlike less privileged schools, the middle-class urban private school I attended had been equipped with a computer lab. It contained some four or five huge wooden desks with three or four desktop computers on each of them, most of them with black and white screens. Once a week, our teacher would walk us through the school to get to the computer lab and have our regular one-hour class with an ICT teacher to learn how to use the computers. As far as I can remember, that was *the* weekly contact I had with computers at the time. We did not have a computer at home and I did not "practice" my technology skills outside of the school lab. Roughly around the same time, my school also introduced EFL (English as a Foreign Language) lessons twice a week. An EFL teacher would come to our classroom for 45 minutes and help us work through some EFL tasks with a printed textbook, some color posters and a cassette. I did not "practice" my foreign language skills outside the school classroom either. In fact, my parents—and even my siblings—had grown up in a time when French and Italian were highly valued in the local community, and thus they hadn't learned English. Moreover, my siblings never had a technology or ICT class throughout their school years. These two "new"

© The Author(s) 2019
G. Canale, *Technology, Multimodality and Learning*, Palgrave Studies in Educational Media, https://doi.org/10.1007/978-3-030-21795-2_1

elements, technology and EFL, being introduced in my school were becoming increasingly visible and valuable in education at a local, regional and probably global scale. Access to these new *educational commodities* was associated with promising professional prospects, a quicker insertion in the globalizing world and more and better economic, cultural and educational opportunities.

Since then, the situation in Uruguay has both changed and remained the same. It has changed because there have been several and more systematic attempts to implement EFL programs and to introduce technology in primary and secondary education. At present, access to both technology and EFL is being universalized across the country by Plan Ceibal, a social, educational and foreign language program set up by the left-wing government in 2007 to bridge social and digital divides. Plan Ceibal is the Spanish acronym for *Project of Educational Connectivity for Online Learning*. Laptops—and more recently tablets—are being handed out to students so that they can use them during class time in any school subject or at home. EFL lessons are being delivered in practically every corner of the country either by an EFL classroom teacher or by the joint work of a Spanish classroom teacher and a remote EFL teacher via a video-conference screen provided by Plan Ceibal. All these phenomena point to a change in local policy and education, which could easily be connected to (relatively) similar trends elsewhere. However, the situation in Uruguay has remained the same in that technology and EFL continue to be highly valued for the future—and present—of local children. Both technology and EFL have actually become *key terms* in education policymaking. Much of the future of local students is discussed around these two key terms, which often times are filled up with meanings of promising innovation, prosperity or even outside-the-box thinking; to a lesser extent, they are sometimes condemned for fostering neo-liberal and highly organized capitalist practices.

This book adopts a particular approach to technology and EFL. It does not center on the ideologically driven discussion of the pros and cons of technology or on whether technology re-skills or de-skills humans. I do take into account ideological aspects of technology in society and in education to better contextualize and understand current trends in policymaking, but instead of focusing on utopian and dystopian views, the book centers on how a nation-wide 1:1 policy (one laptop per child) is being implemented and enacted as an orchestrated attempt to democratize and universalize access to technology and English. In particular, it focuses on how, through enactment, this policy and its key terms come to index different meanings for different stakeholders in particular time/space frames. This, of course, has an effect on how the policy unfolds in time and space. The book also draws attention to the potential implications of education policies which foster the use of new technologies such as this one, in terms of both learning in the twenty-first century and providing meaningful meaning-making opportunities for students. For this to happen, it is required to dig deeper into the ideologies of learning that circulate and still dominate mainstream education and technology implementation. Are current education policies accompanied by a change in our conception of learning? Are these policies accompanied by a shift in views of how learning happens? And about how learning can be demonstrated? Questions like these underlie the discussion and analysis presented in this book to better understand how ideologies of learning shape interaction, communication and learning in the classroom; recognizing or misrecognizing the semiotic work students do with technology or with other educational media and artifacts.

Throughout the book I shall argue that attending to how policy key terms such as technology and EFL come to index particular meanings as they move in time/space scales is important to capture the semiotic processes through which policy-making and policy enactment achieve cultural, socio-political and ideological cohesion in society by articulating meanings at different scales. The trajectories of meaning across scales cannot be entirely predicted a priori; neither can they be entirely shaped by top-down policy actions. And yet, these trajectories impact classroom interaction, communication and learning. As will be argued throughout the book, focusing on policy as meaning-making (i.e. as a complex set of semiotic practices occurring at different time and space frames) and its trajectories is much needed in education not only to better explore the links between technology and learning but also to reflect on what is legitimated as learning, and its implications on students' semiotic processes.

As I shall explain in more detail in Chap. 4, in its broadest form, the policy I investigate—Plan Ceibal—revolves around universalizing and democratizing access to technology. This is by no means strange to current trends in education and social policy-making. Debates over the role of new technology in formal learning settings have permeated discussions in education research, governments, mass media, domestic and international policy and legislation, as well as the political and ideological views of lay citizens.

Technology is both a social process and a social product, ubiquitous in social life. In particular, the wide array of social practices and events in which the dyad *technology-education* is being semiotized and re-semiotized points to two main aspects of technology that research should not neglect.

1. Technology operates in complex discursive networks which comprise political, ideological, social, economic and cultural struggles over the meanings of social reality, the spread of technology, its use and its interaction with individuals in particular environments. In the twenty-first century, these struggles call for research to adopt a *critical* stance, but not necessarily in terms of a *negative critique* of the role of technology in society and education and the ideological implications of the discourse of its supporters. Instead, I believe it calls for what can be framed in broader terms as a *generative critique* (Macgilchrist 2016), which to my mind requires a dynamic, situated approach to analyzing the connections between technology and education in such a way that a better future can be designed (The New London Group, TNLG 1996) for students and for society at large. Needless to say, a *better* future is, by definition, ideological; but it has the advantage of being overtly ideological, seeking to bridge cultural, social and economic gaps that at present might be widening due to unequal access to technology, its commodification and the many asymmetries it can (re)produce in diverse social scenarios, most of which were asymmetrical to begin with.
2. Mono-causal explanations or one-dimensional research approaches to technology and education might not be able to capture the complexity of technology given the diverse, dynamic, complex and heterogeneous scenarios in which individuals make sense *of* and *with* technology in society. For this reason, research must draw on different disciplines, approaches and techniques in an attempt to grasp the complex nature of the phenomenon at hand.

The stance I take in this book attempts to address technology and education as delineated in points 1 and 2. It seeks to offer both conceptual and empirical insights into policy enactment and technology in current education. Conceptually, the study sheds light on the ongoing process of policy recontextualization across scales. This adds new insights to existing research focusing on macro and meso issues education faces in terms of policy-making, implementation and enactment, such as: introducing and integrating technology into the curricula, bridging in-school and out-of-school practices, providing equal access to technology, balancing out top-down and situated agency or even shaping attitudes (Apple and Jungck 1998; Apple 2003; Boody 2001; Muffoletto 2001; Schofield 1995; Setzer and Monke 2001; to name a few). Central to the theoretical discussion is the concept of learning and the type of change in ideology required to better recognize what learning is (Bezemer and Kress 2016; Kress 2003, 2004) and—in particular—what learning with technology is in formal education in the twenty-first century. For such a change to take place we need to dig deeper into curricular and pedagogical relations in schools and classrooms to uncover how these implicate—and are implicated in—interaction, communication and learning with technology artifacts, and how these relations are embedded in larger and more distant policy scales.

As an empirical case study, I adopt a scalar approach to the implementation and enactment of Plan Ceibal as the current nation-wide social, educational and foreign language policy in Uruguay. Designed after the 1:1 model (One Laptop Per Child, OLPC), in its broadest scope the policy has resulted in the adoption of an orchestrated set of curricular and pedagogical actions for students to access and use new technology regardless of their socio-economic status and their (lack of) social and economic privileges in mainstream society. In a narrower sense, the policy has more recently set out to universalize and democratize EFL learning across the country. To investigate this policy and its enactment empirically, the book draws on multimodal social semiotic accounts of learning (*vid.* Bezemer and Kress 2016), ethnographic approaches to discourse (*vid.* Macgilchrist and van Hout 2011), and the partnership between multimodal social semiotics and ethnography (*vid.* Kress 2011, 2015). These approaches are articulated to focus on meaning-making and policy across time/space scales. As I shall define in Chap. 4, *scale* is a useful concept in that it can substitute other approaches to space, power and agency in policy analysis (such as macro, meso, micro *or top-down vs bottom-up*). Unlike other metaphors used in policy research, scale allows for an articulation of different events (for instance, a classroom task, a mass-mediated text or a policy-making decision) without necessarily assuming a monocausal and unidirectional trajectory of meaning across them. Some theoretical and methodological implications of this are outlined in Chap. 2.

Framing the Study

Much of the literature on the introduction of new technology in education (and language education) has foregrounded the ins and outs of policy implementation (stakeholders' attitudes to technology and their effect on use, frequency of use, technical problems). It has also focused on what I call *policy bright spots*, that is, units of analysis (students, schools, classrooms, districts) which—for different reasons—are the center of attention of policy-makers or stakeholders. The approach adopted in this book, however, is somewhat different. In the first place, I focus on the different scales of policy design, implementation and enactment through which the meanings of technology and EFL become recontextualized: from broader scales outside the school (national education policy, national foreign language policy and policy-making institutions) to scales inside the school (school policing, classroom work and interaction). Complementary—albeit not identical—approaches to scales in (language) policy and education can be found in Hult (2010a, b, 2015), Mortimer (2016) and Mortimer and Wortham (2015), to name a few.

Secondly, the view adopted in this book is also different in that the focal EFL classroom I study is not a policy *bright spot*. Instead, I choose to study what I call—in Chap. 4—a *blind spot*: a classroom which is not highly regulated by the policy and which has not been the center of attention of policy-makers or society at large. In other words, a case about which we do not know much or even have expectations about. As will be described in more detail in Chap. 2, the site in which the empirical research was conducted is a small private school and the participants are working-middle-class students. Given that the main aim of Plan Ceibal is to cater for public schools and the underprivileged sector of society, this research site is also a *blind spot* for the policy because there is no official discourse as to what democratization and universalization might/should mean in this particular type of school. Choosing this blind spot, then, is particularly significant for two main reasons: on the one hand, it allows us to investigate how the policy is enacted in a school where—in principle—discourses of democratization and universalization do not operate in the same manner as expected by official policy discourse. This opens a door for exploring unpredicted paths for recontextualization of policy aims and learning goals. What does it mean to access and use technology in a context in which learners were not necessarily deprived of it to begin with? What does it mean to learn EFL with technology in a context in which the language was already available? Does this new type of availability through Plan Ceibal bridge or widen existing gaps? Does it create any new gaps? In other words, what does the policy mean in this particular context? What social, economic, political and ideological meanings become attached to the policy and to using technology in this scenario? How do students position themselves and others with regard to policy key terms such as technology and EFL? On the other hand, choosing this research site is also significant in that a *blind spot* provides a learning environment in which teachers and students have—to some extent—a higher degree of situated agency, as shall be explored in Chaps. 6 and 7. This agency calls for an exploration of the potential of education policy in opening up spaces for socially meaningful meaning-making processes in the classroom.

From the point of view of policy research, looking into this blind spot can eventually inform other 1:1 policies by accounting for unexpected ways of enacting the policy and of enacting curriculum and pedagogy. Although target students' age, the degree of coverage and the actual artifact handed out[1] vary substantially across 1:1 programs, these are being implemented in many countries (Argentina, Brazil, Ethiopia, Australia, Canada, Colombia, Nepal, Peru, Rwanda, South Korea, among many others[2]); therefore, a detailed ethnographic account of the enactment of 1:1 in a blind spot is required to start a conversation between the *expected* and the *unexpected*, the *highly regulated* and the *unregulated*, the *standardized* and the *unstandardized*, between the *more* and the *less* visible scales in which meanings are made. My aim in framing the study this way is not to make a case for comparing the enactment of the policy in *bright* and *blind* spots, in the sense that I do not intend to say that one is better or more adequate than the other. On the contrary, my intention is to offer an alternative narrative to reflect on education policy and its current key terms from a space that has not been explored thus far and a space that has not been strictly designed by official policy discourse and action.

Situating the Policy

In 2007, the Uruguayan government passed a decree to set up Plan Ceibal (Spanish acronym for *Project of Educational Connectivity for Online Learning*),[3] which since then has become a social, educational and also a foreign language policy aiming at the *universalization* and *democratization*[4] of access to technology across the country (Ministry of Education and Culture 2013).

At the social level, the policy seeks to introduce technology to all Uruguayan families with a view to promoting positive attitudes toward it and also to foster its use in various social spaces. This has required a set of orchestrated actions such as setting up centers across the country for adults to learn computer skills, offering free wi-fi connection to all schools and progressively expanding wi-fi to houses and shops across the country and, more recently, starting to hand out free tablets to retired citizens and school children. These actions have been carried out by different governmental offices.

As an education policy, Plan Ceibal has handed out free laptops to all students and teachers in primary and secondary public school[5] education. It has also expanded the policy to some sectors of private education. In public education, all these actions have been accompanied by workshops to train public school teachers on digital skills and the appointment of groups of teachers and programmers to design digital materials, to name a few.

At the level of language learning, in 2011 Plan Ceibal launched a new EFL program: Ceibal en Inglés (*Ceibal in English*). The aim is to *universalize* and *democratize*[6] access to EFL in primary education (Comisión de

Políticas lingüísticas para la Educación Pública CPLEP 2008; Brovetto 2011, 2013). Due to the lack of certified EFL teachers (Administración Nacional de Educación Pública-ANEP Official Census 2007),[7] the policy has set up a blended program[8] for in-site and remote EFL lessons in primary schools. Through a video-conference screen in equipped schools, a remote EFL teacher delivers a weekly lesson in coordination with a classroom teacher, who does not need to have advanced (or even intermediate) skills in the target language.

Plan Ceibal works rather differently for private schools. If a private school opts in, it needs to pay for their students to get the laptops, which are used for in-site teaching and learning purposes. They do not have access to the EFL blended program, nor can they purchase the video-conference screen, the lesson plans or the EFL curriculum specially designed for Plan Ceibal en Inglés. In other words, curricular and pedagogical designs are in charge of private schools themselves. A more detailed account of Plan Ceibal in public and private education settings can be found in Chap. 4.

Situating the Perspective

The overarching approach used in this book comes from multimodal social semiotics and ethnographies (see Chaps. 3 and 4). A partnership between both is promising in terms of better understanding the situatedness of meaning-making processes (Dicks et al. 2006, 2011; Kress 2011, 2015) and, for the purposes of the book, for exploring policy as meaning-making and its ongoing recontextualization across scales.

As I announced earlier, the stance I take lays emphasis on participants, in *what* meanings they make and in *how* they make such meanings in the implementation and enactment of the policy. Inspired by previous works in the field of multimodality and technology in the classroom (Jewitt 2006, 2008), I do not orient the discussion toward questions such as whether technology favors or hinders democratization processes, or whether technology de-skills students and teachers. I do not mean to say these issues are not important. On the contrary, I think these are critical aspects of education and new technology that have been—and still are being—addressed. Instead, I choose to focus on other issues which are intimately related to the actual scenarios in which the policy under study is being enacted, the technology artifacts offered by this new policy and the affordances the laptop offers students to learn in the EFL classroom.

In orienting to the topic from this perspective, I explicitly intend to avoid reproducing a sort of "toxic narrative of crisis" (McCarty 2010, 2) which surrounds educational matters and which may—unwillingly—reinforce long-ingrained stereotypes about local education and policy processes in Uruguay or in other countries from the periphery. As McCarty (2010, 5) reminds us, policy narratives have material consequences in the social world and therefore the way we narrate these stories does have an impact on institutions and on social actors as well.

This does not mean that I do not consider broader aspects of policy-making. The implementation of Plan Ceibal—as well as other education policies—requires considerable funding, which from the point of view of (language) education programs raises questions about feasibility, scalability and sustainability (Donato and Tucker 2010; Tucker 2010; Tucker and d'Anglejan 1971). A detailed account of policy enactment can also be useful in these terms. Findings can potentially address these issues by answering the question of what uses can technology be put to in the classroom to meet the demands of education in the twenty-first century, for which language is not *the only* mode of communication but just one of the many modes of communication students need to engage in. It can also provide substantial insights into what the profile of success (Donato and Tucker 2010) of a policy like this should be in the current century. In other words, findings can shed light on what can/should be the desired or expected outcomes for both EFL and digital literacy[9] goals in this type of policy implementation and enactment.

Finally, exploring meaning-making processes in the EFL classroom within Plan Ceibal policy can eventually inform other language policy processes and pedagogies as well. Findings can inform other 1:1 models implemented in other countries to contribute to a better understanding of differences and similarities across technology-enhanced education programs, how they work and what type of learning they (should) favor, as discussed in the Chap. 8. Along these lines, the discussion does not only pertain to EFL but to any school subject, since 1:1 programs are being used to teach very different types of school contents and subjects.

Organization of the Book

Adopting the stance and perspective delineated above, I organized the theoretical and empirical discussions in different chapters.

Chapter 2 argues for the use of scales in social research and, more specifically, policy research. It discusses some of the theoretical and analytical advantages of adopting scales while at the same time it acknowledges some of its problems. It also discusses why I choose a partnership between multimodal socio-semiotics and ethnographic approaches to investigate scales and meaning-making. Finally, the chapter describes the research site, participants, methods and tools employed.

Chapter 3 delineates learning from a multimodal socio-semiotic perspective. It adds to previous literature in the field to argue for a shift from traditional to alternative ideologies of learning. This requires expanding what we consider learning to be, in what modes and media we believe learning takes place, how we assume students can demonstrate learning, the role we assume learners have in learning and what tools can or should be used to assess such learning. In particular, the chapter discusses how technology can fit this new agenda, what learner-technology artifact interaction can mean in terms of making and demonstrating meanings and the potential this has for designing students' futures.

Chapter 4 provides a more detailed description of Plan Ceibal and the 1:1 policy design, implementation and enactment, as well as a contextualization of local Uruguayan education to the reader. It also discusses the concepts of policy blind and bright spots from both a theoretical and an empirical perspective and explains in what ways the research site is a blind spot and why attending to this is relevant for research and for policy. It also addresses these issues in terms of Plan Ceibal and foreign language teaching.

Chapter 5 adopts an ethnographic outlook at Plan Ceibal policy design, implementation and enactment. Drawing on several sources of data, the chapter centers around the complex meanings the two key terms in Plan Ceibal policy (technology and EFL) make and how these terms come to index different things in broader and narrower policy scales, even within the focal school. Findings give evidence of the complex socio-political, economic and cultural meanings at stake when considering policy as meaning-making and looking at policy from a scalar approach.

Chapters 6 and 7 focus on micro-analytical issues by investigating two aspects of the focal classroom and its enactment of Plan Ceibal. Chapter 6 explores how the introduction of the Plan Ceibal laptops calls for a particular distribution of semiotic labor between the laptop and the printed EFL textbook as curriculum artifacts and the effect this division of semiotic labor has on how the EFL lesson is framed, constructed and negotiated. This contributes to our understanding of the role different policy audiences (i.e. students, school and EFL supervisors, parents, etc.) have in shaping enactment and in guiding semiosis of what the policy is and what it means. It also sheds light on the complex ecology the laptop comes to inhabit, as the classroom is reorganized and rearranged by the introduction of this new educational tool. Along these lines, the chapter shows the role of teacher's agency in framing the lesson, framing the use of the artifact, and legitimating particular ways of interacting and learning with it.

Chapter 7 investigates what meanings students make with the laptop in the EFL lesson, what learning with this artifact means and how learning is assessed and recognized in this particular context. Unlike the previous chapter, it focuses on students' agency as sign-makers and on how they demonstrate their learning by transforming available signs with the technology. Such transformations go far beyond the written and oral modes or traditional EFL goals. On the contrary, these transformations entail several modes and media of representation and communication and need to be looked at multimodally in order to better account for all the semiotic work that takes place in the classroom.

Chapter 8 provides the theoretical and empirical conclusions of the study. It focuses on what data analysis and findings of different policy scales can tell us about learning and how to recognize it in the classroom. It also sheds light on the role education policy and technology can play in helping us expand our notion of learning to better account for students' meaning-making in the twenty-first century. The chapter discusses what paths future research and praxis can take to make sure we transition from traditional to alternative ideologies of learning or, in other words, to make sure we find appropriate ways to recognize students' semiotic work at its fullest.

Attempting to better capture and recognize students' semiotic work in formal education settings is key to current education policies. However, it is indeed a hard task to embark on, and it requires the close collaboration of social actors and disciplines. The outcome, however, can be highly beneficial to students, teachers and, in broader terms, to society at large. Hopefully, the existing and growing body of work in multimodal social semiotics and the ethnographic accounts of education policy—together with current and future studies—can lead us in that direction. Rather than presenting a set of principles and solutions to this issue, this book attempts to open up spaces for research and praxis to look at twenty-first century education policy and learning from an alternative angle.

Notes

1. While some countries still hand out laptops, others have decided to hand out tablets, or both.
2. More information and a list of countries can be found at: www.one.laptop.org (Last accessed: 2/6/2017).
3. This action is embedded in a set of steps promoted by the left-wing party in Uruguay, which took office in for the first time in the history of the country in 2005 and, to date, has been re-elected twice. This fact in interesting from the point of view of education and language policies because the shift from right-wing to left-wing ideologies in the government resulted in a much more explicit way of addressing social and political positionings in education by, for instance, opening up several ideological and implementation spaces (Hornberger and Johnson 2007) to discuss educational matters. Some of these spaces incorporated the voices of lay citizens (such as the National Educational Debate in 2006), while others incorporated the voices of experts and other stakeholders (the Commission of Language Policies in Public Education 2005–2007, the group of Language Policies in 2009, among others). Along with these new spaces

also came new official discourses that made explicit connections between education, social equity and democratization, as shows the analysis of official documents and syllabuses (Canale 2015). This was also accompanied by a substantive growth in educational regulations, legislation and documents in which these ideas became instantiated, such as the General Law of Education (Law 18.437 in 2009), the new National Syllabus for Preschool and Primary Education (2008) and new teaching training programs (2008), just to name a few. This new scenario made the incorporation of new technology in education one of the main symbols of the left-wing government.

4. While in official discourse *universalization* mainly refers to the spread of technology and EFL all over the country, *democratization* mainly refers to providing equal opportunities to all socio-economic groups within society. Both terms belong to the same policy, the difference being the emphasis laid on one facet of the policy or the other.

5. Public education in Uruguay is free, so students do not have to pay any tuition or fee, while students attending private education do pay a fee, which varies substantially depending on the profile of the school.

6. Current educational documents and legislation dictate that at least two additional languages be taught in public schools in Uruguay (CPLEP 2008). However, the implementation of Plan Ceibal has only focused on EFL to date. There have been some discussions around implementing Ceibal also for teaching French as a foreign language, but the idea was soon abandoned. The decision to prioritize EFL is based on many factors: the social demand to learn EFL (CPLEP 2008; López 2013), the higher rates in TEFL certification compared to other foreign language (even though the rate of TEFL certification is low compared to other teaching certification rates), the fact that English is the foreign language with the longest teaching and learning tradition in both public and private education in the country, as well as the regional and international trends in education favoring TEFL.

7. While in Uruguay there is a long standing tradition of TEFL education for teaching at secondary schools, it was not until the past decade that attempts have been made to introduce new TEFL education programs (in public and private institutions) to certify EFL professionals for primary schools (Brovetto 2011). In the past there have been several trial programs to introduce EFL: English for Primary Schools Program (1993), Partial Immersion in English Program, Teaching English Through Content

Program (2006). However, most of these programs did not last for long (Canale 2015).
8. To date, participation in the Ceibal in English program is voluntary at both primary and secondary level, that is to say, the head of the school and the teacher (Spanish teacher in primary school and Spanish teacher in primary school) need to opt in the program. If they do so, then the Ceibal equipment is installed in a room which is used for those video-conference sessions. However, Plan Ceibal intends to universalize this program in the near future.
9. In the last decades, many terms have been coined to identify and specify particular sub-sets of literacy/ies, as reviewed in Potter and McDougall (2017). I prefer to think of *literacy* (with no specification or adjective) to foreground that meaning-making processes are always context bound and situated while—at the same time—unique (Other arguments for using *literacy* as a general term can be found in Kress 2003, 23-ff). However, I decide to refer to "digital literacy" throughout the study to refer to how participants themselves (teachers, educational or school authorities, parents, etc.) seem to orient to literacy within the context of Plan Ceibal. In my data collection process it is frequently the case that stakeholders make a distinction between the textbook and the laptop as artifacts for print and digital literacy, respectively. Hence, I keep this distinction to be as faithful to participants' own voices as much as possible, even when it does not echo my own understanding of literacy.

References

ANEP: Administración Nacional de Educación Pública (National Administration for Public Education). (2007). *Official Census (Censo Nacional Docente)*. Montevideo, Uruguay.

Apple, M. W. (2003). The State and the Politics of Knowledge. In M. W. Apple (Ed.), *The State and the Politics of Knowledge* (pp. 1–23). New York: Routledge Falmer.

Apple, M. W., & Jungck, S. (1998). "You Don't have to be a Teacher to Teach this Unit": Teaching, Technology and Control in the Classroom. In H. Bromley & M. W. Apple (Eds.), *Education/Technology/Power. Educational Computing as a Social Practice* (pp. 133–155). New York: State University of New York Press.

Bezemer, J., & Kress, G. (2016). *Multimodality, Learning and Communication. A Social Semiotic Framework.* London and New York: Routledge.
Boody, R. M. (2001). On the Relationship of Education and Technology. In R. Muffoletto (Ed.), *Education and Technology: Critical and Reflective Practices* (pp. 5–22). Cresskill: Hampton Press.
Brovetto, C. (2011). Alcances y limitaciones del uso de tecnologías para la enseñanza de inglés en educación primaria. In L. Behares (Ed.), *V encuentro internacional de investigadores en políticas lingüísticas* (pp. 37–41). Montevideo: Asociación de Universidades Grupo Montevideo.
Brovetto, C. (2013). "Ceibal en Inglés": Enseñanza de inglés por videoconferencia en Educación Primaria. In *Aprendizaje Abierto y Aprendizaje Flexible. Más allá de formatos y espacios tradicionales.* Montevideo: Plan Ceibal.
Canale, G. (2015). Mapping Conceptual Change: The Ideological Struggle for the Meaning of EFL in Uruguayan Education. *L2 Journal, 7*(3), 15–39. https://doi.org/10.5070/L27323707
CPLEP: Comisión de Políticas Lingüísticas en la Educación Pública. (2008). *Documentos de la Comisión de Políticas Lingüísticas en la Educación Pública.* Montevideo: Administración Nacional de Educación Pública.
Dicks, B., Bambo, S., & Coffey, A. (2006). Multimodal Ethnography. *Qualitative Research, 6*(1), 77–96. https://doi.org/10.1177/1468794106058876
Dicks, B., Flewitt, R., Lancaster, L., & Pahl, K. (2011). Multimodality and Ethnography: Working at the Intersection. *Qualitative Research, 11*(3), 227–237. https://doi.org/10.1177/1468794111400682
Donato, R., & Tucker, G. R. (2010). *A Tale of Two Schools. Developing Sustainable Early Foreign Language Programs.* Bristol, Buffalo and Toronto: Multilingual Matters.
General Law of Education. (2009). Ley General de Educación, 18.437. Presidencia de la República Oriental del Uruguay.
Hornberger, N. H., & Johnson, D. C. (2007). Slicing the Onion Ethnographically. Layers and Spaces in Multilingual Language Education Policy and Practice. *TESOL Quarterly, 41*(3), 509–532. https://doi.org/10.1002/j.1545-7249.2007.tb00083.x
Hult, F. M. (2010a). Analysis of Language Policy Discourses across the Scales of Space and Time. *International Journal of the Sociology of Language, 202,* 7–24.
Hult, F. M. (2010b). The Complexity Turn in Educational Linguistics. *Language, Culture and Curriculum, 23*(3), 173–177. https://doi.org/10.1080/07908318.2010.515992

Hult, F. M. (2015). Making Policy Connections across Scales Using Nexus Analysis. In F. M. Hult & D. Cassels Johnson (Eds.), *Research Methods in Language Policy: A Practical Guide* (pp. 217–231). Malden: Wiley.

Jewitt, C. (2006). *Technology, Literacy and Learning. A Multimodal Approach.* London and New York: Routledge.

Jewitt, C. (2008). Multimodality and Literacy in the School Classrooms. *Review of Research in Education, 32*(1), 241–267. https://doi.org/10.3102/0091732X07310586

Kress, G. (2003). *Literacy in the New Media Age.* London: Routledge.

Kress, G. (2004). Learning, a Semiotic View in the Context of Digital Technologies. In A. Brown & N. Davis (Eds.), *Digital Technology, Communities & Education* (pp. 15–39). New York: Routledge Falmer.

Kress, G. (2011). 'Partnership in Research': Multimodality and Ethnography. *Qualitative Research, 11*(3), 239–260. http://dx.doi.org/10.1177.1468794111399836

Kress, G. (2015). Designing Meaning. Social Semiotic Multimodality Seen in Relation to Ethnographic Research. In S. Bollig, M. S. Honig, S. Neumann, & C. Seele (Eds.), *MultiPluriTrans in Educational Ethnography. Approaching the Multimodality, Plurality and Translocality of Educational Realities* (pp. 213–233). Verlag: Transcript.

López, C. (2013). El lugar del inglés en relación a otras lenguas extranjeras: Análisis de encuesta a montevideanos. In G. Canale (Ed.), *Adquisición, Identidades y Actitudes Lingüísticas. El inglés como lengua extranjera* (pp. 13–49). Montevideo: Cruz del Sur.

Macgilchrist, F. (2016). Fissures in the Discourse-scape: Critique, Rationality and Validity in Post-foundational Approaches to CDS. *Discourse & Society, 27*(3), 262–277. http://dx.doi.org/10.1177.0957926516630902

Macgilchrist, F., & van Hout, T. (2011). Ethnographic Discourse Analysis and Social Science. *Forum: Qualitative Social Research, 12*(1). https://doi.org/10.17169/fqs-12.1.1600

McCarty, T. (2010). Enduring Inequalities, Imagined Futures—Circulating Policy Discourses and Dilemmas in the Anthropology of Education. *Anthropology & Education Quarterly, 43*(1), 1–12. https://doi.org/10.1111/j.1548-1492.2011.01152.x

Ministry of Education and Culture MEC: Ministerio de Educación y Cultura. (2013). *Desarrollo Profesional docente y Mejora de la Educación. Informe País.* Presidencia de la República: Montevideo, Uruguay.

Mortimer, K. (2016). Producing Change and Stability: A Scalar Analysis of Paraguayan Bilingual Education Policy Implementation. *Linguistics and Education, 34*, 58–69. http://dx.doi.org/10.1016.j.linged.2015.08.001

Mortimer, K. S., & Wortham, S. (2015). Analyzing Language Policy and Social Identification Across Heterogeneous Scales. *Annual Review of Applied Linguistics, 35*, 160–172. https://doi.org/10.1017/S0267190514000269

Muffoletto, R. (2001). The Need for Critical Theory and Reflective Practices in Educational Technology. In R. Muffoletto (Ed.), *Education and Technology. Critical and Reflective Practices* (pp. 285–299). Cresskill, NJ: Hampton Press.

Potter, J., & McDougall, J. (2017). *Digital Media, Culture & Education. Theorising Third Space Literacies.* London: Palgrave Macmillan.

Schofield, W. J. (1995). *Computers and Classroom Culture.* New York: Cambridge.

Setzer, V. W., & Monke, L. (2001). Challenging the Application: An Alternative View on Why, When and How Computers Should Be Used in Education. In R. Muffoletto (Ed.), *Education and Technology. Critical and Reflective Practices* (pp. 141–173). Cresskill: Hampton Press.

The New London Group. (1996). A Pedagogy of Multiliteracies: Designing Social Futures. *Harvard Educational Review, 66*(1), 60–92.

Tucker, G. R. (2010). Some Thoughts Concerning Innovative Language Education Programmes. *Journal of Multilingual and Multicultural Development, 17*(2/4), 315–320. https://doi.org/10.1080/01434639608666285

Tucker, G. R., & d'Anglejan, A. (1971). Some Thoughts Concerning Bilingual Education Programs. *The Modern Language Journal, 55*(8), 491–493. https://doi.org/10.1111/j.1540-4781.1971.tb04611.x

2

Analyzing Meaning across Scales

The environments in which sign-makers make, transform and interpret meanings are made up of time/space frames that interact with, affect and implicate one another. The social world and the meanings we make in it operate in scales. Whether our focus is a policy and its enactment—as is the case of this book—or any other social practice, meaning is made and interpreted *in* and *across* scales. To be sure, meaning means *in* scales, and it might mean differently *within* and *across* scales as it moves in time and space.

To adopt a notion of scale and to assume that it relates to meaning-making processes—as I will throughout this chapter—can have profound theoretical and methodological implications for research. This chapter discusses the concept of scale from a socio-semiotic perspective and its relevance to the study of meaning-making processes in any social activity or practice. It also discusses why the concept of scale fits the agenda of a close partnership between a multimodal socio-semiotic and an ethnographic approach to policy as meaning-making, that is to say, as a complex set of semiotic practices occurring at different time and space frames. The main argument for this is that in order to theoretically and analytically articulate the concept of scale and its effect on meaning-making we need to bring to the analysis various and varied sources of data—as ethnographers usually do—and to consider meaning as sign-makers' transformative actions on the available modes and media of representation and communication, as shown by work in the field of multimodal social semiotics. A partnership between both disciplines is key to understanding the situated and scalar nature of meaning.

This chapter will first provide a working definition of scale and argue for its use in research by addressing some theoretical and methodological implications of scalar analysis. Then, it will discuss the need to consider scales as a fundamental theoretical and analytical concept for investigating education policy, and what its benefits are when compared to other approaches to policy studies. Thirdly, the chapter will conclude with a section in which scalar analysis is discussed at the intersect of the multimodal socio-semiotic approach and the ethnographic approach to policy. Finally, the chapter will contextualize the policy under investigation (Plan Ceibal in Uruguay) and will delineate the methodological and analytic choices I made to investigate meaning across Plan Ceibal policy scales and its implications for learning, which will be addressed in more detail in later chapters.

Scales

Terms such as *scale*, *scalarity* and *scalar analysis* are becoming more frequent as metaphors used in education and policy research, discourse analysis, and social semiotics, among other socially driven disciplines engaged in understanding *meaning-making in context*. Adopted from the fields of social geography and World Systems Analysis (*vid* Blommaert 2007), the metaphor of scales has great potential for the analysis of meanings in social life. However, there is no unified definition or full agreement as for the definition of scales or how they should be used in analysis.

In broad terms, scales can be thought of as semiotized space/time (Blommaert et al. 2015), or as the instrument through which sign-makers organize and arrange the semiotic world around them. The assumption that there is a close or even intrinsic relation between time and space (as a *time/space* complex) is also present in previous notions which have been highly influential, such as that of *chronotope* (Bakhtin 1981). In particular, the notion of scales assumes that organization of the social world is by no means a given fact; instead it is the result of sign-makers' constant scaling processes, which are certainly a laborious (Carr and Lempert 2016) albeit not always intentional task (Gal 2016).

However, it is fair to ask: what is it that the concept of scale can add to the discussion of meaning-making? Unlike the traditional notion of context, the definition of scale opens a door to exploring the several co-articulated and co-operating types of organizations and hierarchies in which, for instance, power relations are dynamically constructed, exposed or even presupposed (Blommaert 2015; Coronado and Hodge 2017). It is for this reason that scale works as both a horizontal and a vertical metaphor (Blommaert 2007): scales are not only a matter of scope, but also a matter of implication or even hierarchy. For the purposes of my argument, suffice it to say that this horizontal/vertical metaphor points to the fact that time/space is hierarchically—and contextually—organized and arranged: in a given time/space event a sign might index particular meanings while its trajectory across other time/space scales might transform *how* and *what* it indexes and *for whom* it does so. This is true of layers of apparent events and circumstances as well as of layers of events which are less apparent (Canagarajah and De Costa 2016). However, hierarchy and implication are not linear or mono-causal. For instance, scales interact in such ways that two time/space events that might seem distant can be culturally closer than two neighboring events, a process to which Lemke (2001) refers as *heterochrony* and which is key to understanding how events are linked in structurally complex environments such as the classroom (Bloome et al. 2009).

As Canagarajah and De Costa (2016) argue, scales foreground the traditional problems education research has found in identifying and defining units of analysis and in conceptualizing the relation between language and context (or, for the purpose of this book, meaning and context). Oftentimes this relation is either undertheorized or taken as a given. Similar problems have been encountered by traditional approaches to other social disciplines, such as sociolinguistics (Blommaert 2007), for which tradition has proposed linear explanations of the links between language, time and space. To briefly illustrate this, let us consider the broad topic under investigation: education policy. Emically or etically defining the unit of analysis of a policy—that is, defining it from the perspective of participants or from the perspective of the outsider, respectively—is indeed a complex task, since the very notion of policy implies a set of social, political, cultural and educational interconnected practices which entails different stakeholders making meanings in different time/space frames. Conceptualizing the fields of actions in which a policy takes place, its organization, hierarchies and trajectories has been a complicated task for researchers in education and language policies, as I shall discuss later in the chapter.

While it does not entirely solve the problem of identifying a unit of analysis, drawing on the concept of scale certainly allows research to capture the complexity of meaning-making trajectories and how social objects and phenomena relate to such trajectories by theorizing and empirically analyzing the connections between meaning and time/space frames, and by assuming that relations and hierarchies among them are not necessarily linear, structurally determined or mono-causal.

The organization of scales depends on the complex connections between sign-makers and the environment and this seems key to understanding that hierarchies might not be predetermined. However, it is fair to say that how and whether scales are hierarchically implicated is up for debate: while for some authors broader scales (for instance, the macro, the global) are of higher order than narrower ones (for instance, the micro, the local) (Blommaert 2007), others argue that no hierarchy should be assumed a priori since scales are not ontologically different realities, but part of a whole which is broken down for analytical purposes (Hult 2010b).

For the purposes of the analysis provided in Chaps. 5, 6 and 7, where I consider several scales in which Plan Ceibal policy social actors make sense of and with technology, three methodological aspects of scales and scalar analysis shall be brought to the discussion.

- The main focus of using scales for analytical purposes is not to analyze scales themselves but rather to explore how scales relate to each other

and/or to sign-makers (Canagarajah and De Costa 2016; Hult 2010a, b; Scollon and Scollon 2004); in other words, the interest is more on the *scaling process* than on scales themselves.
* The researcher may take any scale as a starting point for the analysis. As Hodge (2017) explains in his discussion of *multiscalar analysis*, while some authors in the social disciplines are inclined to start from traditional top-down larger-scales and *move down* to more narrow scales others prefer to *scale up*. (Hodge himself uses both paths). Rather than making assumptions about scales and the origin of meaning-making processes or assuming particular trajectories of meaning across scales, the task of the researcher is to identify the relevant scales for the phenomenon at hand and to study how these scales are implicated (Hult 2010b).
* In analytical terms, there is always the danger of wrongly assuming that each meaning-making instance—as experienced by sign-makers or as defined *a posteriori* by the researcher—is an instantiation of a particular scale (Blommaert et al. 2015).

In this book, I do not claim that each event selected from the larger data is in fact representative of a scale. On the contrary, I assume—theoretically and methodologically—that each focal event I analyze is embedded—and operates—within an immediate scale and as well as within the broader scales with which it is interrelated. The scales I identified in the data are *enacted, lived, embodied* or even *talked about* by sign-makers as highly institutionalized social activities such as *policy text writing, advertising, a language lesson, a classroom, a classroom task, framing a lesson, an interview*, and so on. However, this is a personal methodological choice and not a tentative solution to the problem of how to define scales in social research. It should be noted that the problem is not only how to identify and conceptualize scales or who defines them (sign-makers/researcher); it is also that scaling is different for different sign-makers and so they might not share the same sense of scaling,—since orientation to meaning and to scales is dynamically negotiated in social life (Carr and Lempert 2016).

Policy and Scales: Meanings Moving through Space/Time

Conceiving policy as meaning-making allows researchers to explore the many mechanisms by which semiotic, discursive and textual processes operate at different scales to make policies culturally coherent in space and time. Such processes always entail some sort of change, instability or transformation in meaning; what is referred to in broad terms as recontextualization (Bernstein 2000).

Policy as meaning-making implicates the idea that meaning is instantiated in particular ways at different time and space coordinates, depending on how it becomes recontextualized. As it is taken from its original context of production (dislocation) to new contexts (relocation), policy can acquire new meanings to stakeholders who appropriate it (Johnson 2013). Recontextualization to some extent ties meaning to its original context but, at the same time, transforms it so that it can make new meanings in the new contexts in a chain of ongoing semiosis. For this reason, the concept has played an important role in education policy research (Wodak and Fairclough 2010). However, several authors have paid attention to this phenomenon from different disciplines, and many interconnected concepts cater for this fact.

For instance, the concept of entextualization (Silverstein and Urban 1996) attends to how particular pieces of (abstract) discourse may become *entextualized* so that their continuous nature becomes crystallized in meaningful instantiations. In terms of policy research, what discourses become entextualized is in itself meaningful since this points to what abstract discourses policy-makers choose to foreground and what the ideological implications of such choice might be. In Chap. 5 I will look into the implications of Plan Ceibal's foregrounding of technology and EFL as the goals of the left-wing government's democratization and universalization process. Depending on what policy scale is considered, technology can have equal or lower socio-political status than EFL and it might, in fact, be seen as a "problem" rather than as an actual aim of the policy.

For its part, the concept of intertextuality (Kristeva 1986) foregrounds how texts draw on previous texts to instantiate particular meanings. This is also relevant in terms of policy to understand how texts reinforce, contest or reject previous meanings (Lemke 1995), but also to understand how power relations are dynamically constructed and reconstructed in discourse and in meaning-making (Fairclough 1992).

Resemiotization (Iedema 2001, 2003) refers to how meanings migrate from one practice to the next and from one stage of meaning production to the next, this is also key to policy research. For instance, Chap. 5 shows how meanings about the policy come to index different states of affairs in different practices, such as policy texts, mass media advertising text and their design, teachers' and students' appropriation of the policy, and so on.

In particular, within resemiotization practices we can also place the concept of *transduction* (Kress 2011), that is to say transformations from one semiotic mode to another. Studying how the meanings of a policy can be transducted and its implications in the resources used for representation and communication (Kress 2005) is of paramount importance in a growingly visual, digital world. Chapter 5 shows a change of focus between official written documents if compared to an official TV advertisement for the policy. Such changes respond to both the resources available in each mode and the particular social purposes each text pursues in representing the policy to particular audiences. Attending to policy as meaning and as meaning transformation opens a space for the analysis of the heterogeneity of policy moving in space and time.

All of these phenomena are, in one way or another, present in the design, implementation or enactment of a policy, which—from a semiotic perspective—makes policy research challenging and demanding. More specifically, from a multimodal socio-semiotic approach a look at policy across scales may be informative of stakeholders' situated agency in interpreting and appropriating the policy through the meanings they make, such is the case of learners and teachers in the classroom. At the same time, attending to scales beyond the classroom also helps us better contextualize and understand meaning-making processes as interactively negotiated across policy time and space.

As I briefly mentioned in the previous section, policy studies—and in particular those regarding education—face the challenge of investigating an object that—by definition—is implicated and implicates various social practices (policy design, implementation, enactment, advertising, legal regulation, etc.), engages numerous stakeholders and is lived and experienced in both short and long-term scales: a micro event, a day, a year, a lifespan, a generation, and so on. As the concept of heterochrony shows (Lemke 2001), we cannot expect all of these large, mid- and small-scale events to relate to one another simplistically or unidirectionally. How they connect, implicate or draw on each other depends on many factors which cannot be always predicted. In the case of policy, this complex scenario is in part the result of how fast it can move (Walford 2002) and how moment-to-moment transformation or recontextualization relates to time and space (Savsky 2016): the ways in which stakeholders make sense of the policy is in continuous transformation.

The unfolding of policy rescales socio-political phenomena, such as policy scope, stakeholders' agency in appropriating the policy, how citizens orient to the policy and how they position themselves and others with regards to it. For this reason, it is important to capture the complex reality of policy and meaning-making both conceptually and analytically.

Several conceptual metaphors have attempted to define the reality of policy, providing particular notions of directionality, trajectory and causality. Perhaps one of the most widely-spread metaphors for understanding policy—as well as for understanding other phenomena in the social sciences (Hodge 2017) is the three dimensional model of macro, meso and micro levels, which roughly speaking can be mapped onto policy design, implementation and enactment, respectively. Metaphorically, this model implies that the higher we climb across levels, the broader the scope of the policy, the more abstract its nature and the more levels it encapsulates. For instance, the macro, which can be said to comprise both the meso and the micro, is by definition of a more abstract nature (since it pertains to social structures rather than to particular social events) and exerts top-down power in terms of structural agency dictating policy implementation and enactment. This characterization is useful to break the policy into several units of analysis, but it also brings about problems, since it tends to assume structural power and agency as well as a monodirectional and perhaps even mono-causal model of policy. As Wortham and Rhodes (2012) explain:

> These terms are useful insofar as they draw attention to processes of emergence and constraint essential to explaining social identification and other important human processes. But the terms are misleading insofar as they focus attention on allegedly homogeneous levels of explanation—individual creativity or interactional improvisation, on the one hand, and widespread ideologies or institutionalized practices on the other. In fact, both emergence and constraint are accomplished at various scales. Our job as analysts is to identify the types of emergence and constraint relevant to a focal phenomenon or process. These relevant processes will vary from case to case, and some will be neither "macro" nor "micro." (81)

Incorporating the notion of scale in policy research, then, does not mean fully abandoning the notions of macro, meso and micro. By adopting scales in our analysis, we can provide a fuller account of how policy is in constant negotiation across time and space (a classroom event, a policy TV spot, the making of a policy document, policy design, etc.) without assuming a priori there is a particular structural or hierarchical relation of dependency among them.[1]

By this I do not intent to claim that other models have failed in placing situatedness and agency in policy research, but that there is an advantage to adding scales to the working metaphors. In fact, other policy metaphors have foregrounded the situated nature of policy as meaning-making, such as the famous *slicing the onion ethnographically* (Hornberger and Johnson 2007; Johnson 2009; Menken and García 2010), or Ball's model (2006) of policy as both *discourse* and *text* to foreground social actors' agency beyond—or despite—the broader discursive relations that make policies produce truth values and knowledge to attempt to exercise structural power. Despite these useful metaphors, the concept of scale is—to my mind—highly operative in that it better conceptualizes the possibility of rhizomatic connections between different types of events (Deleuze and Guattari 1987).

Multimodal Social Semiotics and Ethnography: A Joint Approach for Analyzing Meaning Across Policy Scales

What meanings of a policy are made across scales? How do these meanings impact the ways in which social actors position themselves and others with regards to the policy? How do these meanings impact what learning is for the policy and for social actors? Questions such as these focus on the situatedness of meaning-making processes and their impact on different fields of social life. In fact, these are some of the main questions I had in mind before engaging in fieldwork and classroom observations. A tentative answer to such broad questions can be informative of what *really* happens with a policy (by "really" I mean what happens in everyday meaning-making across social practices), what it means for stakeholders and how it comes to mean different things at different space and time coordinates.

In order to answer such questions, I needed to draw on different sources of data, engage in varied data collection processes, analysis and interpretation. A partnership between complementary disciplines engaged in understanding situated meaning-making processes could be the road to capturing the complexity of meaning-making as social semiotics and the complexity of scales (Blommaert et al. 2015) as a working unit to understand how meaning-making operates in particular (shorter or longer, broader or narrower) meaning-making practices.

The overarching approach adopted in this book draws on multimodal social semiotics and ethnographies. The potential—and even the limitations—of this combination has been previously discussed in the work of Dicks et al. (2006), Kress (2011, 2015), Dicks et al. (2011), to name a few. On the one hand, multimodal social semiotics foregrounds the multiplicity of semiotic modes (speech, writing, design, touch, gaze, etc.) through which meanings are made and interpreted, as well as the historical, cultural and social conditions in which we make meanings to represent experience and communicate with others (Bezemer and Jewitt 2010). The main focus is on the situatedness of meaning-making, the available semiotic resources for making meanings and how these are ensembled and orchestrated by sign-makers. Like ethnography—in the broadest sense of the term—multimodal social semiotics attends to situated social action and situations and to the complexity of everyday social life with a focus on meaning. It can also draw on several sources of data, research artifacts such as notes, transcripts, and so on and cultural artifacts made by participants. However, while ethnography necessarily focuses on processes, multimodal social semiotics might also look into particular instantiation of meaning-making or signs.[2] Despite this and other differences, a partnership between multimodal social semiotics and ethnography is feasible and potentially beneficial as long as we understand the differences in what each discipline goes after (Kress 2011).

As for the use of ethnography, this study is inspired by focused ethnography (Knoblauch 2005) and ethnographic approaches to discourse (Macgilchrist and van Hout 2011). These approaches focus on the fragmented nature of human activities in current times, and so they study particular aspects and scenarios in smaller scales than traditional ethnographies do (Agar 2006). To compensate for the shorter duration of fieldwork, these types of ethnographic work strive for density of data collection (Knoblauch 2005). Ethnographic fieldwork and tools have proven fruitful in providing interpretive notions in the enactment of education and language policies (Hornberger and Johnson 2007; Johnson 2009, 2013; McCarty 2011; Menken and García 2010), as well as in additional language programs (Donato and Tucker 2010; Tucker 1999). Prolonged engagement in the research site and collection of several sources of data also proved fruitful in multimodal studies to better contextualize and describe situated meaning-making processes (Jewitt 2006; Kress 2011; Stein 2008; Unsworth 2008; Kress et al. 2005; van Leeuwen 2011; among others). Thickness and richness of description is particularly relevant in the study under investigation since policies tend to change rapidly (Walford 2002), which imposes certain restrictions as for the length of fieldwork in the same site.

The multiple sources of data the study draws on cannot—and do not intend to—capture *all* of the possible ways of enacting the policy, or all of the possible ways of making meanings within the policy. On the contrary, the study attempts to explore qualitatively *some* of the ways in which this phenomenon is instantiated (Peräkylä 2004).

Methods, Procedures and Data Collection Tools

The research is an empirical case study (Stake 1994). Ethnographic data were collected in a focal school (to which I will refer as Fleetwood School), a focal EFL classroom in that school (Vera's EFL beginner class) and in other schools and Plan Ceibal policy-making spaces. However, systematic collection of data took place at the level of the focal school and classroom.

The design aimed at balancing a thick and detailed description and a broader contextualization so as to make the qualitative study provide a detail account whose results could be transferable to other contexts or studies (Lincoln and Guba 2000; Stake 1994) and to make sure results could realistically migrate to other educational contexts (Brown 1992). It also aimed at achieving ecological validity (Bronfenbrenner 1976; van Lier 2004) by drawing on instruments, collecting and analyzing data in ways that account for participants' meaning-making processes.

Within the seven months of observations in the focal school, I documented five different units of classroom work (see Appendix for a more detail description of each unit and how they unfolded lesson by lesson). Prior to this, students had sat for two other units of classroom work and I observed those lessons, but I did not record them. In general, a complete unit of classroom work lasted around 3–4 weeks long. Data were collected in different ways, as follows.

Observations

Observations in Vera's classroom lasted around seven months, three times a week. These observations were video-recorded as well as documented in a researcher's field notes. Notes were made for different purposes: to record my own reflections and to help me contextualize video-recordings. Less systematic observations also took place at other policy sites: other schools, other classrooms, Plan Ceibal facilities, and official meetings, among others. Unlike the focal classroom, observations in other sites were not recorded.

Video-Recording

Classroom data were video-recorded with two cameras to capture two main angles (teacher's and students' view). When classroom tasks required students to use the laptops, textbooks or notebooks, two cameras were placed to capture both the screen or the page and student's faces and bodies. For these purposes, only some students were selected randomly and on the spot. Due to compatibility and software issues, I could not record directly from the laptop screens. Instead, these recordings were made from an actual camera.

Interviews

Two types of interviews were conducted: interviews within the focal research site and interviews elsewhere. The first type refers to those interviews carried out with stakeholders at Fleetwood School (i.e. students, teachers, parents, head of the school). Non-focal interviews refer to those carried out with other stakeholders who do not belong to the school (i.e. Plan Ceibal authorities, experts and educators, students and teachers at other schools, etc.). Throughout the book I present extracts of transcripts that belong to the first type of interviews, while I use information from the second type to contextualize the study. Interviews with students were required to take place inside the school. The teacher, on the contrary, was interviewed both inside and outside the school.

Transcripts

A transcription code was designed based on the requirements of the research study and the sources of data at hand. Interviews were transcribed orthographically because they were used to contextualize the phenomenon under investigation or a particular classroom event. Focal events in the classroom (video-recordings), however, were transcribed in a more narrow fashion. These transcriptions include: the time (as indicated in the recording), a written description of participants' actions (gestures, movements, gaze) and an orthographic transcript of the verbal interaction, with the English translation when the interaction took place in Spanish. When the event under investigation required the use of the laptop, I also included an "artifact action" label in the transcript, to show—simultaneously—what humans and non-humans participants were doing. I also include images. To maintain the anonymity of participants of the school, I do not show their faces and I erase identifiable features. These pictures are used to better illustrate how the events unfold. Also, throughout the study the teacher is addressed as Vera (V) and focal students are addressed as S1, S2, S3, S4, S5, S6, S7, and S8. The following numbers (S9, S10…) belong to non-focal students who also attend the school.

Needless to say, transcripts do not intend to capture all the complexity of modes, media and resources in communication, but to offer a glance of salient features which are relevant to the analysis in order to answer my research questions.

Member Checks

As part of the reflexive and iterative process, I did member checks with participants so that they had the chance to review the data and my interpretation. Due to school schedule, this was more often done with the teacher than with students. Member checks did not necessarily aim at classic data triangulation (Maxwell 1996). I did not take participants' opinion at face value either. Instead, I used member checks as another source of data (Lemke 2012).

Cultural Artifacts Collection

As explained earlier, I have been collecting and reviewing Plan Ceibal en Inglés artifacts since it was officially launched in 2011. These artifacts include: official documents and decrees, newspaper articles, Plan Ceibal reports, Ceibal en Inglés TV spots, international documentaries about Plan Ceibal, news broadcasts, EFL syllabuses and lesson plans, newspaper job ads for RTs, teacher unions' minutes and documents, online-forums and news, classroom images, my own notes from participating in related meetings and events, among others. These were reviewed to better contextualize the policy and the enactment process. Classroom artifacts such as students' work were also collected, but for analysis purposes when they pertained to the focal events, such is the case, for instance, of students' final texts for assessment.

Ceibal en Inglés Data Bank

I also reviewed approximately 100 video-recording of EFL classes in public schools, which were available in Ceibal en Inglés data bank. These videos show different lessons in different schools across the academic year in primary school. Although I was granted access to the data bank, I did not have permission to reproduce actual images or classroom interactions from those videos since they are used for Plan Ceibal internal purposes and do not circulate publicly.

Positionality

As a member of the Uruguayan community, I have performed—and still perform—many overlapping roles intimately connected to the topic under investigation. I have been an EFL student in both public and private schools; I have also been an EFL teacher, a TEFL instructor in public and private teacher education institutions, among others. I have also participated as an external consultant for Plan Ceibal for a short period of time.

All of these overlapping roles certainly informed and shaped my understanding of the policy and my data analysis processes, as well as my interest and framing of the topic. Because of all these roles, I have participated in meetings, conferences and other local events in which technology in education, EFL and foreign language instruction were discussed and debated, as well as meetings and conversations with Plan Ceibal stakeholders.

Also, I have had access to the opinions and views of EFL students, teacher education students, and educational authorities in the local community, as they have also had access to my own. I have also participated in teachers' meetings in which the goals of Plan Ceibal and the ins and outs of technology in education were heatedly debated. My own alignment with left-wing ideologies has also granted me more frequent access to the views and opinions of local left-wing political actors as well. Despite this, I made sure I had access to other voices to both see the policy from another perspective and to learn what other voices had to say about it.

Research Site and Participants

The research site is a working-middle-class, private high school in the capital city Montevideo (Uruguay). A full account of the school and the classroom is provided in Chap. 4. Given the goals of the study, the criteria for selecting the school and classroom were based on (i) accessibility to the research site, (ii) participants' willingness to take part in the study so as to ensure their engagement throughout the academic year, (iii) the fact that the school is a "blind spot" of the policy (private schools do not have much regulation from Plan Ceibal, as explained in detail in Chap. 4), and (iv) the teacher's own motivation to use technology in the classroom.

Details about the research were negotiated and finalized with participants (school administrators, teachers, parents and students). After conversations with the teacher and the head of the school and based on my research goals, I decided to select the first-year high-school class (regular EFL stream) of eight students (aged 12).

Students in the focal classroom have no prior formal EFL learning experience, except for one student who was also attending private EFL lessons (S8). As all high-school students at Fleetwood, they also have Portuguese as a foreign language lessons, but in these lessons they do not use Plan Ceibal laptops (known as XO laptops). All of these students had technology at home (desktops, laptops or tablets) except for one student (S4) who could only access a laptop at home when her elder brother visited her.

The teacher (Vera) is an EFL certified teacher. At the time of the study, she had over ten years of experience teaching EFL in private and public schools. She taught (and still teaches) both in the regular and bilingual stream of Fleetwood. Despite her interest in technology, at the moment of the research she had never been involved with Plan Ceibal in public education. However, she is now (2018) engaged in Plan Ceibal en Inglés for secondary education. Vera does not have any formal education in technology, other than one undergrad class she took. Despite this, she is interested in the implementation of new technology in education and in foreign language instruction. Among the other private schools in which she worked at the time of the research, Fleetwood was the only one who had opted in Plan Ceibal. Among EFL teachers at Fleetwood, she was perceived as the one who more often uses technology and who showed more creative ways of using it in the EFL lesson, which also made her a good match for the research.

Notes

1. Another explanation for this can be found in Canagarajah and De Costa (2016).
2. A short and clear description of fundamental differences and similarities can be found in the Ethnography entry on the MODE project website (see Glossary of Multimodal terms): https://multimodalityglossary.wordpress.com/ethnography/ (Last accessed 9/4/2018).

References

Agar, M. (2006). An Ethnography by Any Other Name.... *Forum: Qualitative Social Research, 7*(4). https://doi.org/10.17169/fqs-7.4.177

Bakhtin, M. (1981). *The Dialogic Imagination: Four Essays by M.M. Bakhtin.* Austin: University of Texas Press.

Ball, S. J. (2006). *Education Policy and Social Class.* London and New York: Routledge.

Bernstein, B. (2000). *Pedagogy, Symbolic Control and Identity: Theory, Research, Critique.* London: Taylor & Francis.

Bezemer, J., & Jewitt, C. (2010). Multimodal Analysis: Key Issues. In L. Litosseliti (Ed.), *Research Methods in Linguistics* (pp. 180–197). London: Continuum.

Blommaert, J. (2007). Sociolinguistic Scales. *Intercultural Pragmatics, 4*(1), 1–19. https://doi.org/10.1515/ip.2007.001

Blommaert, J. (2015). Meaning as a Non-linear Effect. The Birth of Cool. *AILA Review, 28*, 7–27. https://doi.org/10.1075/aila.28.01blo

Blommaert, J., Westinen, E., & Leppänen, S. (2015). Further Notes on Sociolinguistic Scales. *Intercultural Pragmatics, 12*(1), 119–127. https://doi.org/10.1515/ip-2015-0005

Bloome, D., Beierle, M., Grigorenko, M., & Goldman, S. (2009). Learning Over Time: Uses of Intercontextuality, Collective Memories, and Classroom Chronotopes in the Construction of Learning Opportunities in a Ninth-Grade Language Art Classroom. *Language and Education, 23*(4), 313–334. https://doi.org/10.1080/09500780902954257

Bronfenbrenner, U. (1976). *The Experimental Ecology of Education*. Paper presented at the American Educational Research Association Annual Meeting, San Francisco. Retrieved March 25, 2019, from https://files.eric.ed.gov/fulltext/ED131025.pdf

Brown, A. L. (1992). Design Experiments: Theoretical and Methodological Challenges in Creating Complex Interventions in Classroom Settings. *The Journal of the Learning Sciences, 2*(2), 141–178. https://doi.org/10.1207/s15327809jls0202_2

Canagarajah, S., & De Costa, P. I. (2016). Introduction: Scale Analysis, and Its Uses and Prospects in Educational Linguistics. *Linguistics and Education, 34*, 1–10. https://doi.org/10.1016/j.linged.2015.09.001

Carr, S. E., & Lempert, M. (2016). Introduction: The Pragmatics of Scale. In E. Summerson Carr & M. Lempert (Eds.), *Scale. Discourse and Dimensions of Social Life* (pp. 1–24). Oakland: University of California Press.

Coronado, G., & Hodge, B. (2017). *Metodologías semióticas para análisis de la complejidad*. Retrieved November 12, 2018, from https://www.westernsydney.edu.au/ics/people/researchers/bob_hodge

Deleuze, G., & Guattari, F. (1987). *A Thousand Plateaus*. Minneapolis: University of Minnesota Press.

Dicks, B., Bambo, S., & Coffey, A. (2006). Multimodal Ethnography. *Qualitative Research, 6*(1), 77–96. https://doi.org/10.1177/1468794106058876

Dicks, B., Flewitt, R., Lancaster, L., & Pahl, K. (2011). Multimodality and Ethnography: Working at the Intersection. *Qualitative Research, 11*(3), 227–237. https://doi.org/10.1177/1468794111400682

Donato, R., & Tucker, G. R. (2010). *A Tale of Two Schools. Developing Sustainable Early Foreign Language Programs*. Bristol, Buffalo and Toronto: Multilingual Matters.

Fairclough, N. (1992). *Discourse and Social Change*. Cambridge: Blackwell.

Gal, S. (2016). Scale-Making: Comparison and Perspective as Ideological Projects. In E. Summerson Carr & M. Lempert (Eds.), *Scale. Discourse and Dimensions of Social Life* (pp. 91–111). Oakland: University of California Press.

Hodge, B. (2017). *Social Semiotics for a Complex World*. Cambridge: Polity Press.

Hornberger, N. H., & Johnson, D. C. (2007). Slicing the Onion Ethnographically. Layers and Spaces in Multilingual Language Education Policy and Practice. *TESOL Quarterly, 41*(3), 509–532. https://doi.org/10.1002/j.1545-7249.2007.tb00083.x

Hult, F. M. (2010a). Analysis of Language Policy Discourses Across the Scales of Space and Time. *International Journal of the Sociology of Language, 202,* 7–24.

Hult, F. M. (2010b). The Complexity Turn in Educational Linguistics. *Language, Culture and Curriculum, 23*(3), 173–177. https://doi.org/10.1080/07908318.2010.515992

Iedema, R. (2001). Resemiotization. *Semiotica, 137,* 23–39. https://doi.org/10.1515/semi.2001.106

Iedema, R. (2003). Multimodality, Resemiotization: Extending the Analysis of Discourse as Multi-semiotic Practice. *Visual Communication, 2*(1), 29–57. https://doi.org/10.1177/1470357203002001751

Jewitt, C. (2006). *Technology, Literacy and Learning. A Multimodal Approach*. London and New York: Routledge.

Johnson, D. C. (2009). Ethnography of Language Policy. *Language Policy, 8*(2), 139–159. https://doi.org/10.1017/S0261444817000428

Johnson, D. C. (2013). *Language Policy*. New York: Palgrave Macmillan.

Knoblauch, H. (2005). Focused Ethnography. *Forum: Qualitative Social Research, 6*(3).

Kress, G. (2005). Gains and Losses: New Forms of Texts, Knowledge, and Learning. *Computers and Composition, 22*(1), 5–22. https://doi.org/10.1016/j.compcom.2004.12.004

Kress, G. (2011). 'Partnership in Research': Multimodality and Ethnography. *Qualitative Research, 11*(3), 239–260. https://doi.org/10.1177/1468794111399836

Kress, G. (2015). Designing Meaning. Social Semiotic Multimodality Seen in Relation to Ethnographic Research. In S. Bollig, M. S. Honig, S. Neumann, & C. Seele (Eds.), *MultiPluriTrans in Educational Ethnography. Approaching the Multimodality, Plurality and Translocality of Educational Realities* (pp. 213–233). Verlag: Transcript.

Kress, G., Jewitt, C., Bourne, J., Franks, A., Hardcastle, J., Jones, K., & Reid, E. (2005). *English in Urban Classrooms. A Multimodal Perspective on Teaching and Learning*. London: Routledge Farmar.

Kristeva, J. (1986). *The Kristeva Reader* (T. Moi, Ed.). New York: Columbia University Press.

Lemke, J. (1995). *Textual Politics. Discourse and Social Dynamics*. London and Bristol: Taylor & Francis.

Lemke, J. (2001). Discursive Technologies and the Social Organization of Meaning. *Folia Linguistica, 35*(1/2), 79–96. https://doi.org/10.1515/flin.2001.35.1-2.79

Lemke, J. (2012). Analyzing Verbal Data: Principles, Methods, and Problems. In J. Barry, K. T. Fraser, & J. Campbell (Eds.), *The Second International Handbook of Science Education* (pp. 1471–1484). London: Springer.

Lincoln, Y. S., & Guba, E. G. (2000). The Only Generalization Is: There is No Generalization. In M. R. Gomm, M. Hammersley, & P. Foster (Eds.), *Case Study Method* (pp. 27–44). London: Sage.

Macgilchrist, F., & van Hout, T. (2011). Ethnographic Discourse Analysis and Social Science. *Forum: Qualitative Social Research, 12*(1). https://doi.org/10.17169/fqs-12.1.1600

Maxwell, J. A. (1996). *Qualitative Research Design: An Interactive Approach*. London: Sage.

McCarty, T. (2011). Introducing Ethnography and Language Policy. In T. McCarty (Ed.), *Ethnography and Language Policy* (pp. 1–28). New York and London: Routledge.

Menken, K., & García, O. (Eds.). (2010). *Negotiating Language Policies in Schools. Educators as Policymakers*. New York and London: Routledge.

Peräkylä, A. (2004). Reliability and Validity in Research based on Naturally Occurring Social Interaction. In D. Silverman (Ed.), *Qualitative Research: Theory, Method and Practice* (pp. 283–304). London: Sage.

Savsky, K. (2016). State Language Policy in Time and Space: Meaning, Transformation, Recontextualisation. In E. Barakos & J. W. Unger (Eds.), *Discursive Approaches to Language Policy* (pp. 51–70). London: Palgrave Macmillan.

Scollon, R., & Scollon, S. W. (2004). *Nexus Analysis. Discourse and the Emerging Internet*. London and New York: Routledge.

Silverstein, M., & Urban, G. (1996). The Natural History of Discourse. In M. Silverstein & G. Urban (Eds.), *Natural Histories of Discourse* (pp. 1–17). Chicago: Chicago University Press.

Stake, R. (1994). Case Studies. In N. K. Denzin & Y. S. Lincoln (Eds.), *The Handbook of Qualitative Research* (pp. 236–247). Thousand Oaks: Sage.

Stein, P. (2008). *Multimodal Pedagogies in Diverse Classrooms. Representations, Rights and Resources*. London and New York: Routledge.

Tucker, G. R. (1999). The Applied Linguist, School Reform and Technology: Challenges and Opportunities for the Coming Decade. *CALICO Journal, 17*(2), 197–222.

Unsworth, L. (2008). Multimodal Semiotic Analyses and Education. In L. Unsworth (Ed.), *Multimodal Semiotics. Functional Analysis in Contexts of Education* (pp. 1–13). London and New York: Continuum.

van Leeuwen, T. (2011). Multimodality. In J. Simpson (Ed.), *The Routledge Handbook of Applied Linguistics* (pp. 669–682). London and New York: Routledge.

van Lier, L. (2004). *The Ecology and Semiotics of Language Learning. A Sociocultural Perspective*. New York: Kluwer Academic Publishers.

Walford, G. (2002). When Policies Move Fast, How Long Can Ethnography Take? In B. A. U. Levinson, S. L. Cade, A. Padawer, & A. P. Elvir (Eds.), *Ethnography and Education Policy Across the Americas* (pp. 23–38). London: Praeger.

Wodak, R., & Fairclough, N. (2010). Recontextualizing European Higher Education Policies: The Case of Austria and Romania. *Critical Discourse Studies, 7*(1), 19–40. https://doi.org/10.1080/17405900903453922

Wortham, S., & Rhodes, C. R. (2012). The Production of Relevant Scales: Social Identification of Migrants During Rapid Demographic Change in One American Town. *Applied Linguistics Review, 3*(1), 75–99. https://doi.org/10.1515/applirev-2012-0004

3

Toward a Multimodal Socio-Semiotic Account of Learning

The previous chapter made a case for a close partnership between a multimodal socio-semiotic approach and ethnography to explore meaning-making processes. More specifically—and in connection to the topic of this book—it argued that there are theoretical and practical advantages to investigating education policy as situated meaning-making processes. Since meaning-making is by definition situated, that is to say bound to time/space scales, scalar analysis or a multi-scalar approach is useful for both theory and empirical analysis. Throughout this chapter, connections will be made between the previous arguments and the study of learning as meaning-making from a multimodal socio-semiotic approach. Given the ubiquitous role of technology in current education policy-making, emphasis will be laid on what a multimodal socio-semiotic approach—in partnership with ethnography—has to offer to the study of technology and meaning-making in education, that is to say, how learners make meanings with technology in classrooms and how we can approach this to acknowledge their agency as sign-makers.

Many studies in the field of social semiotics underscore the relationship between multimodality and new technology, as well as its relevance for education and learning in the new century (Jewitt 2006, 2008, 2013,

2014; Lemke 2011; Scollon and Levine 2004; TNLG 1996; Unsworth 2008). Such studies foreground the fact that communication and learning are not monomodally achieved, and therefore they should not be conceived as solely linguistic work, but instead as multimodal work comprising several modes and media. The chapter will introduce social semiotics as an overarching approach to learning and meaning-making processes, and multimodality as a framework to explore both how modal resources and media are deployed to make meanings with technology and also to analyze the resulting complex signs made with such technology. This focus on how sign-makers interact with technology contributes to the understanding that semiosis is not achieved in isolation, but instead it is achieved in a particular environment and in collaboration with other human or non-human entities. In other words, the chapter characterizes learning from a multimodal socio-semiotic approach. To do so, it explores some of the many connections between technology, meaning-making and multimodality in the understanding that new technology plays a fundamental role in modern formal education and that the interaction, communication and learning that take place with such technology in schools needs to be approached multimodally. The chapter also discusses the potential benefits of approaching learning from a multimodal socio-semiotic perspective as an alternative to traditional—and to some extent still dominant—ideologies of learning which permeate many school and classroom practices and which obscure much of the meaning-making that takes place within school and classroom walls (as well as outside of them).

Social Semiotics and Meaning-Making

Social semiotics underscores the situatedness of meaning-making processes and the various ways in which humans make meanings by drawing on several modal resources and media in particular situations and for particular purposes.

In opposition to traditional notions of the sign as a socially agreed upon and arbitrary construct (Saussure 1967) social semiotics underscores the idea that the very nature of the sign is culturally motivated

(Kress 1993) or ideological (Vološinov 1973). This foregrounds the fact that neither meaning-making processes nor signs are stable or fixed (Lemke 1995a, b). Signs and meaning-making processes are constitutive of situated social practices in which participants make sense of the world, represent experience, communicate with others and establish social relations, and as such they are situated and context-bound. Meaning-making processes serve three *meta-functions* (Halliday 2001, 2014), in that each instance of meaning-making realizes three types of functional meaning: representation, orientation and organization. These meta-functions were originally posited to explain how meaning-making operates in verbal language, but they were later expanded to account for other semiotic resources and meaning-making in general (Kress and van Leeuwen 2006). To put it simply, the ideational meta-function pertains to how social experience is construed (i.e. representation); the interpersonal meta-function pertains to how social relations are constructed and enacted (i.e. orientation); the textual meta-function to how information is organized to achieve textual cohesion and coherence (i.e. organization). All three together constitute the main functions semiotic resources come to serve for creating meanings.

The situatedness of meaning-making processes accounts for the agentive role of sign-makers in making meanings in particular social contexts. However, agency is also restricted. Within this framework, context is a constitutive aspect of meaning-making processes (Hodge and Kress 1988) and not just as something external to such processes. Meaning is then the result of how sign-makers draw on resources available to them (Kress 2005, 2010; van Leeuwen 2005) in a particular context and for particular purposes (Adami and Kress 2014). However, the resources they deploy are the result of the dialectics between history and culture, which shape—and in time are shaped by—how meanings can be made socially. In other words, the resources available to sign-makers are restricted to some extent by culture (the cline of potentiality, Halliday 2014) and by what resources are able to mean in particular instantiations. Resources are the reflection of how semiotic systems have historically and culturally developed for specific meaning-making potentials (van Leeuwen 2005). Culture does not only provide a set of affordances and resources but, at the same time, restrictions and constraints.

In the understanding that "even a rich socially and semantically based linguistic analysis of contemporary texts can provide only a partial description of how they work to create meaning" (Painter et al. 2012, 2), a socio-semiotic approach favors the analysis of how semiotic resources are intertwined in meaning-making processes (Kress 2010; Kress and van Leeuwen 2001, 2006; Unsworth 2008). To attend to such processes, the notion of multimodality is highly useful, since—as will be discussed below—it allows us to (i) de-center language as *the* sole mode of communication, and concomitantly (ii) foreground the multiplicity of modes (visual, aural, graphic, etc.) engaged in making meanings to (iii) focus on how modes and resources become orchestrated and divide labor to make complex meanings which cannot be captured by looking into a particular mode in isolation.

Multimodality

The study of meaning-making processes has traditionally been atomized (Jewitt 2008; van Leeuwen 2004), resulting in the lack of a coherent and unified—but yet multidisciplinary—method for analyzing how semiosis is socially and culturally achieved (Hodge and Kress 1988; Kress and van Leeuwen 2006; Machin and Mayr 2012; Machin and van Leeuwen 2007). It was not until the past few decades that more systematic attempts were made toward a coherent approach to analyzing semiotic processes in a global manner.[1] Multimodality is a framework on the making that aims to unify such attempts (O'Halloran 2012) demonstrating that all discourses and signs are, by definition, multimodal (Jewitt 2011; Kress 2010; Kress and van Leeuwen 2001, 2006; Scollon and Levine 2004). This claim may seem obvious at first sight (Stockl 2007); however, it underscores both the traditional hegemony of discourse analysis—focused on verbal language—and the need to consider semiosis as a multimodal process to capture the complexity of meaning-making processes. Along the same lines, it must be noted that although multimodality has proven very fruitful for better capturing the complexity of communication in our current social world, it is also true that communication has always been by definition multimodal (Hodge 2017). The main difference lies in how we now approach it theoretically and methodologically.

What multimodality foregrounds, then, is the fact that resources for making meanings are of many kinds and not only verbal (Hodge and Kress 1988; Kress and van Leeuwen 2006; van Leeuwen 2005). One of its fundamental contributions is to explore the ways in which modal resources orchestrate to make meanings or, as van Leeuwen(2005, 4) puts it, how "[a]lmost everything we do or make can be done or made in different ways and therefore allows, at least in principle, the articulation of different social and cultural meanings".

Multimodality leads us to analyze how complex meanings are created in the articulation of both *modal resources*—or *modes*—and media. Modal resources are semiotic resources that can be selected to make meanings, depending on the particular context and interest of the sign-maker (e.g. verbal, visual, aural, etc.). Media are the materials through which modal resources become instantiated (e.g. printed page, computer screen, palette, human voice, etc.) (Kress and van Leeuwen 2001). Choices made by sign-makers take place at both the level of modes and the level of media, and they are shaped by the interest of the sign-maker, what the context offers for representation and communication and the cultural functionalization of modes.

Functionalization of modes refers to the fact that modal resources historically and culturally become specialized for particular social purposes and functions (Kress and van Leeuwen 2001, 2006). For instance, some highly codified societies have specialized writing for legal affairs and legal regulation (legislation, laws, reports, etc.). This is an example of the process to which Kress et al. (2001, 16) refer as *functional specialization* of a semiotic mode, and it explains why for particular purposes a mode may play a more salient role than others. Through the process of specialization a semiotic mode becomes associated with particular social functions and particular media, specializing its functionality and also providing sign-makers with particular affordances (Kress 2011). However, functionalization is never thoroughly determined *a priori* since historical, social and ideological forces are dialectically intertwined with semiotic modes and media. The development of a new technology, for instance, offers potential new uses and orchestrations of modal resources. Such potential can be studied at the intersect of multimodality, technology and education, since all three are key for a better understanding of learning in the new era.

Multimodality, Technology and Education

From its inception, multimodal socio-semiotic studies have engaged in exploring the relation between discourse and (new) technology (Scollon and Levine 2004). As a result of rapid changes and transformations in modern societies, there currently is a "burgeoning variety of texts forms associated with information and multimedia technologies" (TNLG 1996, 9). New technology gives way to new configurations and reconfigurations of texts, new ensembles and orchestration of modal resources and media. Along these lines, some of the challenges of education are—as shall be discussed later in the chapter—how to incorporate these new phenomena into the curriculum and classroom practices so as to bridge the gap between what the school legitimates as *literacy* and other social practices that take place inside and outside of the school.

In the past decades, the massive incorporation of new technology in education has brought about a heated debate among scholars. In a continuum of perceptions and arguments that range from utopian to dystopian views, some studies have underscored covert hegemonic intentions of social reproduction and control, blaming technology for deskilling teachers, mechanizing practices and reproducing social, economic and cultural access inequality (Apple 2003; Apple and Jungck 1998; Boody 2001; Muffoletto 2001). Others have explored how social actors may— through individual or collective agency—transform the spaces they live in by resisting or resignifying hegemonic practices (Bromley and Apple 1998; Sung and Apple 2003).

Oftentimes, these views about technology in education have been criticized either for romanticizing classrooms and human practices before new technologies were introduced or for being highly uncritical of the role of technology in education (Alexander 2006; Setzer and Monke 2001). It has also been claimed that debates surrounding technology need to critically evaluate the environment in which technology is introduced, since the sole introduction of a technology artifact does not necessarily mean it will be used in the way and for the purposes it was designed (Hakkarainen et al. 2013; LeBaron 2002; Stahl et al. 2006), neither does it mean that it will be used at all (Schofield 1995).

As announced in Chap. 1, in this book I deliberately shift the discussion from the traditional *yes/no* question about technology in education (and for learning) toward the description and explanation of meaning-making processes that take place in the classroom and their potential (Jewitt 2006, 2008). To my mind, this approach has a lot to offer to research on education, policies and learning in that it foregrounds how technology artifacts interact with other curriculum artifacts, teachers and students to construct classroom and institutional ecologies in which meanings are made at the same time that it allows us to better capture learners' situated agency in interacting with technology, communicating and learning at different scales, as discussed in Chaps. 5, 6 and 7.

Multimodality, Technology and Literacy

The focus on multimodality, technology and literacy has been clearly delineated by the work of TNLG (1996). Around two decades ago, the group advocated revisiting traditional concepts in education, such as *literacy* and *skills*. This was needed due to a rapid change in our societies.

Traditionally, education has looked at literacy and skills as something students either possess or lack in terms of verbal resources. As Kress (2003) and Jewitt (2008) explain, *literacy as a linguistic achievement* mainly restricts the focus on verbal language as the sole indicator of failure or success, failing to see that literacy as meaning-making allows us to understand how individuals construct and represent the world around them[2] through different modal resources and media.

Traditional—and to a great extent still dominant—literacy practices in schools, however, focus on verbal language and on decontextualized individual cognitive skills (Gee 2000). Works in the field critical literacies, multimodality and social semiotics have attempted to bridge school and out-of-school practices. These studies foreground that children's out-of-school activities seem to involve a lot of multimodal doing (Gee 2007) while school practices still revolve around linguistically dense printed-pages

(Jewitt 2008; Serafini 2014). In this respect, traditional school practices—which became dominant during the industrial age and for industrialization purposes—are not able to account for the new ways of making meanings, the new multimodal ensembles and the higher multimodal density in text production in post-industrial societies (Matthiessen 2014; Norris 2011). In this chapter as well as in the remainder of this book I will refer to these traditional schooling practices as *traditional ideologies of learning*. Later chapters (Chaps. 6 and 7) will show how, through a multimodal socio-semiotic account of learning, alterative practices or *alternative ideologies of learning* can be designed and fostered.

Ideologies of Learning and Literacy

The introduction of new technology—or, in general, new artifacts—in education does not represent in itself a change in educational practices (Kalantzis et al. 2010; Kress 2013). On the contrary, while the new artifact may be socially regarded as an innovative element in education, it may co-exist with or even reproduce traditional practices due to teaching style, preference, lack of policy support, motivation, among other reasons. A significant change in practices does occur when the orientation to learning also changes, or in other words when participants themselves do not assume they are doing the same activity with different artifacts but rather that they are doing a different activity. A significant change in terms of how we—researchers, practitioners, stakeholders and students—orient to learning requires us to review what we are doing in schools, how we are doing it and for what purposes.

For the purpose of this book, two main ideologies of learning can be said to be available—coexisting and even competing—in current education: a traditional ideology and an alternative one. Of course there are some important variations within each of these, as there is in any ideology. These ideologies of learning permeate different spaces, curriculum artifacts (textbooks, new technology, etc.) and instruments (assessment rubrics, tests, etc.) and operate at different scales from classroom interaction to wider institutional and official policy spaces. My characterization of these two ideologies goes back to Kress (2013), who defines *traditional* and *alternative views of learning*. In this book, however, I opt to call them *ideologies* of learning to foreground the fact that each of these views implies and entails ideological work and assumptions (Fairclough 2003) about what learning is, what it is for, how it works, how it can and should be demonstrated, and so on. In turn, these assumptions can shape school practices at the level of classroom interaction, policy-making, school policing, curriculum and pedagogy.

For the traditional ideology of learning, power and authority in teaching are a given; assessment is an instrument to estimate "acquisition" through metrics, and the curriculum is "content" (Kress 2013), or a set of socially valuable information and facts to be delivered by the teacher and acquired by the student. In this respect, learning can be characterized as a set of practices (with a clearly delineated path or route) that aims at the transmission of facts, values and behaviors, generally in a mechanical manner, with a focus on achievement in a particular time and space. These notions correspond to the tradition of schooling in previous times, which prepared students for an industrializing world, but still dominate many curriculum and teaching practices nowadays. What this ideology of learning entails is clearly conveyed by the metaphor of *learning as acquisition* (Kress et al. 2001). In its most radical form, the metaphor of acquisition characterizes learners as passive recipients of knowledge (generally in the form of a set of highly organized abstract rules) which are internalized for subsequent "use" or "application" by the learner (or, in these terms, the "user").

On the contrary, an alternative ideology of learning focuses on the learner's *interest* and *agency*, as will be defined later in the chapter. The focus is not on measuring "learning outcomes" based on the "accumulation of facts and information". Instead, the focus is on what students can do with modes and media, and what this tells us about their interest and agency as sign-makers (Bezemer and Kress 2016). The alternative ideology of learning conceives learning as a situated social process that takes place in/as communication, regardless of whether the context or participants orient to it as such. This means that as school policy and documents, assessment instruments and tools can dictate what we are expected to orient to as learning (and concomitantly what we are expected to leave out), there is a lot of semiotic work of the students which is not being captured. This ideology also draws on notions of collaboration (among humans and artifacts) in communication and interaction, as foregrounded—for different purposes—in social frameworks such as: actor network theory (Latour 2006), activity theory (Engeström 1987, 2001), and distributed and situated cognition (Resnik et al. 1997; Schnotz 1997). This allows us to account for the fact that humans do not make meaning in isolation and, in the same way, they do not learn in isolation, as semiotic labor is distributed among humans, artifacts and the environment.

The next section discusses a socio-semiotic multimodal account of learning, which attempts to capture, theorize and potentially put into practice the underlying assumptions of an alternative ideology of learning, one for which recognizing the learner and their agency is essential. Such ideology—as shall be seen next—requires us to conceive learning through a metaphor of transformation, as has been posed in various modern theories. However, our notion of transformation pertains to the field of social semiotics. The remaining sections will articulate the notion of learning as transformation—and other satellite concepts—within the alternative ideology of learning, foregrounding the benefits of this ideology in terms of how learners are fully recognized as social and cultural agents.

Toward an Alternative Ideology: Learning as Transformation

In this section I shall discuss the multimodal socio-semiotic account of learning I adopt in this book, that of learning as transformation (Kress 2015a, b; Bezemer and Kress 2016). To better understand and contextualize this notion I will briefly discuss the traditional conception of learning as meaning-making in Systemic Functional Linguistics—SFL—(Halliday 1993) from which it derives. However, I will also point out some key differences between learning as transformation in this framework and other approaches to learning among SFL-oriented accounts.

Halliday (1993) saw learning as a semiotic process, that is to say, as a process of making meanings. This is key to shifting from a traditional

3 Toward a Multimodal Socio-Semiotic Account of Learning

ideology of learning (for which learning is passive reception) to an alternative one that is able to foreground learners' agency. Halliday's definition opened a door to exploring the process of learning (and also language learning) by situating learning and use in the context of semiotic systems and semiotic resources, respectively. Unlike other language-based theories of learning that assume learning to be an inner process of accumulation of information and syntactic rules, Halliday's definition of (language) learning conceptualizes learning through the metaphor of development (Halliday 1974/2004). This metaphor is by no means exclusive to his approach in language theory, theories of learning and education. However, learning as development has a particular meaning in Halliday's theory. By this metaphor language learning can be understood as the process of developing a semiotic system (i.e. language). Such a semiotic system can be said to develop dialectically in the individual and in culture. Through this process, both the individual and culture influence and change each other as learning expands both the sign-maker's *repertoire* (their semiotic resources for making meanings) and the cultural *reservoir* (the overall meaning-making potential as historically and culturally shaped). Learning—in Hallidayan terms—is "learning to mean, and to expand one's own meaning potential" (Halliday 1993, 113). Such semiotic expansions pertain to verbal resources (i.e. language learning) as well as to other non-verbal semiotic resources. Transformation is necessary for expansion, since it is through transformation that the child can turn experience into meaning and it is through transformation that meanings are exchanged (Halliday 1998/2004). Although this notion of learning foregrounds meaning potential in general, much of the work in SFL—and Halliday's own work—focused on the expansion of verbal resources until multimodality became established as one of the main topics in the SFL agenda.

The idea that learning implies developing the semiotic system and expanding our potential to mean through transformation was highly influential for other SFL-oriented approaches to learning, such as the Sydney School. Their approach to learning (and teaching) was specifically designed as interventionist (Rose 2010), that is to say, as an attempt to intervene teaching and learning practices at the level of classrooms and schools. Both historically and contextually, the Sydney School responded to a socio-political problem in terms of how learning was conceived of: the school practices that dominated the literacy scene of the 80s in Australia—and in many other countries—which favored students' "own exploration" of reading and writing without explicit instruction or even modeling. Grounded in situated findings from educational linguistics, genre and grammar analysis, the point of departure of the Sydney School was the observation that access to verbal (and other non-verbal) meaning-making resources is not distributed equally among students within the education system (Martin and Rose 2008). Far from righting this wrong, traditional school practices played a key role in reinforcing such ill-distribution of resources. For instance, Christie (2002) discusses how often times in the teaching and learning of writing an expected curricular outcome (e.g. learning to write a particular type of text) can be achieved through several disconnected classroom events, providing no curricular or pedagogical cohesion among them, and even lacking a set of explicit pedagogical/instructional strategies for achieving such goal. In this type of school practice students are generally not provided with the tools and explicit scaffolded instruction to succeed and so success actually depends on their prior experience and access to certain texts and genres.

The theoretical and political positioning by the Sydney School has far reaching implications if seen from our discussion of traditional versus alternative ideologies of learning. It shows that instead of re-designing instructional tools and school practices as to better distribute meaning-making resources and to favor the development of resources in the classroom, traditional ideologies of learning reinforce the unequal distribution of resources. In such terms, students who already "possess" such resources are legitimated as successful learners because they can already perform accordingly, whereas the others continue to be excluded because they are not able to perform within the expectations of canonical literacy norms and often times implicit curricular expectations.

In this respect, one of the main goals of the Sydney School and its characterization of learning was to "prepare" students—rather than to "repair" (Dreyfus et al. 2016). Preparing students implies helping them build up representation and communicative resources for participation in social practices. Understanding genre as a semantic concept, as "patterns of meaning" and as "a staged goal oriented social process" (Martin and

3 Toward a Multimodal Socio-Semiotic Account of Learning 53

Rose 2007, 2008) this approach assumes culture to be "a system of genres" (Martin 2000, 52). Explicit teaching of genre, then, is understood as a door to empowering students from disadvantaged backgrounds by providing them with the (canonical) resources for making meanings in a given culture (Dreyfus et al. 2016) or, in other words, by providing them with the (valued) resources for enacting particular social practices and relations in a culture (Martin and Rose 2008, 6).

In this model, learning is designed through different stages which require particular skills and ways of (inter)acting with texts. One of the main aims of such design is to account for teachers' (pedagogical) agency in favoring learning. For instance, through cycles of deconstruction, joint construction and independent construction (*vid* Rothery and Stenglin 1995), agency in meaning-making is gradually released to students. In the deconstruction stage the teacher exposes students to at least one cycle of support and engagement with a text (or texts) to explore, for example, patterns of meaning in the text (which represents an instantiation of the genre at hand). In the joint construction stage, students collaborate (with peers and or "experts") by distributing expertise and semiotic labor for creating their own text. Finally, in the independent construction stage students reconstruct the text independently, based on what s/he has gained in the previous stages. In this manner, students are exposed to various types of scaffolded tasks before they are actually required to—let's say—write their own texts independently. In terms of meaning-making, then, learning is expansion in that it is the process through which semiotic resources that were not available to sign-makers now become available, at the same time that they can make new meanings with them.

Both the notion of development and expansion foreground the agentive nature of meaning-making. However, a multimodal socio-semiotic approach to learning moves forward and posits a quite different metaphor: learning as transformation. Albeit to some extent compatible with the notion of expansion, this metaphor has further theoretical implications for shifting toward an alternative ideology: learning cannot be just understood *in communication*, but rather *as communication*. Any material transformation in a sign can, in fact, be taken as evidence of learning. From this particular perspective, learning is the agentive transformation of signs (available to meaning-makers) that takes place in any communicative event and social practice. Thus, learning may—or may not—lead to the expansion of resources, but it certainly does have a transformative effect on the environment (i.e. the available signs), on the sign-maker (who does the actual transformation), on the interpreter and on the actual materiality of the sign, all of which come to change as transformation takes place. To restate, from this perspective learning is transforming signs and their materiality for particular communicative purposes regardless of whether such transformation leads—or not—to expansion. This continuous transformative nature of meaning-making, signs and learning is key to a multimodal socio-semiotic approach.

Previously in the chapter, it was made explicit that meaning-making is in itself multi-semiotic and multimodal: a sign is, in fact, the actual materialization of such multi-semiotic work (Stein 2008). Along these lines—and to restate—we can assume that learning is the agentive production of signs in a given environment and the actual instantiation of choices through available semiotic modes and media. I use *agentive* here in the sense that the sign-maker's design of a sign responds to the ideological purposes of sign-making and to what they want to represent and communicate to others (Bezemer and Kress 2016), as will be explained later in the *Learner as Sign-Maker* section.

Sign-making does not represent the reproduction of previously established meanings (Kress 2000a, b). On the contrary, learning is evident in the transformation of previous meanings into new meanings which represent the (ideological) interests of the producer (Bezemer and Kress 2016; Kress 2000a, b; Kress et al. 2001) in a given time and place: no two signs are identical, neither are identical the contexts of sign production and interpretation.

In the work of Kress (2015a, b) learning as transformation foregrounds the sign-maker's agency in this transformative process in which they make decisions about the design and materiality of the sign as designed for a particular audience. However—as explained earlier—it also considers how agency is restricted by the way resources have historically and culturally developed, as addressed in the works of Hasan (1984) and Halliday (2014) for verbal resources, and Kress and van Leeuwen (2001, 2006) and van Leeuwen (2005) for semiotic resources in general. The focus on both *affordances* and *restrictions* semiotic resources provide sign-makers allows us to understand that meaning is created within choices. Choices and meaning-making potentials are closely linked since semiotic resources provide us with meaning potentials which can, in turn, be put to infinite uses.[3] The notions of *repertoire* and *reservoir* previously defined clearly illustrate this. The overall meaning-making potential (reservoir) belongs to culture as a collective system while the individual resources for meaning-making (repertoire) are drawn from this collective system that develops socially and historically (Halliday 2001; Martin and Rose 2007; Matthiessen et al. 2010).

Learning as transformation, then, brings into the picture the sign-maker, the interpreter, the environment and the resources available for sign-making. Through noticing and engaging with particular aspects of the complex environment, sign-makers engage in sign transformation giving way to for interaction/communication/learning. Noticing, engaging and transforming particular aspects of an available sign occur as a sort of "prompt" that can be initiated by the sign-maker themselves or by a shaping agent. In this manner, two different routes of learning can be identified.

Bezemer and Kress (2016) state that route A is the learning that occurs by self-initiation, while route B is originated by a shaping agent who initiates and shapes the process of another's learning, as typically occurs in formal instruction. For both cases, the authors state that what can count as "evidence of learning" within this view are *signs of engagement* and *signs of learning*.

Signs of engagement are the socially and interactively meaningful ways in which sign-makers respond *to* and *in* the environment, and in which they demonstrate their attention or interest at a particular moment. For instance, Bezemer and Kress (2016) discuss how a student's change in posture during a lesson can be indicative of her engagement, demonstrating attention. They also underscore the fact that *signs of engagement* are also multimodal (gaze, gesture, speech, etc.) and they can even be originated by non-human participants. For instance, a cursor and its placement within the computer screen can be a sign of a learner's engagement with a particular element.

Signs of engagement offer cues on signs of learning by demonstrating sign-makers' orientation and/or attention to particular elements of their environment. When exploring signs of engagement over time, Bezemer and Kress (2016) suggest, we can reflect on learning, or the socially meaningful transformation of signs. In other words, for a sign-maker to appropriate and transform an available sign, they need to first have attended to and engaged with it in a particular environment.

Learning and Recognition

As was stated previously, learning can be initiated by the very learner (route A) or by a shaping agent (route B), as the case of formal education. Route B implies that—at least—two sign-makers (let us say, teacher and student) come together and that one of them shapes or prompts learning. In formal education, this shaping of learning takes place in many ways and at many different scales (see Chaps. 5, 6 and 7): shaping occurs in classroom interaction, policies, curriculum, students' interaction with curriculum artifacts, prompts and task designs, among many others. All these elements and circumstances offer signs for students to respond to and transform in a continuous semiotic chain of meaning-making. Such notion of learning as transformation is desirable—in theory and in practice—as a means to recognize all the semiotic labor students do (with peers, experts, artifacts, etc.), but at the same time it conflicts with traditional agenda of schools in reinforcing authority, power and control. Here, we stumble upon a practical—but fundamental—problem: while full recognition of students' semiotic work is needed to account for learning, such full recognition is usually impeded by the notions of learning that cut across many classrooms and schools and that permeates curriculum artifacts such as tests, metrics and assessments.

One of the biggest challenges of positing learning as agentive transformation is that it differs greatly from (still) dominant teaching and learning practices or, in other words, that the implications of this alternative ideology of learning do not fit the purposes of traditional schooling in reproducing power relations and identities. Learning is usually perceived as something that happens once in a while, something that can be completely engineered by external (usually teacher's or textbooks') design, something that does not happen to everyone to the same extent, something that can be completely grasped and measured by metrics. Such sort of fetishism contributes to reinforcing the power and authority of the shaping agent in causing or at least helping to cause a qualitative or quantitative change in the learner. My point here is not to criticize the teacher's role in assisting learning. On the contrary, such role as a shaping agent is paramount in formal education and is also paramount in an alternative ideology of learning. On the contrary, my purpose is to reflect on the fact that traditional ideologies of learning are not innocent in reproducing power relations and authority; not fully recognizing the learner is a way of complying (and assuring they will keep on complying) to the established authority and power. Such ideologies are not fair to teachers either in that they place them in an uncomfortable role in which they are not equipped with the instruments to recognize all—or at least a lot—of the learning that takes place in their classrooms which, in turn, does not give full recognition to their own work as teachers. The question we should ask as researchers and practitioners is not *what or how do students learn?* but instead *what can we recognize about their learning and how?*

This radical change in perspective is clearly illustrated by Bezemer and Kress (2016), who provocatively begin Chap. 3 of their book by turning around the traditional question of what learning is. Instead of asking *what is learning* (a question that at first sight might identify us with a particular theory or paradigm depending on what our response is), they ask *what is not learning*. This leads us to another key concept for a multimodal socio-semiotic approach to learning as transformation: recognition. According to Kress (2013), still dominant school practices tend to capture only a small portion of all the transformative semiotic work students do in the classroom. Present forms of assessment and metrics respond to what I call here traditional ideologies of learning, focusing on learning as acquisition and competence. This, according to the author, leads to a sort of misrecognition: learning, teaching practices and their effects are not captured to its fullest by traditional school practices. To recognize learning, then, requires us to design forms of assessment which allow us to account for students' agency in meaning-making (learning) as well as to account for the underlying principles students draw on when transforming signs.

This view implies a radical change in what is conceived or legitimated as learning in both formal and informal learning contexts. For this reason, a *culture of recognition* (Kress and Selander 2012) or a *generosity of recognition* (Bezemer and Kress 2016) is required to underscore the semiotic work by learners across modes and media. As expressed by Kress (2013, 124), educational research—and teaching practices—still lacks *tools for recognition*, that is, organized and institutionalized ways to (appropriately) recognize the semiotic work of students in different modes, media, genres, and so on to account for the actual learning (as transformation). In general, the tools and instruments employed to "assess" learning are highly standardized tests which aim to quantify the learning process or the learning outcomes. These tools are dominant within the traditional ideology of learning and still govern assessment practices in schools. In terms of theory—but also in terms of praxis—recognition has the potential to make visible most of the semiotic transformative work students do in the classroom (Manghi 2017) and to provide an ethical framework for education in which the semiotic work of a group is not privileged over others (Kress 2015a). To date, attempts to further recognize students' semiotic work might occur at the level of classroom practices or may be initiated by teachers, generally without planned or systematic support by other stakeholders, tools and instruments. However, policy can eventually play a key role in this.

Learning and Recognition: An Example from the Classroom

The idea that a lot of the meanings students make in the classroom passes unnoticed may not be new to a teacher: policy regulations, school expectations, curriculum design and many other phenomena pose structural constraints on teacher's agency and shape classroom goals. Any teacher knows that not all of students' actual semiotic work is valuated and recognized. However, what might be new is to think that all semiotic work requires transformation and therefore involves learning. The question, then, is what researchers and practitioners can do to expand our notion

3 Toward a Multimodal Socio-Semiotic Account of Learning

of learning so as to appraise students' semiotic work in its full potential. Chapters 7 and 8 address this issue in more detail. This section presents a brief illustrative classroom example that offers just a hint on how micro events which might appear irrelevant at first sight are in fact revealing of the transformative semiotic work of students engaged in making meanings.

The EFL teacher, Vera, uses the language textbook to explain the concept of daily routines in her beginners' lesson. In terms of the official foreign language curriculum, this implies providing students with the required vocabulary (action verbs, adverbs of time and frequency), functions (telling the time) and some grammar structures (declarative sentences in the present tense, SVO order in English), all of which pertain to verbal resources in the foreign language and not to any other semiotic resources. After completing many tasks and activities in which students are exposed to all these points of the EFL curriculum, Vera requires students to use their laptops to make a short comic strip with their own routines. Image 3.1 shows one of the comic strips that one student (S7) made with the *PlayComic* software.

As a final assessment activity, Vera would go to each student's desk and ask them to explain how they made their comic and in what ways the comic represented their daily routine. In other words, she asked students to somehow overtly recall their own meaning-making processes and make them available to her. Extract 3.1 is part of her interaction with S7 in which they are going over the comic strip that reads *"I go to high school at 7:30 am"*.

Image 3.1 S7's *"I go to high school at 7:30"* with PlayComic

Extract 3.1 Vera and S7 during S7's explanation of her daily routine comic (Unit 2, Day 12)

V: And what about this one? (points to a strip in the comic)
S7: Ah, I go to school early…very early (laughs)
V: At what time?
S7: Seven-thirty.
V: Oh, it is early. So you walk to school, you don't go by car or bus?
S7: Eh, yes. Walk. Very…Very rápido (*fast*) because always late. Very very rápido (*fast*) (points to the smoke next to her feet in the cartoon) ¿Viste? El humo… corro para no llegar tarde (*the smoke is because I run so as not to be late*)
V: Oh, I see. So you go running, not walking.
S7: Yes.

S7's sign visually depicts her rushing. This can easily be noted by the way her feet and arms are positioned in the representation, by how she is out in the street but still she is still holding her bag-pack (as if she still hasn't got time to put it on) and also by the smoke next to her feet, which is frequently used in cartoons to indicate rapid movements. However, the written declarative statement reads: *I go to high school at 7:30 am*. This statement in itself complies with a lot of the expectations as far as she uses a declarative structure to offer new information to the audience, she uses the expected preposition (*at*) for telling the time, she uses present tense to signal a daily routine, among other things. However, the meanings S7 made are far more complex than this.

What does this brief classroom extract tell us about a multimodal socio-semiotic approach to learning and about recognition as a key concept to such approach? Or, in other words, what does this tell us about the alternative ideology of learning I have been describing? From a traditional perspective, an EFL curriculum focuses on verbal meanings, and it might even focus exclusively on verbal meanings which are made in the target language. Non-verbal modal resources are not taken into account or are considered mere ornaments to verbal communication. Verbal resources which do not belong to the foreign language might not even be considered either. Neither are taken into account the many ways in which writing and speech can ensemble, orchestrate and interact with other modes in particular signs, such as the way semiotic labor is divided in the cartoon.

3 Toward a Multimodal Socio-Semiotic Account of Learning

In Extract 3.1 it becomes clear that for S7 it is important to tell her audience that she has to rush to school in the morning, as she explains to the teacher. By her choice of the verb *go* to represent her experience as she moves from her house to her school and her visual choice of representing herself rushing or running to school (by adding the smoke next to her feet), S7 is dividing semiotic labor among modes to make a complex sign which needs to be considered as a whole. If the interpreter—in this case the teacher—only foregrounds writing against the interview with S7, then the student will be characterized as not being able to make certain specific meanings since *go* seems too general to index *rushing* (*go* is by definition an umbrella term for many *ways of going* which include more specific verbs, such as *run*, *rush*, etc.). This type of interpretation draws on the traditional deficit ideology which focuses on what a sign-maker does not seem to be able to do (verbally). Such interpretation would lead the teacher to think that S7 does not have the required "competence" or "ability" to communicate such delicate meanings in the foreign language, regardless of the fact that for the genre at hand visual resources are more specialized for such purposes. This interpretation can be said to carry two main problems in terms of recognition: on the one hand it seems to view communication exclusively as linguistic achievement, and on the other hand it fails to grasp the actual situatedness of meaning-making processes. Upon appraising what the environment offers–as the available signs, modes, media and artifacts for making meanings, the student divides semiotic labor among modes so as to represent and communicate what she wants to her audience. The fact that she goes to school at 7:30 (and not to any place else) is communicated by writing and the fact that she has to rush so as not to be late (and therefore she cannot, for instance, walk or stroll to school) is communicated visually.

An alternative ideology of learning foregrounds what the student as sign-maker was able to do and how she was able to do it. This would require recognition of as much of her agency and semiotic work as possible. It would also require us to foreground the multimodal orchestration and the underlying principles that shape her sign-making process and to recognize the fact that not all of the semiotic work is done by written or oral resources. In fact, an alternative ideology of learning focuses on the fact that the student is able to draw on her experience with previous cartoons to cater for the fact that in this genre it is not only possible—but also expected—to specify certain meanings—like ways of doing things—visually, such as is the case of the smoke next to her feet to indicate rushing.

As can be noted from this brief example, such alternative ideology foregrounds the fact that the student is not a *user* of a semiotic system (a system that already exists in full, is fixed and stable); on the contrary, she is a *sign-maker* who draws on contextual and environmentally bound affordances to make new meanings. To better explain this, I will next describe the notions of *interest* and *criticality* in sign-making, which account for the ways in which S7 decides how and what to represent in her cartoon to her audience.

Learner as Sign-maker: Interest and Criteriality

From what was discussed in the previous sections, it becomes evident that to better capture learning we need to attend to signs of engagement and signs of learning that may pass unnoticed in traditional education. This is fundamental for teaching practices to recognize actual signs of learning in learners' meaning-making processes.

Along these lines, there are two concepts entailed in sign-making processes which account for the agentive nature of sign transformation: *interest* and *criteriality* (Kress 2015a). Interest refers to the particular uses to which modes are put with regards to what the sign-maker wants to communicate and to whom. Criteriality refers to how representation is made based on what is considered—by the sign-maker—to be "enough" in representation. As Kress (2004, 18) puts it: "it is the interest of the sign-maker which determines what is regarded as criterial about an entity to be represented; that which is criterial determines what is to be represented about that entity; and only what is seen as criterial is represented".

Sign-makers' interest and criteriality, however, are restricted by the modal resources and media available to them. Restrictions, again, occur both historically and contextually. Historically, the culture shapes what modes will be used and for what purposes, resulting in the functionalization of modal resources (Kress and van Leeuwen 2001). On the other hand, sign-makers also make meanings with the resources a particular environment offers for representation and communication in a particular place and time (Kress 2010; van Leeuwen 2005). From the point of view of formal learning environments, these two restrictions on meaning-making processes need to be taken into account in assessment (Bezemer and Kress 2016). In other words, in trying to design tools for recognition such as assessment instruments, we need to consider both the modes chosen for representation and communication, as well as the purposes modal resources serve. For instance, in the previous example of making a comic about her daily routine, we can argue that written resources for specifying the meaning of "go" may not have been made available in the environment for the student to draw on or simply that it was not available to her at that particular time and space. There is no further evidence to analyze this, but there is evidence to further analyze what she actually did: to use some available visual resources to specify certain meanings. The way in which she used these visual resources requires an understanding of the artifact and its affordances as well as an understanding of the genre at hand and what can/should be done to comply with certain genre expectations, and even an understanding of what and how one can communicate to the audience.

The remainder of this chapter focuses on three key concepts for a multimodal socio-semiotic account of learning in formal education: the classroom, sign-maker's agency and artifacts.

The Classroom from a Multimodal Socio-semiotic Perspective

Far from being just a physical space, the classroom constitutes a designed environment for teaching and learning which responds to values and ideologies of learning attempting to shape the behavior of those inhabiting such space, namely teachers and students (Kress et al. 2005; Lawn 1999). Classroom practices, then, are embedded in historical and cultural processes which shape—from the perspective of design—what classrooms are to be and what classrooms participants are to do. What meanings can be made, or what meanings are legitimated as learning, depend on these historical and cultural processes.

Actual classrooms, however, negotiate these meanings, since they may accept or to some extent re-shape, contest or reject expectations/impositions by school administrators, policy-makers and other stakeholders. The actual classroom, as an instantiation of potential classrooms constructed historically and culturally, can be understood as a site in which pedagogical discourse mediates top-down policies and its enactment.

For the purpose of this book, I am particularly interested in drawing on two notions of the classrooms from—what I believe to be—two complementary approaches to social semiotics. These notions are: the classroom as a (multimodal) sign (Kress 2005) and the classroom as an ecology (Tudor 2001; van Lier 2004a, b).

To my mind, the classroom as *sign* shows two aspects of the classroom: the classroom as instantiation (or the classroom as a complex "text") and the classroom as a potentiality (the classroom as a more abstract social practice). Along these lines, by stating that the classroom is a multimodal sign it becomes clear that the classroom responds to wider social and historical structures and practices (Kress et al. 2005) while, at the same time, as an instantiation it also has the potential to change them. In every classroom, design, display, visuals, sitting arrangement, furniture arrangement, among others, make up a complex sign that multimodally shapes—and is shaped by—meaning-making processes and pedagogical practices. This notion of the classroom foregrounds it as semiotic sediment of practices of different orders (cultural, social, institutional) over time, which respond to particular expectations about social relations, roles, power differences, among others.

Complementarily, I also draw on the notion of the classroom as an *ecology*. The classroom—as a site—belongs to wider ecosystems which interact with it and operate on it—while at the same time are operated by it, such as institutions, homes, and so on. The metaphor of the classroom as an ecology helps to debunk traditional notions in teaching which see the classroom as a space that attempts to represent or mirror the outside world, instead of as a space of its own right, with particular values, practices and discourses (Tudor 2001). By drawing on the *ecology* metaphor I intend to foreground the historical, cultural and contextual complexity of semiotic work, as entailed in the notion of ecosystems (Lemke 2000; van Lier 2004a). At the same time, the metaphor accounts for the many scales which interact with the classroom: society at large, policy-making processes, school policing, and so on represent interacting and overlapping ecosystems.

The classroom as both sign and ecology foregrounds the idea that participants are not in themselves the unit of analysis; instead the unit of analysis is the interaction of participants, artifacts and the spaces they co-habit in the process of making meanings, which are key elements to understanding the signs they produce in particular contexts.

Artifacts and Sign-makers in the Classroom

Artifacts are products of human culture which, at the same time, produce and reproduce culture. As such, artifacts can be conceptualized as either physical (material) or cognitive objects. They are experiential mediators between humans and objects (Vygotsky 1978) and they help us perform certain tasks and make sense of the world around us. For the purposes of this study, I am particularly interested in the fact that artifacts are semiotic objects that represent the sedimental history of previous meaning-making processes. Along the same lines, the significance of these artifacts is linked to the social and cultural norms that govern the uses artifacts can/will be put to. However, the restrictions artifacts producers may impose on users interact with users' agency as well (Hakkarainen et al. 2013). In other words, part of a sign-maker's situated agency lies in the possibility to negotiate how design and use shape one another.

The concept of artifact, as Engeström (1987, 2001) puts it, overcomes the theoretical notion of the individual in isolation. It helps us to understand that individuals cannot be captured without their cultural means and that social practices cannot be understood without the individual and collective agency in producing and using artifacts. Throughout the book, I will refer to artifacts in their material manifestation only (as *material semiotic artifacts*, Lemke 2000, or *object-artefact*, Bezemer and Kress 2008). Although I do acknowledge the existence of mental artifacts and their importance for other types of analyses, the book mainly focuses on artifacts of material nature as manifested in classrooms, and in particular it focuses on two: textbooks and laptops, which seem to distribute a lot of the semiotic work in many classrooms.

The classroom environment is inhabited by many material artifacts which can interactively be framed and oriented to by participants as *curriculum artifacts*, that is, as pertaining to the pedagogy and ends of schooling and formal education. Artifacts help to mediate (authorized) meaning-making processes in the lesson and in curriculum enactment. From this perspective, it becomes clear that artifacts are not just tools for transmitting curricular content. Instead, they are tightly linked to the educational processes in which they are implicated, and so "their effects on education are described as transformation processes in which both human practice, but also the material objects themselves are changed" (Röhl 2015, 122).

Some of these artifacts—mainly, the printed textbook—have a long tradition of authorization for learning (Luke et al. 1989) and still continue to be widely used in education despite the rise of digital tools and platforms (Bezemer and Kress 2015). Other artifacts, on the other hand, have been introduced much more recently; this is the case of laptops in Uruguayan education (see Chap. 4). According to Blyth (2009), such technology artifacts are *marked* in (foreign language) teaching and learning practices, unlike the printed textbook which—for its long-standing tradition—has been naturalized as an everyday curriculum artifact. Despite this difference, each of these artifacts provides learners with particular affordances for learning and for experiencing what is known as the *lived curriculum* (Lemke 1990).

Throughout the book I will use *technology artifact* to refer to the XO laptops. All material artifacts are, in some way, technological, since they represent the dialectics between human action and culture. However, students, teachers, policy-makers and society at large do not orient to all artifacts as being *technological*. For that reason, I choose to use the expression *technology artifacts* to describe the artifacts to which participants orient as such.

To understand how artifacts contribute to meaning-making, an important issue to discuss is human-artifact interaction, or how sign-makers and artifact distribute labor to make meanings in the classroom. Both activity theory and actor network theory underscore this. Activity theory assumes artifacts and humans have *asymmetrical* relations and statuses (Engeström 1987; Kaptelinin and Nardi 2006; Sannino et al. 2009; van Oers et al. 2008), favoring human's agency. Actor network theory, on the contrary, assumes both builder—or user—and object need to be theoretically and methodologically addressed as equals (Latour 1987, 2006). More recently, practice theory has drawn on Latour's actor network theory, but prioritizes human agency while still positing material artifacts also have agency (Röhl 2015; Schatzki 2001).

Despite some differences, all these approaches to human-artifact interaction highlight the cultural and social relevance of artifacts in making meanings, taking into account events of different scales, avoiding simplistic mono-causal explanations and underscoring that action is distributed among humans and artifacts (Miettinen 2009). These are the theoretical assumptions that underlie my analysis of learner-artifact interaction in Chap. 7.

Agency and the Learner: Artifact Interaction in the Classroom

Generally defined in the social sciences as the effect agents have on the social world through their actions (Dowding 2011), agency has become a key issue in education. This definition, albeit simple, has proven problematic because it leaves many questions unanswered, mainly those regarding whether agents need to be human, whether they need to be individuals (and not collective groups), whether their actions need to be consciously planned and intentional, among others (Ahearn 2001). To complicate things further, it is also important to bear in mind that agency becomes instantiated in both what people do and what people resist doing or do in a different way from what is expected (Giddens 1984).

Throughout the book I will consider agents as either individual, collective or even institutional entities which act (considering both acting and resisting action as forms of action) in the social world to make meanings.

Their agency is necessarily influenced and shaped by many structural and environmental factors (Dowding 2011), which are constitutive of the spaces in which they act. In light of the previous section, I shall discuss agency as linked to two aspects of technology in classrooms: *artifact use* and *sign-making*.

Critical studies that attack the use of technology in education view agency from a top-down perspective, focusing on structural relations of power and top-down policies and actions. However, there are other critical—and more situated—ways to explore the ways in which technology can be used in education, such as focusing on what users (teachers, learners, etc.) do and what they can potentially do with it (Jewitt 2006), as well as exploring the affordances artifacts offer them. This allows us to foreground individual and situated agency, at the same time that environmental factors that shape the classroom ecology and that may restrict agency are also considered.

An important aspect of exploring agency in the classroom has been the analysis of how users interact with semiotic (Lemke 2000), curriculum (Guerrettatz and Johnston 2013) artifacts such as textbooks and laptops, but also how they interact with other aspects of classroom design. As an example, Kress et al. (2005) have shown how the design and architecture of space in a classroom does not completely shape how users will interact with it. Instead, they show how meaning-making processes are dialectically intertwined in design and practice. In the same vein, a study in an English as a Second Language classroom by Guerrettatz and Johnston (2013) shows the ways in which curriculum artifacts (such as the textbook, classroom tasks, lesson plans), classroom activities and classroom interactions are in a dialectical relation, showing that meaning-making processes in the classroom depend on the interplay of many artifacts and social actors within the ecology. Attending to the ecology of the classroom, then, is fundamental to understand artifact-user interaction and agency.

As for how agency relates to sign-making in the classroom, multimodal socio-semiotic analyses have demonstrated that learning requires students to appropriate previous signs in order to transform them into new signs that fit the ideological interests of sign-makers (Kress 2000a, b; Kress et al. 2001), as posed by the definition of learning previously discussed.

3 Toward a Multimodal Socio-Semiotic Account of Learning

The question of what affordances technology artifacts provide sign-makers to make meanings also pertains to agency, since meaning-making processes are mediated by these artifacts. New technology allows for new ways of producing meanings (Lemke 2011). There are new possibilities to create, disseminate and distribute their own multimodal texts in more mobile contexts of production and reception (Leander and Vasudevan 2009). I believe one of the potential contributions of teaching as recognition of students' learning, in this respect, is to account for these contexts for production, circulation and interpretations of the signs students make in the classroom (see Chap. 7).

In the following chapters I will discuss students' agency as sign-makers, that is to say, as learners. This will allow me to look into students' agency from two complementary—albeit not identical—perspectives. On the one hand, by looking at classroom events in which learners interact with and upon the technology in classroom tasks carefully designed by the teacher, I will be able to look into how such design opens a space for students to become agents by exploring, for instance, different features, affordances and limitations the technology (and the environment in which it is used) offers. This is probably more aligned with how the School of Sydney orients to agency, by looking at the role of the teacher in designing pedagogy and curriculum for their students. On the other hand, I will explore students' agency as evinced in the signs they make by analyzing the principles underlying these signs. This foregrounds students' interest and criteriality regardless of whether this complies—or not—with the expectations by the teacher, the school or the curriculum. Both ways of approaching agency in learning will allow me to explore the two sides of recognition: teacher/student; shaping agent/learner; interpreter/sign-maker.

Multimodal Socio-semiotic Approach to Learning and Additional Language Studies

The discussion of Image 3.1 and Extract 3.1 hints to some of the main differences between traditional and alternative ideologies of learning. Such shift is in fact a challenge to any content subject and certainly a bigger challenge for language education because it requires us to de-center language to re-center communication as a multimodal phenomenon and to foreground sign-makers' agency in representing and communicating with others.

The analyses and discussions throughout this book draw on empirical data of an EFL classroom in which educational policy dictated students should learn the foreign language with technology (laptops). Choosing to explore learning from a multimodal socio-semiotic perspective in a foreign or additional language classroom is by no means innocent or random. A language classroom is potentially an excellent—and at the same time challenging—site to explore the tensions between traditional and alternative ideologies of learning. One of the main reasons for this, as I shall explain next, is the fact that "teaching and learning a language" has traditionally resulted in foregrounding and legitimating verbal (written and oral) resources as the sole modes engaged in communication and learning. In fact, this is done by backgrounding the role of other semiotic resources. This tension may—in principle—not be so apparent in other content subjects and a multimodal socio-semiotic approach to learning has a lot to offer to elucidate this issue. This does not mean that further recognition of semiotic work is only required in language classrooms, it only means that historically and culturally teaching a language has reinforced long-ingrained traditional ideologies of learning in particular ways.

A close partnership between theoretical and practical knowledge of a school subject and a multimodal socio-semiotic framework allows us to explore how meaning-making is achieved through various modal resources in the classroom. This is important for researchers and practitioners to better understand the socio-semiotic and multimodal nature of communication and learning in formal education. However, it is fair to

3 Toward a Multimodal Socio-Semiotic Account of Learning

say that so far some disciplines have lent themselves more than others to such partnership.

There are detailed accounts of social semiosis, multimodality and learning in school subjects as English, Composition, Rhetoric (Bowen and Whithaus 2013; Jewitt 2006; Kress et al. 2005; Miller and McVee 2012), science education (Kress et al. 2001; Lemke 1998), history and biology (Manghi Haquin 2013), to name a few.

In the field of additional language education studies, the need to underscore multimodality as key to fully understanding literacy is now advocated more strongly (Block 2013; Lin 2012; Royce 2002). However, the articulation of social semiotics, multimodality and additional language studies has not been easy, and the field of additional language studies has had a quite different turn if compared to other disciplines. Whereas multimodality becomes a common term in the field, it is usually part of theoretical constructs that draw on rather traditional notions such as that of *(multimodal) communicative competence* (Royce 2002, 2007; Lotherington and Ronda 2012).

This is not to say that multimodality has not started to permeate the field—on the contrary, the term has become very popular in a short amount of time, but it is fair to say that still the field draws on constructs that derive from traditional ideologies of learning. This problem seems logical, since adopting a socio-semiotic and multimodal approach to learning requires, by definition, that we de-center writing and speech as the modes of communication and learning to focus on the vary many modal resources, ensembles and orchestrations engaged in any social practice. Such an approach, then, seems to attempt against the traditional identity of additional language studies built upon the notion that language played a key role in communication and learning and that all other semiotic resources were either subjected to it or mere ornaments to verbal communication. This point becomes clear if we consider the discussion around Image 3.1 and Extract 3.1. From a traditional approach, we could argue that the fact that the student chooses the verb "go" while visually represents her action as rushing and running to school shows that she is lexically unable to specify certain meanings; or we could even suggest that she is using visuals *strategically* to compensate for her lack of more specific vocabulary.[4] All these ways of looking at S7's sign atomize communication by presupposing writing is the main mode engaged in meaning-making processes and by concomitantly assuming non-verbal resources are either ornamental or strategic to paper over the cracks of a deficiency in (linguistic) communication.

In this complicated disciplinary context, a main fact emerges as fundamental to understand how and why multimodality is—to my mind—finding it hard to call for its legitimate place in language education and additional language studies. Language—speech and writing—is to a great extent still thought of as the legitimate and sole instrument of communication and learning. Block (2013) calls this a *linguistic bias* or "a tendency to conceive of communicative practices exclusively in terms of the linguistic (morphology, syntax, phonology, lexis) although the linguistic is often complemented with a consideration of pragmatics, interculturalism and learning strategies" (56). In broader terms, Kress (2000a) had also noted this when he stated that the field of language education holds a rather conservative view about communication, for which understanding the compositionality of verbal language alone seems to be enough.

Along these lines, this book hopes to contribute to our current understanding of learning as transformation from a socio-semiotic perspective and, at the same time, to contribute to the field of second and additional language studies and its shift from traditional to alternative ideologies of learning so as to foster more and better recognition of students' semiotic work in the classroom. Current education policies—which foster the use of technology in schools—can play a key role in this shift, as long as the use of technology artifacts is framed in ways in which students' situated agency in sign-making can be better recognized and as long as the multimodal transformative nature of their semiotic work is accounted for.

Conclusions

While there are apparent advantages to expanding our notion of learning and communication in multimodal terms, this book argues that this is not enough and attempts to demonstrate that such change in the fields of education and language studies should be accompanied by a shift from the traditional notion of competence to the socio-semiotic notion of transformation. It is only through such adoption that students' meaning-making processes will begin to be better recognized by means of coherent and more generous accounts of learning, school practices and instruments of assessment.

Along these lines, in Chap. 4 I will present Plan Ceibal and Plan Ceibal en Inglés policy as well as the socio-political and demographic profile of Uruguayan education. This will provide the reader with a detailed context of the education and language policy under investigation. Chapters 5, 6 and 7 will investigate different scales of Plan Ceibal implementation and enactment and how within and across these scales meanings are made about and with technology inside and outside of the EFL classroom. Such meanings contribute to framing the policy, framing learning and even positioning individuals in different ways with regards to the political, social and educational aspects of the policy. Throughout the analysis chapters I will explore what technology, EFL and learning means across several scales of the policy. This will shed light on the enactment of the policy and, in more general terms, on recognition and how learning is recognized in different ways and to different extents depending on what scale is considered and how each scale makes meaning of technology and EFL.

Notes

1. There were, of course, previous approaches to discourse that catered for how modes intersect, such as visuals and writing. See, for instance, the work of Barthes (1977) and Angenot (1985), just to name a few.
2. For a thorough theorization of the role of schools and their potential in favoring literacy as meaning-making, see Kalantzis and Cope (2000) and Luke (2000), just to name a few.
3. For a discussion on verbal language, see Hasan (1984) and for a wider discussion on semiotic resources in general, see van Leeuwen (2005).
4. Often times in additional language learning theories, non-verbal resources have been considered to be used strategically to compensate for the lack of verbal resources in communication, as a sort of compensatory strategy. For instance, in the traditional definition of *communicative competence* (Canale and Swain 1980; Canale 1983), *strategic competence* is a sub-

component which accounts for verbal and non-verbal resources used to compensate for communication problems in the target language, pointing to what the individual hasn't still acquired or learned.

References

Adami, E., & Kress, G. (2014). Introduction: Multimodality, Meaning Making and the Issue of Text. *Text & Talk, 34*(3), 231–237. https://doi.org/10.1515/text-2014-0007

Ahearn, L. (2001). Language and Agency. *Annual Review of Anthropology, 30*, 109–137.

Alexander, B. (2006). A Threat to Professional Identity? The Resistance to Computer Mediated Teaching. In M. Hanrahan & D. L. Madsen (Eds.), *Teaching, Technology, Textuality. Approaches to New Media* (pp. 27–35). New York: Palgrave Macmillan.

Angenot, M. (1985). *Critique de la raison sémiotique*. Montréal: Presses de L´Université de Montréal.

Apple, M. W. (2003). The State and the Politics of Knowledge. In M. W. Apple (Ed.), *The State and the Politics of Knowledge* (pp. 1–23). New York: Routledge Falmer.

Apple, M. W., & Jungck, S. (1998). "You Don't Have to be a Teacher to Teach this Unit": Teaching, Technology and Control in the Classroom. In H. Bromley & M. W. Apple (Eds.), *Education/Technology/Power. Educational Computing as a Social Practice* (pp. 133–155). New York: State University of New York Press.

Barthes, R. (1977). *Image, Music, Text*. London: Fontana.

Bezemer, J., & Kress, G. (2008). Writing in Multimodal Texts: A Social Semiotic Account of Design for Learning. *Written Communication, 25*(2), 165–195. https://doi.org/10.1177/0741088307313177

Bezemer, J., & Kress, G. (2015). The Textbook in a Changing Multimodal Landscape. In N. M. Klug & H. Stöckl (Eds.), *Language in Multimodal Contexts* (pp. 21–28). New York: De Gruyter.

Bezemer, J., & Kress, G. (2016). *Multimodality, Learning and Communication. A Social Semiotic Framework*. London and New York: Routledge.

Block, D. (2013). Moving Beyond "Lingualism": Multilingual Embodiment and Multimodality in SLA. In S. May (Ed.), *The Multilingual Turn.*

Implications for SLA, TESOL and Bilingual Education (pp. 54–77). New York and London: Routledge.

Blyth, C. (2009). From Textbook to Online Materials: The Changing Ecology of Foreign Language Publishing in an Era of ICT. In M. Evans (Ed.), *Foreign Language Learning with Digital Technologies* (pp. 174–202). London and New York: Continuum.

Boody, R. M. (2001). On the Relationship of Education and Technology. In R. Muffoletto (Ed.), *Education and Technology: Critical and Reflective Practices* (pp. 5–22). Cresskill, NJ: Hampton Press.

Bowen, T., & Whithaus, C. E. (2013). *Multimodal Literacies and Emerging Genres*. Pittsburgh: University of Pittsburgh Press.

Bromley, H., & Apple, M. W. (Eds.). (1998). *Education/Technology/Power. Educational Computing as a Social Practice*. New York: State University of New York Press.

Canale, M. (1983). From Communicative Competence to Communicative Language Pedagogy. In J. C. Richards & R. W. Schmidt (Eds.), *Language and Communication* (pp. 2–27). London: Longman.

Canale, M., & Swain, M. (1980). Theoretical Basis of Communicative Approaches to Second Language Teaching and Testing. *Applied Linguistics, 1*(1), 1–47. https://doi.org/10.1093/applin/I.1.1

Christie, F. (2002). *Classroom Discourse Analysis. A Functional Perspective*. London and New York: Continuum.

Dowding, K. (Ed.). (2011). *Encyclopedia of Power*. London and Washington, DC: Sage.

Dreyfus, S. J., Humphrey, S., Mahbob, A., & Martin, J. R. (2016). *Genre Pedagogy in Higher Education. The SLATE Project*. London: Palgrave Macmillan.

Engeström, Y. (1987). *Learning by Expanding. An Activity-Theoretical Approach to Developmental Research*. Helsinki: Orienta-Konsuiltit.

Engeström, Y. (2001). Expansive Learning at Work: Toward an Activity Theoretical Reconceptualization. *Journal of Education and Work, 14*(1), 133–156. https://doi.org/10.1080/13639080020028747

Fairclough, N. (2003). *Analysing Discourse*. London and New York: Routledge.

Gee, J. P. (2000). New People in New Worlds: Networks, the New Capitalism and Schools. In B. Cope & M. Kalantzis (Eds.), *Multiliteracies. Literacy Learning and the Design of Social Futures* (pp. 41–66). London and New York: Routledge.

Gee, J. P. (2007). *What Video Games have to Teach Us about Learning and Literacy*. New York: Palgrave Macmillan.

Giddens, A. (1984). *The Constitution of Society: Outline of the Theory of Structuration*. Berkeley: University of California Press.

Guerrettatz, A. M., & Johnston, B. (2013). Materials in the Classroom Ecology. *The Modern Language Journal, 97*(3), 779–796. https://doi.org/10.1111/j.1540-4781.2013.12027.x

Hakkarainen, K., Paavola, S., Kangas, K., & Seitamma-Hakkarainen, P. (2013). Sociocultural Perspectives on Collaborative Learning: Toward Collaborative Knowledge Creation. In C. E. Hmelo-Silver, C. A. Chinn, C. K. K. Chan, & A. O'Donnell (Eds.), *The International Handbook of Collaborative Learning* (pp. 57–73). New York: Routledge.

Halliday, M. A. K. (1974/2004). A Sociosemiotic Perspective on Language Development. In J. Webster (Ed.), *The Language of Early Childhood* (pp. 90–111). London and New York: Continuum.

Halliday, M. A. K. (1993). Towards a Language-based Theory of Learning. *Linguistics and Education, 5*, 93–116. https://doi.org/10.1016/0898-5898(93)90026-7

Halliday, M. A. K. (1998/2004). Representing the Child as a Semiotic Being. In J. Webster (Ed.), *The Language of Early Childhood* (pp. 6–26). London and New York: Continuum.

Halliday, M. A. K. (2001). *El lenguaje como semiótica social*. Buenos Aires: Fondo de Cultura Económica.

Halliday, M. A. K. (2014). *Introduction to Functional Grammar*. London and New York: Routledge.

Hasan, R. (1984). What Kind of Resource is Language? *Australian Review of Applied Linguistics, 7*, 57–86.

Hodge, B. (2017). *Social Semiotics for a Complex World*. Cambridge: Polity Press.

Hodge, R., & Kress, G. (1988). *Social Semiotics*. Cambridge: Polity Press.

Jewitt, C. (2006). *Technology, Literacy and Learning. A Multimodal Approach*. London and New York: Routledge.

Jewitt, C. (2008). Multimodality and Literacy in School Classrooms. *Review of Research in Education, 32*(1), 241–267.

Jewitt, C. (2011). An Introduction to Multimodality. In C. Jewitt (Ed.), *The Routledge Handbook of Multimodal Analysis* (pp. 14–27). London and New York: Routledge.

Jewitt, C. (2013). Multimodality and Digital Technologies in the Classroom. In I. de Saint-Georges & J. J. Weber (Eds.), *Multilingualism and Multimodality. Current Challenges for Educational Studies* (pp. 141–152). Rotterdam: Sense.

Jewitt, C. (2014). Multimodality, "Reading" and "Writing" for the 21st Century. In C. Lutkewitte (Ed.), *Multimodal Composition. A Critical Sourcebook* (pp. 309–324). Boston and New York: Bedford / St. Martin's.

Kalantzis, M., & Cope, B. (2000). Changing the Role of Schools. In B. Cope & M. Kalantzis (Eds.), *Multiliteracies. Literacy Learning and the Design of Social Futures* (pp. 117–144). London and New York: Routledge.

Kalantzis, M., Cope, B., & Cloonan, A. (2010). A Multiliteracies Perspective on the New Literacies. In E. A. Baker (Ed.), *The New Literacies. Multiple Perspectives on Research and Practice* (pp. 61–87). New York and London: Guilford.

Kaptelinin, V., & Nardi, B. A. (2006). *Acting with Technology. Activity Theory and Interaction Design*. Cambridge: MIT Press.

Kress, G. (1993). Against Arbitrariness: The Social Production of the Sign as a Foundational Issue in Critical Discourse Analysis. *Discourse & Society, 4*(2), 169–191. https://doi.org/10.1177/0957926593004002003

Kress, G. (2000a). Multimodality: Challenges to Thinking about Language. *TESOL Quarterly, 34*(2), 337–340. https://doi.org/10.2307/3587959

Kress, G. (2000b). Design as Transformation: New Theories of Meaning. In B. Cope & M. Kalantzis (Eds.), *Multiliteracies: Learning Literacy and the Design of Social Futures* (pp. 153–161). Melbourne: Macmillan.

Kress, G. (2003). *Literacy in the New Media Age*. London: Routledge.

Kress, G. (2004). Learning, a Semiotic View in the Context of Digital Technologies. In A. Brown & N. Davis (Eds.), *Digital Technology, Communities & Education* (pp. 15–39). New York: Routledge Falmer.

Kress, G. (2005). Gains and Losses: New Forms of Texts, Knowledge, and Learning. *Computers and Composition, 22*(1), 5–22. https://doi.org/10.1016/j.compcom.2004.12.004

Kress, G. (2010). *Multimodality. A Sociosemiotic Approach to Contemporary Communication*. London: Routledge.

Kress, G. (2011). What is Mode? In C. Jewitt (Ed.), *The Routledge Handbook of Multimodal Analysis* (pp. 54–67). London and New York: Routledge.

Kress, G. (2013). Recognizing Learning. A Perspective from a Social Semiotic Theory of Multimodality. In I. de Saint-Georges & J. J. Weber (Eds.), *Multilingualism and Multimodality. Current Challenges for Educational Studies* (pp. 120–140). Rotterdam: Sense.

Kress, G. (2015a). Designing Meaning. Social Semiotic Multimodality Seen in Relation to Ethnographic Research. In S. Bollig, M. S. Honig, S. Neumann, & C. Seele (Eds.), *MultiPluriTrans in Educational Ethnography. Approaching the Multimodality, Plurality and Translocality of Educational Realities* (pp. 213–233). Verlag: Transcript.

Kress, G. (2015b). Semiotic Work. Applied Linguistics and a Social Semiotic Account of Multimodality. *AILA Review, 28*, 49–71. https://doi.org/10.1075/aila.28.03kre

Kress, G., Jewitt, C., Bourne, J., Franks, A., Hardcastle, J., Jones, K., & Reid, E. (2005). *English in Urban Classrooms. A Multimodal Perspective on Teaching and Learning.* London: Routledge Farmar.

Kress, G., Jewitt, C., Ogborn, J., & Tsatsarelis, C. (2001). *Multimodal Teaching and Learning: The Rhetorics of the Science Classroom.* London: Continuum.

Kress, G., & Selander, S. (2012). Multimodal Design, Learning and Cultures of Recognition. *Internet and Higher Education, 15*(4), 265–268. https://doi.org/10.1016/j.iheduc.2011.12.003

Kress, G., & van Leeuwen, T. (2001). *Multimodal Discourse. The Modes and Media of Contemporary Communication.* London: Arnold.

Kress, G., & van Leeuwen, T. (2006). *Reading Images. The Grammar of Visual Design.* London and New York: Routledge.

Latour, B. (1987). *Science in Action. How to Follow Scientists and Engineers through Society.* Cambridge, MA: Harvard University Press.

Latour, B. (2006). *Reassembling the Social. An Introduction to Actor-Network Theory.* Oxford: Oxford University Press.

Lawn, M. (1999). Designing Teaching. The Classroom as a Technology. In I. Grosvenor, M. Lawn, & K. Rousmaniere (Eds.), *Silences & Images. The Social History of the Classroom* (pp. 65–82). New York: Peter Lang.

Leander, K., & Vasudevan, L. (2009). Multimodality and Mobile Culture. In C. Jewitt (Ed.), *Handbook of Multimodal Analysis* (pp. 127–139). London: Routledge.

LeBaron, C. (2002). Technology Does not Exist Independent of Its Use. In T. Koschmann, R. Hall, & N. Miyake (Eds.), *CSCL 2: Carrying Forward the Conversation* (pp. 433–439). Mahwah: Lawrence Erlbaum.

Lemke, J. (1990). *Talking Science: Language, Learning, and Values.* Norwood: Ablex Publishing.

Lemke, J. (1995a). *Textual Politics. Discourse and Social Dynamics.* London and Bristol: Taylor & Francis.

Lemke, J. L. (1995b). Intertextuality and Text Semantics. In M. Gregory & P. Fries (Eds.), *Discourse in Society: Functional Perspectives* (pp. 85–114). Norwood: Ablex Publishing.

Lemke, J. L. (1998). Multiplying Meaning: Visual and Verbal Semiotics in Scientific Text. In J. R. Martin & R. Veel (Eds.), *Reading Science* (pp. 87–113). London: Routledge.

Lemke, J. (2000). Across the Scales of Time: Artifacts, Activities, and Meanings in Ecosocial Systems. *Mind, Culture, and Activity, 7*(4), 273–290. https://doi.org/10.1207/S15327884MCA0704_03

Lemke, J. (2011). Multimodality, Identity, and Time. In C. Jewitt (Ed.), *The Routledge Handbook of Multimodal Analysis* (pp. 140–150). London: Routledge.

Lin, A. (2012). Multilingual and Multimodal Resources in Genre-Based Pedagogical Approaches to L2 English Content Classrooms. In C. Leung & B. V. Street (Eds.), *English. A Changing Medium for Education* (pp. 79–103). Bristol, Buffalo and Toronto: Multilingual Matters.

Lotherington, H., & Ronda, N. (2012). Multimodal Literacies and Assessment: Uncharted Challenges in the English Classroom. In C. Leung & B. V. Street (Eds.), *English—A Changing Medium for Education* (pp. 104–128). Clevedon: Multilingual Matters.

Luke, C. (2000). Cyber-schooling and Technological Change: Multiliteracies for New Times. In B. Cope & M. Kalantzis (Eds.), *Multiliteracies. Literacy Learning and the Design of Social Futures* (pp. 67–88). London and New York: Routledge.

Luke, C., de Castell, S., & Luke, A. (1989). Beyond Criticism: The Authority of the School Textbook. In S. de Castell, A. Luke, & C. Luke (Eds.), *Language Authority and Criticism. Readings on the School Textbook* (pp. 245–260). London and New York: Falmer.

Machin, D., & Mayr, A. (2012). *How to do Critical Discourse Analysis*. London: Sage.

Machin, D., & van Leeuwen, T. (2007). *Global Media Discourse. A Critical Introduction*. London and New York: Routledge.

Manghi, D. (Ed.). (2017). *La complejidad de la interacción en el aula, reconociendo significados que transforman*. Valparaíso: Ediciones Universitarias de Valparaíso.

Manghi Haquin, D. (2013). Representación y comunicación del conocimiento en Educación Media: análisis multimodal del discurso de materiales utilizados para la enseñanza escolar de la historia y de la biología. *Onomázwin, 27*, 35–52.

Martin, J. R. (2000). Grammar Meets Genre—Reflections on the 'Sydney School'. *Arts: The Journal of the Sydney University Arts Association, 22*, 47–95.

Martin, J. R., & Rose, D. (2007). *Working with Discourse*. London and New York: Continuum.

Martin, J. R., & Rose, D. (2008). *Genre Relations: Mapping Culture*. London: Equinox.

Matthiessen, C. I. M. M. (2014). The Multimodal Page: A Systematic Functional Exploration. In T. D. Royce & W. L. Bowcher (Eds.), *New Directions in the Analysis of Multimodal Discourse* (pp. 1–62). London and New York: Routledge.

Matthiessen, C. I. M. M., Teruya, K., & Lam, M. (2010). *Keyterms in Systemic Functional Linguistics*. London and New York: Continuum.

Miettinen, R. (2009). The Riddle of Things. Activity Theory and Actor Network Theory as Approaches to Studying Innovations. *Mind, Culture and Activity, 6*(3), 170–195. https://doi.org/10.1080/10749039909524725

Miller, M. S., & McVee, M. (Eds.). (2012). *Multimodal Composing in Classrooms. Learning and Teaching for the Digital World*. New York and London: Routledge.

Muffoletto, R. (2001). The Need for Critical Theory and Reflective Practices in Educational Technology. In R. Muffoletto (Ed.), *Education and Technology. Critical and Reflective Practices* (pp. 285–299). Cresskill: Hampton Press.

Norris, S. (2011). Modal density and Modal Configurations: Multimodal Actions. In C. Jewitt (Ed.), *The Routledge Handbook of Multimodal Analysis* (pp. 78–90). London and New York: Routledge.

O'Halloran, K. (2012). Análisis del discurso multimodal. *Revista de la Asociación Latinoamericana de Estudios del Discurso, 12*(1), 75–97.

Painter, C., Martin, J. R., & Unsworth, L. (2012). *Reading Visual Narratives. Image Analysis in Children's Picture Books*. Sheffield: Equinox.

Resnik, B. L., Pontecorvo, C., & Säljö, R. (1997). Discourse, Tools and Reasoning. In B. L. Resnik, R. Säljö, & C. Pontecorvo (Eds.), *Discourse, Tools and Reasoning. Essays on Situated Cognition* (pp. 1–21). Berlin: Springer.

Röhl, T. (2015). Transsituating Education. Educational Artifacts in the Classroom and Beyond. In S. Bollig, M. S. Honig, S. Neumann, & C. Seele (Eds.), *MultiPluriTrans in Educational Ethnography. Approaching the Multimodality, Plurality and Translocality of Educational Realities* (pp. 122–139). Verlag: Transcript.

Rose, D. (2010). Genre in the Sydney School. In J. P. Gee & M. Handford (Eds.), *The Routledge Handbook of Discourse Analysis*. London: Routledge.
Rothery, J., & Stenglin, M. (1995). *Exploring Literacy in School English*. Sydney: Metropolitan East Disadvantaged Schools Program.
Royce, T. (2002). Multimodality in the TESOL Classroom: Exploring Visual-Verbal Synergy. *TESOL Quarterly*, 36(2), 191–205. https://doi.org/10.2307/3588330
Royce, T. (2007). Multimodal Communicative Competence. In T. Royce & W. Bowcher (Eds.), *New Directions in the Analysis of Multimodal Discourse* (pp. 361–390). Mahwah: Lawrence Erlbaum Associates.
Sannino, A., Daniels, H., & Gutiérrez, K. D. (Eds.). (2009). *Learning and Expanding with Activity Theory*. Cambridge: Cambridge University Press.
Saussure, F. (1967). *Cours de Linguistique Générale*. Paris: Grande Bibliotèque Payot.
Schatzki, T. R. (2001). Introduction: Practice Theory. In T. R. Schatzki, K. K. Cetina, & E. von Savigny (Eds.), *The Practice Turn in Contemporary Theory* (pp. 1–14). London: Routledge.
Schnotz, W. (1997). Strategy-Specific Information Access in Knowledge Acquisition from Hypertext. In B. L. Resnik, R. Säljö, & C. Pontecorvo (Eds.), *Discourse, Tools and Reasoning. Essays on Situated Cognition* (pp. 336–359). Berlin: Springer.
Schofield, W. J. (1995). *Computers and Classroom Culture*. New York: Cambridge University Press.
Scollon, R., & Levine, P. (2004). Multimodal Discourse Analysis as the Confluence of Discourse and Technology. In P. Levine & R. Scollon (Eds.), *Discourse & Technology. Multimodal Discourse Analysis* (pp. 1–6). Washington, DC: Georgetown University Press.
Serafini, F. (2014). *Reading the Visual. An Introduction to Teaching Multimodal Literacy*. New York: Teachers College Press.
Setzer, V. W., & Monke, L. (2001). Challenging the Application: An Alternative View on Why, When and How Computers Should Be Used in Education. In R. Muffoletto (Ed.), *Education and Technology. Critical and Reflective Practices* (pp. 141–173). Cresskill: Hampton Press.
Stahl, G., Koschmann, T., & Suthers, D. (2006). Computer-Supported Collaborative Learning: An Historical Perspective. In R. K. Sawyer (Ed.), *Cambridge Handbook of the Learning Sciences* (pp. 409–426). Cambridge: Cambridge University Press.
Stein, P. (2008). *Multimodal Pedagogies in Diverse Classrooms. Representations, Rights and Resources*. London and New York: Routledge.

Stockl, H. (2007). In Between Modes: Language and Image in Printed Media. In E. Ventola, C. Charles, & M. Kaltenbacher (Eds.), *Perspectives on Multimodality* (pp. 9–30). Amsterdam: John Benjamins.

Sung, Y. K., & Apple, M. (2003). Democracy, Technology, and Curriculum: Lessons from the Critical Practices of Korean Teachers. In M. W. Apple (Ed.), *The State and the Politics of Knowledge* (pp. 177–191). New York: Routledge Falmer.

The New London Group. (1996). A Pedagogy of Multiliteracies: Designing Social Futures. *Harvard Educational Review, 66*(1), 60–92.

Tudor, I. (2001). *The Dynamics of the Language Classroom*. Cambridge: Cambridge University Press.

Unsworth, L. (2008). Multimodal Semiotic Analyses and Education. In L. Unsworth (Ed.), *Multimodal Semiotics. Functional Analysis in Contexts of Education* (pp. 1–13). London and New York: Continuum.

van Leeuwen, T. (2004). Ten Reasons Why Linguists Should Pay Attention to Visual Communication. In P. Levine & R. Scollon (Eds.), *Discourse & Technology. Multimodal Discourse Analysis* (pp. 7–19). Washington, DC: Georgetown University Press.

van Leeuwen, T. (2005). *Introducing Social Semiotics*. London and New York: Routledge.

van Lier, L. (2004a). The Semiotics and Ecology of Language Learning. Perception, Voice, Identity and Democracy. *Utbildning & Demokrati, 13*(3), 79–103.

van Lier, L. (2004b). *The Ecology and Semiotics of Language Learning. A Sociocultural Perspective*. New York: Kluwer Academic Publishers.

van Oers, B., Wardekker, W., Elbers, E., & van der Veer, R. (Eds.). (2008). *The Transformation of Learning. Advances in Cultural-Historical Activity Theory*. Cambridge: Cambridge University Press.

Vološinov, V. N. (1973). *Marxism and the Philosophy of Language*. New York and London: Seminar Press.

Vygotsky, L. S. (1978). *Mind in Society: The Development of Higher Psychological Processes*. Cambridge: Harvard University Press.

4

Plan Ceibal Policy and the 1:1 Model in Uruguay

The previous chapter delineated key concepts for addressing learning from a multimodal socio-semiotic perspective as a theoretical, analytical and ethical requirement to shift from traditional to alternative ideologies of learning. Such shift has the potential for the semiotic work of students to be better attended to and recognized. For this to happen, attention needs to be drawn to both the affordances and limitations the environment offers to learners as sign-makers and how sign-makers make use of resources to represent the social world according to their interest and to communicate with others by dynamically establishing interpersonal relations.

The classroom environment is usually inhabited by many curriculum artifacts employed for making meanings, and particular ideological, socio-political and economic forces have legitimated these artifacts as required for *authorized learning*, that is to say, the type of learning or demonstration of learning expected by the official curriculum. Among these curriculum artifacts, new technology has become the most visible one for stakeholders, policy-makers and researchers as well. The design and implementation of education policies to introduce new technology in schools and classrooms is now common practice and takes place in many forms. Part of our work to better recognize students' semiotic work lies in investigating how students make meanings with technology artifacts in formal education and what role technology—as a material artifact—plays in the social life of sign-makers and their environments.

This chapter provides a brief overview of the educational landscape of Uruguay and the design and implementation of Plan Ceibal as a social, educational and foreign language policy set up to democratize and universalize access to technology across the country. This policy represents one of the many forms in which technology is being introduced in classrooms and in society: the 1:1 or *one laptop per child* model (OLPC, MIT). The chapter concludes with a description of the research site—Fleetwood School—and discusses how it fits the bigger picture of Plan Ceibal and why this site is relevant for an analysis of how the policy is enacted. The chapter also provides background information and context for the analysis developed in Chaps. 5, 6 and 7.

Uruguay: A Socio-educational Profile

Uruguay has around 3,400,000 inhabitants (World Bank Group 2017), being the second smallest country in Latin America. Half of the country's population is concentrated in the capital city—Montevideo—while the rest lives in urbanizing and rural areas. This demographic profile has certainly had an effect on language education, providing—in practice—more and better opportunities for second and foreign language learning to those children who live either in the capital or—to a lesser extent—in any of the urbanizing areas, despite the small size and population of the country.

The literacy rate is considered to be one of the highest in the region (98% according to Index Mundi 2018). Around 85% of the student population attends public schools while the remaining 15% attend private schools (Ministry of Culture and Education 2011). This is by no means a new trend in the country; on the contrary, it follows a historical pattern in which public school has always accounted for much more of the student population than private schools. Public schools are State-sponsored and State-funded. Since the passing of Law of Common

Education (*Ley de Educación Común*) in 1877, the three pillars of Uruguayan public education have been *secular, free,* and *obligatory* (*laica, gratuita y obligatoria*). As for secularity, unlike other countries in Latin America public education in Uruguay is not associated with any particular religion—neither is the State. As for the second, students and their families do not need to pay any type of fee or tuition; they have a right to access public education free of charge. Finally, education is obligatory in that it is considered to be a key instrument for social life; therefore parents have an obligation to enroll their children in primary and secondary school. While tertiary education and university-level education are also secular and free, they are not mandatory.

Despite the fact that public education covers the majority of the school population, private education accounts for around 15%. The latter can be either secular or have a particular religious affiliation. Private schools' fees vary substantially depending on the school. For this reason, private education has traditionally been associated with both middle and upper classes. However, it is fair to say that public education—albeit mostly associated with the working and the working-middle class—cuts across all socio-economic levels of Uruguayan society.

The differences between public and private education has to some extent an impact on official curriculum design and regulations. The National Curriculum is designed by government authorities and all public and private certified schools must follow its guidelines and regulations (in terms of school subject, contents, hours of classroom work, among others). However—as will be discussed in the next section—in general terms private schools have not traditionally been a space of strict State regulation regarding foreign language teaching.

Foreign Languages and English Language Teaching in Uruguay

The origins of private foreign language teaching in Uruguay dates back to middle and upper classes in the early nineteenth century. Foreign language teaching—mostly English and French was carried out by immigrants and private institutions (Monreal 2010). Throughout the nineteenth century several private schools were set up to promote English teaching: the *British College* (1856), the *English College* (1865), *the English High School* (1870). Some of these schools first targeted lower socio-economic immigrants' children as a strategy to maintain the migrant language, while later on they targeted the higher socio-economic sectors of society to teach EFL. By the end of the nineteenth century and the beginning of the twentieth century other schools were also set up, such as the *English and French School*, the *International College*, and the *Flores Collegiate School* (Monreal 2010). Other languages such as French, Italian and German were also popular at the time.

Throughout the twentieth century, many private language institutes and more schools were also founded (Viera 2010): *Instituto Cultural Anglo-Uruguayo* (1934), *Alianza Cultural Uruguay-Estados Unidos* (1939) and the Uruguayan–American private bilingual school (1958). The popularity of EFL teaching in private education reached its peak during the second part of the twentieth century, when more schools and institutes were set up, as happened in many other countries around the globe (Phillipson 1992).

Even though private schools are required to comply with some common guidelines and regulations provided by the central government, they may choose to, for instance, include the teaching of foreign languages other than the ones offered in public education, or even rearrange the contents of official curricula to fit their own purposes, as long as some minimal official requirements are met.

In public education, foreign language policies and programs are regulated by the Central government through educational authorities. The inclusion or exclusion of foreign languages in the curriculum has traditionally been subjected to supervision by the authorities of primary, secondary, tertiary, and university-level education, resulting in a complex linguistic scenario in which a language could be present in one of these levels and not in the others.

As for secondary education, English is the foreign language that has achieved the greatest continuity in the national foreign language curriculum, since its introduction in the nineteenth century, together with Latin and French. All other languages, however, have been in and out of the curriculum: Italian, French, Portuguese, Latin, German, and so on. Given the current foreign language teaching scenario around the globe, it comes as no surprise to learn that while official statistics show that toward 1854 only 21% of the students in high schools took English (Gabbiani 1995; Ranguis 1992), nowadays the language covers all high schools across the country.

EFL gained even more momentum in the 1990s when local and regional neoliberal governments reproduced discourses about the need to speak English for becoming citizens of the world, accessing "first world" information, culture and technology, as well as to having more and better job opportunities regionally and globally. Similar discourses were deployed in the Latin American region through the development of *Mercado Común del Sur* (MERCOSUR), which constitutes—since the beginning of the 1990s—an economic bloc in the southern region of South America.

By 1996, EFL was officially the only mandatory foreign language across the whole secondary school curriculum. As a way to make up for the increasing supremacy of English, a few public foreign language centers *Centros de Lenguas Extranjeras* (CLE) were established in 1996 after English became the official mandatory language for all six years of secondary education. Since the inception of CLEs, public education high school students can opt to attend these centers after class time and learn other foreign languages. CLEs, however, have a very narrow reach: according to official statistics, by 2012 their student body did not exceed 4% of the total public secondary school population.

As for public primary education, traditionally it did not include any foreign languages in the curriculum, with the exception of a few schools that had signed agreements with embassies, and so offered some foreign languages. These mostly depended on funding by each embassy. It was not until late in the twentieth century that several trial programs were implemented to expand EFL in primary education: *English for Public Primary Schools program* (1993), the *Partial Immersion in English program* (2001), and the *Teaching English through Content program* (2006). The design and official discourses surrounding these programs usually drew on the growing importance of English worldwide and also on the early age acquisition trends that underscored potential benefits of younger access to a foreign language. Most of these programs were discontinued after a short time. However, EFL teaching coverage in public primary education changed substantially with the advent of Plan Ceibal in Uruguay, as will be described in the following sections.[1]

Plan Ceibal and the 1:1 Model

In 2005, for the first time in the history of Uruguay, the left-wing party Frente Amplio took office after winning the national elections. This party was founded in 1971 as a coalition of several left and left-wing inspired ideologies. At the moment of writing this book (2019), the party is in office after having won national elections three consecutive times.

By 2007, the Uruguayan government passed a decree to set up Plan Ceibal (Spanish acronym for *Project of Educational Connectivity for Online Learning*), a local model of the *one laptop per child* initiative (OLPC or 1:1). Since then, it has become known as one of the most ambitious left-wing government policies.

In broad terms, Plan Ceibal can be characterized as a social, educational and also a foreign language policy aiming to *universalize* and *democratize* access to technology across the country (Ministry of Culture and Education 2013). In official discourses, *universalization* refers to the spread of technology throughout the country while *democratization* mainly refers to providing equal opportunities to all socio-economic groups within society. Both terms belong to the same actions in terms of policy-making, the difference being the discursive emphasis laid on one facet of the policy or the other.

At the social level the policy seeks to bring technology to all Uruguayan families as a means to bridge the so-called digital divide. To do this, a set of orchestrated actions have been carried out. For instance, the government—through the Ministry of Education and Culture—has set up Centers in different parts of the country for adults to have the possibility of learning computer skills. The government has also set up wi-fi connections in all public schools and progressively expanded wi-fi connectivity to homes and shops across the country. As for the technology offered to citizens, Plan Ceibal has handed out laptops (locally known as

XO laptops or *Ceibalitas*) to public school students—and teachers—and more recently has started to hand out tablets to students as well as to retired citizens.

As an educational policy, Plan Ceibal has handed out these laptops for free to students and teachers in primary and secondary public school education, and has also expanded the policy to some sectors of private education as well, as shall be discussed later. These actions have been accompanied by some short workshops to train public school teachers on digital skills, the formation of groups of teachers and programmers to design digital materials, among others. The aim is for technology to permeate school practices across the curriculum.

Within this broad policy, *Plan Ceibal en Inglés* (or *Ceibal in English*) is perhaps the program that has received the most attention in the past years. Ceibal en Inglés is a language program that was officially launched in 2011 and started running in 2012. Official discourses framed this EFL program amidst the problems public education has traditionally encountered, such as covering available TEFL positions or being able to fill those positions with certified and qualified EFL teachers. Due to the lack of certified EFL teachers and the low TEFL graduation rate (ANEP, Official Census 2007), Plan Ceibal expanded its scope by attempting to *universalize* and *democratize* access to EFL in primary education (CPLEP 2009; Brovetto 2011, 2013) by incorporating technology as means to reach the full primary school populations (given that EFL was already universalized in secondary school). The specifics of this language program are described in the next section entitled *Plan Ceibal en Inglés*.

The broad program of Plan Ceibal entailed a substantial change in policy-making strategies because of the many levels (social, educational, and foreign language) it comprises and its ambitious aims: to democratize and universalize access to technology and bridge the digital divide both in society at large and between private and public schools. A previous attempt to introduce technology in local public education had been made in the 1900s by a right-wing government to equip public schools with desktop technology. This policy, however, did not universalize access and only catered for in-school practices (at the time of this policy desktops were also new technology at hand), while Plan Ceibal has a broader social aim and has come to exist in a time where portability and mobility are highly valued.

Expanding the use of technology throughout the country did not come without political and ideological struggles. Providing an exhaustive list of the debates around the program is far beyond the scope of this book, so I will briefly mention some. By no means do I intend to foreground some debates and background others; the reader can easily find a more exhaustive list of these debates by browsing local newspapers online.

The first years of implementation, there was resistance inside and outside of the local educational sphere. Teacher unions demanded to be better prepared for the technology and a slower implementation that would give them time to become more familiarized with the technology. In fact, one of the main debates between unions and the government was whether the laptops should have been introduced gradually and after preparing teachers, school directors and other stakeholders or whether they needed to be introduced rapidly—as they were—and wait for schools to integrate this new artifact in a "grass-root" fashion. Teachers also complained salaries should be raised before such huge investments were made on technology. They also complained about the little participation they had in the design and implementation process. Anecdotally, at one point unionized teachers called for a strike which consisted on their not turning on the Plan Ceibal XO equipment (laptops) for the whole school day, a "digital strike".

Right-wing political opponents drew on broader and sometimes more general arguments to resist the implementation of the program. Some claimed technology was not the road to a better and higher-quality education; one politician was highly criticized for claiming the program would "make students more stupid" while others argued that other basic needs had to be fulfilled before technology was universalized. After 11 years of implementation of the program, a lot of these debates seem to have come to a halt. Debates do remain, but now they mostly revolve around learning assessment, quality evaluation and standards, all aspects that pertain to a more advanced stage of implementation. In fact, Plan Ceibal has become one of the key symbols of the left-wing governments and their social, political and educational orchestrated actions to democratize and universalize education.

As in other regions of the world, broader discussions as for how and when to use technology in education also remain. Such debates have been particularly heated when debating the 1:1 model for introducing technology in education worldwide. This model has been implemented in many other countries in Latin America and in other regions as well. It is perhaps the most frequent frame of thought for policy-making and the introduction of technology in education nowadays. Despite this, implementation and enactment of the 1:1 model has varied substantially in terms of the degree of coverage within the population, its uses and purposes (in-school and out-of-school practices, for instance), the scope of the policy and even the actual technology artifact handed out (laptops, tablets, etc.). With local adaptations, the 1:1 model has been adopted by Chile (Hepp et al. 2004), Italy, Ethiopia, Brazil (Pischetola 2014) and some states of the United States (Clark n.d.), just to name a few. However, one of the most striking differences in implementation is that due to its small population, the small size of Uruguay and its political and economic stability, Plan Ceibal has been able to spread throughout the country in only a couple of years. Another difference is that while most programs focus on school children or the younger generation in general, Plan Ceibal has also targeted older generations such as retired citizens. Along these lines, the policy has a broader social aim that includes—but goes beyond—the strictly instructional and educational. These—along with other reasons—make Uruguay a potential "laboratory for Latin American educational policies" (Vaillant 2015, 405), as well as for other regions.

As review syntheses have shown, there are some important differences not only in the ways in which 1:1 models have been implemented and enacted around the globe, but also in the ways in which these have been investigated (Sell et al. 2012; Zheng et al. 2016). For the sake of my argument, I will only present a brief contextualization of local research about Plan Ceibal. As for Plan Ceibal as a general social and educational policy, local research has mostly focused on top-down actions and the macro level of policy design, including some aspects of implementation (Barboza Norbis 2013; Ferreira Cabrera et al. 2010; Larrouqué 2013; Rodríguez Zidán 2010; Rodríguez Zidán and Bochia 2010).To my knowledge, no study has yet addressed in a systematic manner what Plan Ceibal technology means across different scales (inside and outside of classrooms and schools), how the laptops as technology artifacts shape and are shaped by classrooms, how these artifacts interact with other curriculum artifacts, what affordances these artifacts provide for learning in the local context or what it means to learn in this new ecology in local classrooms. It should be noted, however, that a few studies have engaged in grounded perspectives, which better capture the daily reality of local classrooms and social actors. Gabbiani (2010) analyzes micro events within two classrooms in which the laptops are used with a view to characterizing interactions between peers in learning processes. Her focus is on describing patterns of verbal interaction. The author also interviews learners to explore their attitudes toward Plan Ceibal. In a similar vein, Kachinovsky et al. (2013) describe interactions among students when using the laptops, how they construct knowledge and how this fits into the bigger picture of the classroom.

Plan Ceibal en Inglés

Within Plan Ceibal, Ceibal en Inglés is a technology-enhanced program for primary education which was launched in 2011 and started to be implemented in schools in 2012. Its main aim is to universalize and democratize access to EFL in primary education to bridge the divide between public and private schools. Unlike Plan Ceibal, Ceibal en Inglés is strictly educational (it only pertains to formal instruction). Since one of the problems of public education has been to cover available TEFL positions, the program sought ways to introduce EFL lessons in the content Spanish lesson (taught by primary teachers in Spanish). A new teaching figure was introduced for these purposes: a remote EFL teacher who delivers the EFL lesson with the assistance of the Spanish teacher.

By 2017, Ceibal en Inglés had been implemented in around 3300 classrooms in public primary schools and 344 classrooms in public secondary schools all over the country (Kaiser 2017), covering 4th, 5th and 6th graders. Even though this EFL program has gained the most attention, some schools remain in which EFL is taught without Plan Ceibal.[2]

However, by 2015 Ceibal en Inglés already accounted for 73% of primary school students' access to EFL across the country (Kaiser 2015).

Given that primary public education had traditionally not offered foreign languages, the main focus of the program has been on primary students. In public primary schools, the EFL class in Ceibal en Inglés consists of the following: an EFL remote teacher (RT)—who can be in Uruguay or abroad—video-conferences a group of students and a Spanish teacher (CT, classroom teacher) who does not need to have advanced skills in the language. Through a video-conference screen (see Table 4.1), the RT delivers a 45-minute lesson (lesson A) to introduce new linguistic points which are afterwards reviewed by the CT in two in-site weekly sessions (lessons B and C). It should be noted that while the CT is actually a school and State employee, the remote teacher is outsourced (hired via Ceibal and not via the school or educational authorities).

The physical space of the classroom for lesson A is usually not the same classroom in which they have their regular lessons or lessons B and C. This is because the video-conference equipment requires a specific room which is generally only used for Plan Ceibal en Inglés purposes: each school equips one room with the technology and students go to that room once every week when they have the lesson with the RT (lesson A). Students attend this classroom once a week (when they video-conference with the RT who is the EFL expert[3]) while twice a week the CT (non-expert in TEFL) is in charge of delivering the lesson (generally not in the Ceibal classroom where the equipment is).

All three lessons are highly standardized and scripted, and both scripts and classroom materials are provided by the British Council in Uruguay (although now Ceibal en Inglés is starting to design local lesson plans). This decision to partner with the British Council has met with both positive and negative reception in the local EFL teaching community. While some consider it is beneficial for the program to partner with an international agency and some even heavily draw on nativist and culturist arguments to underscore the role of English native-speakers in lesson design, others have been more critical of the role of the British Council and the politics of outsourcing lesson and material design. Regardless of particular ideological positionings, this partnership has a rescaling effect on the policy

(Lingard and Rawolle 2011) since transnational social actors, their aims and agendas have been incorporated into Ceibal en Inglés implementation.

The design of the three lessons per week unfolds as follows. While lesson A mostly makes use of the video-conference screen, lesson B and C may include (albeit not frequently) the use of XO laptops by students. In this respect, students can access an educational online platform (CREA2) with extra EFL material, which offers the possibility to contact other teachers via online fora. This platform is used for students, teachers and other Plan Ceibal stakeholders to share materials and ideas. It is also used for students to complete some online tasks, among other things.

RTs are hired via local EFL institutes and also via the British Council. They can be locals or they can reside abroad. In both cases, they need to attend a *teaching point* equipped with Ceibal technology: computer, speakers, microphone, connection to the school site, and so on. Teaching points are found at Plan Ceibal facility, at some local language institutes and also abroad.

More recently, Ceibal en Inglés has also started to offer lessons for secondary education. However, they are not content lessons (since secondary schools do have in-site EFL teaching), but conversation classes through video-conference, which are held once a week. Its implementation is still lower than Ceibal en Inglés in primary education: by 2018 around 300 classrooms (in 150 secondary schools) were using Ceibal en Inglés in secondary education. At the time of writing, there are also other initiatives within Plan Ceibal to use the video-conference equipment for other purposes (for instance to teach Mathematics, Physics or other subjects for which there is a shortage of in-site teachers across the country). However, these are still being discussed.

Ceibal en Inglés is optional in that each school needs to opt in the program. This, as stated by Ceibal Policy stakeholders, was a strategy to make sure the program would have "enthusiastic and motivated" CTs and school principals. However, there have been recent discussions as for whether to make Ceibal en Inglés mandatory.

As for learning assessment, Ceibal en Inglés in primary schools offers a standardized computer-based adaptive test for EFL learners. As of 2018, the test assesses three main components: (i) reading comprehension, grammar and vocabulary; (ii) listening comprehension; (iii) writing. For these purposes, the XO laptop is used as a means to complete the test, but students are not required to demonstrate any ability in using or interacting with the technology. In 2016, scores indicated that around 40% of the students who took part in the program for a complete year achieved A1 level of proficiency (according to the CEFRL n.d., *online*), while the remaining students got either lower (−A1, A0) or higher scores (−A2, A2).[4]

Local research has not looked into Ceibal en Inglés in enough detail yet. A few studies representing the official discourses and voices of Ceibal en Inglés and the British Council have outlined the theoretical and methodological foundations of this EFL program (Banegas 2013, Brovetto 2011, 2013). A qualitative study (Frade 2018) looks at interaction patterns in teacher-student in-class conversations and how these come to shape their roles within this program. Frade finds that since the classroom teacher can have a basic or more advanced knowledge of English, the role and identity of the CT—compared to the RT—can vary depending on many circumstances. The classroom teacher can be a mere spectator of the EFL lesson, she can help the RT regulate classroom behavior or even assist in the delivery of the lesson and its content.

Plan Ceibal in Private Education

Plan Ceibal has expanded its scope to private education as well, even though this is not the main aim of the policy and this aspect of the policy is not advertised and rarely talked about. For private schools, the program works in a substantially different way. Private schools willing to be part of Plan Ceibal pay for their participation. If they opt in, they are offered Plan Ceibal's wi-fi connectivity and are also handed out laptops for students. These laptops have access to the CREA platform in which educational Plan Ceibal software and programs are available, but private schools do not follow any other specific educational guidelines as for what purposes or how to use the laptops, or depend on Plan Ceibal in any other way (other than for fixing broken laptops or potential connectivity issues). Also, since schools pay for the laptops, they usually decide for students not to take them home, unlike public education in which the XO laptop actually belongs to the student. This aspect in particular depends on each school and its laptop distribution policy.

Schools which have opted in Plan Ceibal have done so in two different modalities. From 2012 to 2014 (modality 1) schools could buy the Aula Ceibal package, which includes technology equipment (XO laptops), maintenance service and technical training. One hundred and twelve private schools remain in this modality, with around 23–35 laptops per school. Since 2014 (modality 2), private schools can buy laptops and connectivity separately (around 535 schools have opted in this modality by 2018).

Since private education is not the main scope of the program—and thus it is not highly regulated—other specifics about implementation and enactment depend on each school. Even the EFL curriculum is not associated with the policy. As well as public schools in which Ceibal en Inglés is not being run, private schools follow the guidelines of an EFL curriculum which was designed and approved before the program was set up. As a result, for these spaces the use of the XO laptop—or technology in general—is not strictly regulated in a top-down fashion.

These differences between public and private schools and how they implement Plan Ceibal also shape their enactment. It is along these lines that I chose to make a distinction between bright and blind policy spots, as I announced in Chap. 1. In the next section I will briefly discuss bright and blind policy spots; then I will describe the focal research site, Fleetwood School, as well as the focal classroom.

Policy Bright and Blind Spots

Policy is always designed with an audience in mind and, in general, at some point policy decisions require policy-makers to include and exclude sectors of the population for which the policy might or might not apply. In the same way, official policy discourse usually foregrounds and backgrounds particular audiences as potential beneficiaries—or not—of the policy. From a socio-semiotic and an ethnographic perspective this is relevant since meaning-making and sense-making of the policy is an ongoing semiotic activity that takes place at many scales and which cannot be entirely shaped by top-down forces. However, policy texts usually attempt to guide the semiosis of the audience and shape meaning-making processes so that the policy will be thought of and perceived in particular ways. Beneficiaries are also expected to make sense of the policy in particular ways and to attach particular meanings to the policy with regards to the social world around them and their social lives.

During the ethnographic fieldwork, this phenomenon emerged as recurrent and apparent in the data. Since Plan Ceibal is designed by a left-wing government as a means to universalize and democratize access to technology, its implementation and enactment in public education is the focus of attention of official discourse and reports, government spokespeople, local education authorities, newspapers and mass media, and even lay citizens. This makes sense in that by foregrounding public education we can evaluate the policy, its success and drawbacks in achieving its main goals. However, there is an open space in which the policy also operates and which has not been visualized until now. What do discourses of universalization and democratization of technology mean in a private school? How do private school students orient to this technology and what it represents socially and ideologically? How are these laptops used for learning in a school for which there is no scripted lessons, no standardized EFL material and no standardized assessment tests? Looking into this sort of black hole seemed interesting in order to investigate what the policy can do, what technology can do in formal education and more importantly to recognize what students do with technology in less constrained environments.

My characterization of public school classrooms as policy bright spots and private school classrooms as blind spots responds to this phenomenon. By this characterization I do not intend to claim that one is better than the other, that regulation is intrinsically wrong or that both types of enactments of the policy should be compared. On the contrary, this characterization intends to capture the reality of the policy and to explain why it might be relevant for policy research in general to focus on blind spots as well.

As for Ceibal en Inglés in particular, and based on what I have discussed so far, there are several points that characterize bright and blind spots, as illustrated in Table 4.1.

Table 4.1 Characterization of bright and blind spots, based on the ethnographic fieldwork and data

Policy bright spots	Policy blind spots
Universalization and *democratization* of access foregrounded as the aim of the policy	*Universalization* and *democratization* of access backgrounded as the aim of the policy
Officially recognized as the main audience of the government and the beneficiaries of the policy	Not documented in the data as being considered policy beneficiaries in official discourse, mass media or by lay citizens
Its implementation has been advertised locally and abroad (mass media advertisements, documentaries, etc.)	Its implementation has not been advertised
Curriculum is highly standardized and its enactment is supervised	Curriculum follows basic guidelines but is not frequently supervised in enactment
Lesson design usually outsourced and scripted, although there are some new initiatives to design local lesson plans	Lesson design depends on teachers and to a lesser extent on school authorities
Conference screen and—to a lesser extent—XO laptop as the most representative curriculum artifacts in lesson enactment	XO laptop and printed textbook as the most representative curriculum artifacts in lesson enactment
The use of technology is top-down mandated (and scripted in the lesson plan)	The use of technology can be mandated by the school but in general depends on each teacher
Two teachers: a Spanish classroom teacher assisting the enactment of the lesson and an EFL remote teacher	An EFL classroom teacher
Students "own" the laptop	The school "owns" the laptop
Learning is demonstrated by standardized tests and quantified in scores and metrics used for official purposes and for evaluating the policy	Learning is demonstrated in the manner the teacher or the school decides. However, education authorities provide baseline guidelines and recommendations, which can be adapted

The tentative list of points raised in Table 4.1 explains the specifics of Plan Ceibal enactment at Fleetwood School, as described in the next section.

Fleetwood School as a Policy Blind Spot

Fleetwood is a small private school with a population of around 180 students: 71 are high school students (1st through 4th) while the remaining students are primary school students. The school is located in a middle-class neighborhood in Montevideo.

In general terms, the school has a strong sense of itself as a small community, and it becomes engaged in several activities which pertain to the local social life and involves other social actors as a way to engage students. For instance, during the time I conducted the ethnographic fieldwork at the school, students took part in several fund raising events, third- and fourth-year students also participated in local plans to improve the environment and cleanliness of the neighborhood. The school principal also got other social actors to come to the school and engage students in several activities. For instance, small business owners and government stakeholders offered talks and presentations to fourth-year students on how to start up their own business, how to become more organized with money and information, among others. Also, former students were engaged in activities to enhance the school building, such as painting murals on some of the classroom and school walls.

The school offers both primary and secondary education in two language streams: bilingual and regular. Students on the bilingual stream attend the school for around 6–7 hours a day and have EFL lessons every day. As most bilingual schools in Uruguay, these lessons are oriented to international examination tests (such as *Cambridge First Certificate in English*). Students on the regular stream attend school for around 4–5 hours a day and have EFL lessons three times a week (around 3 hours per week). These students do not take international exams and their classes do not revolve around test practice or test-taking strategies. For parents, the decision whether to make their children attend one or the other stream mostly depends on money, since the monthly fee for bilingual stream is considerably higher than the fee for the regular one. A majority of students usually opt in the bilingual stream. For instance, in the focal classroom there were 8 students because these chose the regular stream and were taking EFL lessons for the first time. However, other 15 attended the bilingual stream. All students have access to the XO laptops whether they attend the regular or the bilingual stream. However, students attending the bilingual stream have a separate room for their EFL lessons.

In Fleetwood School XO laptops are kept in a computer lab room, which was initially designed for desktops (years before Plan Ceibal was set up). Teachers have a key to this room and so they can pick up the XO laptops—or request a student to pick them up themselves—whenever a laptop is to be used. The school has around 30 laptops.

The computer lab room is generally used for ICT classes (for which students surprisingly use desktops but not the XO laptops) and occasionally for some content subjects. The use of XO laptops also varies substantially across subjects, often times based on the teacher's interest and motivation to use it since the school itself does not have strict policies on teaching practices.

As for EFL lessons, the extent to which XO laptops are used in the classroom mostly depends on teacher motivation and willingness to plan lessons around the use of this technology. The school favors the use of the XO laptops but does not have any policy as for how, when or how much teachers need to make use of this artifact. In fact, my ethnographic fieldwork in the school indicates that the focal teacher—Vera—uses the XO laptops considerably more often and for more varied purposes than most EFL teachers in the school. Together with Vera, teachers of school subjects such as geography, design and mathematics are the ones who seem more actively engaged in XO laptop use. As I discussed in Chap. 1, both EFL and technology have been and still are key terms in local education. Therefore, the presence of either one suffices to fulfill some educational purposes. For this reason, school authorities did not insist that EFL teachers used XO laptops since the EFL lesson in itself served such purposes. They did expect more XO laptop use for other content subjects.

Conclusions

The introduction of new technology in the landscape of formal education is an everyday practice in current policy-making. Among the many ways in which technology can be introduced, the 1:1 model is one of the most frequent ones. However, this model has been implemented in different ways and for different purposes in many parts of the world. For several reasons exposed in this chapter, Plan Ceibal seems to be particularly interesting in the way in which it implemented this policy and in the way this policy becomes implicated in official discourse by the government. This makes Plan Ceibal a rich site for detailed ethnographic research to study policy as meaning-making and eventually inform other policies or migrate findings to other local realities.

This chapter outlined some fundamental aspects of both EFL education and Plan Ceibal in Uruguay. It also described Fleetwood School and how it fits the bigger Plan Ceibal picture with a view to offering the reader a contextualization of the phenomenon under investigation and the research site of the study. The contextualization provided is essential for the situated interpretation of findings and discussions in Chap. 5 through Chap. 7 of the book. Chapter 5 shows the complexity of the two keywords in Plan Ceibal policy (technology and EFL) and how both key terms come to index different meanings across broader and narrower policy scales, including Fleetwood School-wise. Chapters 6 and 7 will focus on more micro-analytical issues by investigating two aspects of Vera's classroom and its enactment of Plan Ceibal: (1) How the introduction of the XO laptop calls for a particular distribution of semiotic labor between the laptop and the printed EFL textbook and the effect this has on how the EFL lesson is framed, constructed and negotiated; (2) What meanings students make with the laptop, what learning with this artifact means and how learning is assessed and recognized in this particular context.

Notes

1. A detailed account of English in Uruguayan education can be found in Kaiser (2017).
2. Initially, these were schools that had adopted a partial-immersion language program designed to teach curricular content through the target language. After the 2008 reform, though, the aim has changed and now these schools teach EFL through curricular content. To date, the coverage of this program is rather low since most of the governmental attention is now focusing on Ceibal en Inglés.

3. "TEFL expert" is the most common denomination. However, certifications and credentials for foreign language teaching vary substantially within the program.
4. A full report on the administration of this assessment test and scores can be found in the EFL Adaptive Assessment Test Executive Summary: http://ingles.ceibal.edu.uy/wp-content/uploads/2015/08/Evaluacion-adaptativa-Ingl%2D%2Ds-2014_Resumen-Ejecutivo1.pdf (Last access: 02/13/2017).

References

ANEP: Administración Nacional de Educación Pública. (2007). *Censo Nacional Docente (Official Census)*. Montevideo, Uruguay.

Banegas, D. L. (2013). ELT through Videoconferencing in Primary Schools in Uruguay: First Steps. *Innovation in Language Learning and Teaching, 7*(2), 179–188. https://doi.org/10.1080/17501229.2013.794803

Barboza Norbis, L. (2013). Plan CEIBAL: Procesos de planificación y desarrollo de la política educativa de TIC en el sistema educativo uruguayo. In C. M. de Rennie (Ed.), *Políticas y Experiencias Innovadoras en Educación: Uruguay y Brasil* (pp. 100–149). Montevideo: Arca.

Brovetto, C. (2011). Alcances y limitaciones del uso de tecnologías para la enseñanza de inglés en educación primaria. In L. Behares (Ed.), *V encuentro internacional de investigadores en políticas lingüísticas* (pp. 37–41). Montevideo: Asociación de Universidades Grupo Montevideo.

Brovetto, C. (2013). "Ceibal en Inglés": Enseñanza de inglés por videoconferencia en Educación Primaria. In *Aprendizaje Abierto y Aprendizaje Flexible. Más allá de formatos y espacios tradicionales*. Montevideo: Plan Ceibal.

CEFRL (Common European Framework Reference for Languages). (n.d.). Retrieved March 30, 2019, from https://www.coe.int/en/web/common-european-framework-reference-languages/level-descriptions

Clark, J. (n.d.). *OLPC and the US: The Factors Design for Development* (pp. 1–14). Stanford University.

CPLEP, ANEP: Administración Nacional de Educación Pública Comisión de Políticas Lingüísticas para la Educación Pública. 2005–2007. (2009). Documentos oficiales. Retrieved November 2, 2017, from http://www.anep.edu.uy/plinguisticas/phocadownload/publicaciones/comisionpoliticasling-uisticaseducacion%20publica.pdf

Ferreira Cabrera, G., Teliz, F. A., & Rodriguez Zidán, E. (2010). Gestión del cambio y nuevas tecnologías en Uruguay. Análisis de las percepciones docentes sobre el Plan Ceibal en Salto (pp. 250–263). In *Primer Foro Nacional de Ciencias de la Educación en Formación Docente. El rol del conocimiento en escenarios educativos en transformación*. Montevideo, Uruguay.

Frade, V. (2018). (Des)construcción de la identidad docente. Estudio de caso de enseñanza de inglés por videoconferencia en Uruguay. *Linguagem & Ensino, 21*, 121–146.

Gabbiani, B. (1995). Situación de la enseñanza del español y el portugués como lenguas extranjeras en el Uruguay. In *Anais do encontro sobre políticas lingüísticas* (pp. 81–87). Curitiba, Brasil: UFPR.

Gabbiani, G. (2010). Interacción entre pares y realización de tareas en edad escolar. Actas de las III Jornadas de Investigación y II de Extensión de la Facultad de Humanidades y Ciencias de la Educación. n/p.

Hepp, P., Hinostroza, E., & Laval, E. (2004). A Systemic Approach to Educational Renewal with New Technologies. In A. Brown & N. Davis (Eds.), *Digital Technology, Communities & Education* (pp. 299–311). New York: Routledge Falmer.

Index Mundi. (2018). Retrieved February 17, 2017, from http://www.indexmundi.com/

Kachinovsky, A., Martínez, S., Gabbiani, B., Gutiérrez, R., Rodríguez Rava, B., Ulriksen, M., & Achard, P. (2013). Impacto de Plan Ceibal en el funcionamiento cognitivo y lingüístico de los niños. In A. Rivoir (Ed.), *Plan Ceibal e Inclusión Social. Perspectivas Interdisciplinaria* (pp. 99–151). Montevideo: Plan Ceibal y Universidad de la República.

Kaiser, D. J. (2015). Ceibal en Inglés Report. Retrieved March 28, 2017, from http://ingles.ceibal.edu.uy/wp-content/uploads/2015/12/Ceibal-en-Ingl%2D%2Ds-Report-DJ-Kaiser-September-2015.pdf

Kaiser, D. J. (2017). English Language Teaching in Uruguay. *World Englishes, 36*(4), 744–759. https://doi.org/10.1111/weng.12261

Larrouqué, D. (2013). La implementación del Plan Ceibal: Coaliciones de causa y nueva gerencia pública en Uruguay. *Revista Uruguaya de Ciencia Política, 22*(1), 37–58.

Lingard, B., & Rawolle, S. (2011). New Scalar Politics: Implications for Education Policy. *Comparative Education, 47*(4), 489–502. https://doi.org/10.1080/03050068.2011.555941

MEC: Ministerio de Educación y Cultura (Ministry of Culture and Education). (2011). *Uruguay en Cifras*. Montevideo: Instituto Nacional de Estadística.

MEC: Ministerio de Educación y Cultura. (2013). *Desarrollo Profesional docente y Mejora de la Educación. Informe País.* Montevideo, Uruguay: Presidencia de la República.

Monreal, S. (2010). La educación británica. In J. A. Varese (Ed.), *Influencia británica en el Uruguay. Aspectos para su historia* (pp. 97–132). Montevideo: Cruz del Sur.

Phillipson, R. (1992). *Linguistic Imperialism.* Oxford: Oxford University Press.

Pischetola, M. (2014). Teaching with Laptops: A Critical Assessment of One-to-one Technologies. In M. Stocchetti (Ed.), *Media and Education in the Digital Age. Concepts, Assessments, Subversions* (pp. 203–214). Frankurt: Peter Lang.

Ranguis, C. A. (1992). Panorama histórico de la enseñanza de lenguas extranjeras en el Uruguay. In U. Kühl & M. Stephan (Eds.), *Las lenguas extranjeras en la enseñanza pública* (pp. 11–16). Montevideo: Instituto Goethe.

Rodríguez Zidán, E. (2010). El Plan Ceibal en la Educación Pública Uruguaya: Estudio de la relación entre tecnología, equidad social y cambio educativo desde la perspectiva de los educadores. *Actualidades Investigativas en Educación, 10*(2), 1–25.

Rodríguez Zidán, E., & Bochia, F. (2010). Estudio exploratorio sobre la percepción del impacto del Plan Ceibal ¿Cambian las prácticas de los docentes? In *Primer Foro Nacional de Ciencias de la Educación en Formación Docente. El rol del conocimiento en escenarios educativos en transformación* (pp. 264–280). Montevideo.

Sell, G. R., Cornelius-White, J., Chang, C. W., MacLean, A., & Roworth, W. R. (2012). *A Meta-synthesis of Research on 1:1 Technology Initiatives in K-12 Education.* Ozarks Educational Research Initiative. Retrieved March 30, 2019, from http://education.missouristate.edu/assets/clse/Final_Report_of_One-to-One_Meta-Synthesis__April_2012_.pdf

Vaillant, D. (2015). Uruguay: The Teacher's Policies Black Box. In S. Schwartzman (Ed.), *Education in South America* (pp. 405–421). London: Bloomsbury.

Viera, M. G. (2010). El instituto cultural Anglo-uruguayo. In J. A. Varese (Ed.), *Influencia británica en el Uruguay. Aspectos para su historia* (pp. 133–141). Montevideo: Cruz del Sur.

World Bank Group. (2017). Retrieved March 28, 2017, from http://www.worldbank.org/

Zheng, B., Warschauer, M., Lin, C., & Chang, C. (2016). Learning in One-to-One Laptop Environments: A Meta Analysis and Research Synthesis. *Review of Educational Research, 86*(4), 1052–1084.

5

Technology and EFL across Policy Scales

Chapter 2 underscored some of the theoretical and methodological implications of using scales to analyze meaning-making processes and, in particular, to analyze how meanings circulate—in different ways and directions—across policies in education. In broad terms, a scalar approach to social semiosis has the advantage of capturing the situated, dynamical, unexpected trajectories of meaning-making processes and to explore these trajectories through different—and yet complementary—time/space lenses. In particular, a scalar approach to policy in education has the advantage of better capturing the semiotic, ideological and discursive conflicts and struggles for meaning inherent in any policy design, implementation and enactment. By adopting this approach, we can study policy as a set of recontextualization practices (Wodak and Fairclough 2010) which entail ongoing transformation of meanings. These complex trajectories of meaning cannot be theorized solely in terms of institutional agency and overt power (such as *top-down* and *bottom-up* policies) or in terms of the stage and scope of action (such as macro, meso, micro aspects of a policy), because meaning-making is shaped and reshaped across scales.

The present chapter looks into how different scales dynamically operate in making and shaping meanings within and across Plan Ceibal policy. In particular, it looks into how two ideologically highly charged elements in the policy (technology and EFL) come to index different—and even conflicting—meanings across scales. Both technology (the broader Plan Ceibal) and EFL (Plan Ceibal en Inglés) appear—in different ways as I shall show later in the chapter—as the main goals of the policy. Technology and EFL, then, can be considered to operate as what other theoretical frameworks call *ideologemes* (Angenot 1977, 2010; Kristeva 1986), *keywords* (Williams 1983) or *concepts* (Gadamer 2002) of the policy, in that through these terms particular representations and positionings to social reality are defined, established, disputed, contested or even rejected. My argument is that these key policy terms are highly charged—socially, politically and ideologically, and therefore they scale jump (Blommaert 2007), making it evident that they are intertextually asymmetrical (ibid. 2007, 9) and that they constitute a site for defining what the introduction of technology in education might or should mean.

The fieldwork, visits to different schools and classrooms, as well as the conversations and interviews held with different stakeholders and the review of documents, mass mediatized texts, and so on point to something which may seem obvious about the meanings of the policy: EFL and technology (and in particular the XO laptop) in Plan Ceibal do not *mean* the same *across* policy scales. They also point to a less obvious fact: they do not mean the same even *within* the same scale. However, the focus of this chapter is not on *why* things do not mean the same across scales. The very notion of situated meaning-making processes makes the answer apparent: meanings are not fixed or stable. For this reason, my focus is in on *how* EFL and technology do not mean the same across and within scales or, in other words, on the instability of meaning (Lemke 1995) which allows for acceptance, contestation and rejection of representations, and at the same time provides political, cultural and semiotic cohesion to the policy across time and space.

It should be clearly stated that the aim is not to offer an example of how to do scalar analysis to investigate policies in education or any other social affairs. One of the main advantages—and biggest challenges—of ethnographic and socio-semiotic approaches lies in foregrounding the uniqueness and situatedness of context (Kress 2011, 2015), which requires the researchers to iteratively design questions, tools and research strategies that will help them deal with such uniqueness while at the same time will allow their research to be as transparent and transferable as possible. With this in mind, the focus is on how meanings are made and remade across scales in the particular policy under investigation.

Taken in isolation, the chapter offers an example of how key policy terms become a site of dispute and struggle to make sense of the policy, and how this is particularly complex when various scales are considered. Together with the rest of the book, the present chapter offers a narrative that contextualizes and describes what meanings several policy scales construct with regards to EFL and Plan Ceibal technology, to understand heterogeneous scales (Lemke 2000; Mortimer and Wortham 2015; Wortham 2006) through which the meaning(s) of EFL and technology are negotiated. This paints the big picture of how meanings circulate outside the focal classroom. Chapters 6 and 7, however, will adopt a more micro-analytical stance and will focus on smaller policy scales to explore the construction of EFL in the particular classroom under investigation.

XO Laptops in Society

Some five or six years ago, when Plan Ceibal policy was still gaining momentum, it could still catch the attention of locals to see six-year-old children turning on their XO laptops while sitting at the bus stop or riding on their way to school. It could also call our attention to see children during summer break sitting right outside a closed school trying to get a signal to play games on their XO laptops. In only a few years the policy grew so fast that such scenarios probably do not call our attention anymore. In fact, we now see how other social actors—such as retired citizens—also make use of Plan Ceibal technology (such as XO tablets) without finding it strange, as it once might have appeared to us. Such is the visibility of Plan Ceibal policy—and of the material artifacts associated with it—that regardless of the different opinions and attitudes people might hold toward technology and toward the policy, the presence of Plan Ceibal in everyday life is taken as a fact.

As a material artifact used inside and outside of Uruguayan schools, the XO laptop has become an iconic object of universalization and democratization discourses in public education. This makes the XO laptops more visible, and—metonimically—it also makes Plan Ceibal policy more visible in larger social scenarios outside of the educational realm. In general terms, lay citizens are aware of the policy and its aims, and the XO laptop represents Plan Ceibal to them, even though other technology artifacts are also involved in the policy (e.g. tablets or video-conference screens). Most students and parents, for instance, are aware of what the different models and designs of XO laptops are in terms of shape, size, color and some functionalities.

A quick look at the ethnographic data also points to this fact: XO laptops are visually represented in many different types of documents and texts, accounting for a wide array of social practices which range from official reports to authorities to international audio-visual documentaries and local TV advertisements. Plan Ceibal policy merchandise (stickers, book covers, website page, etc.), policy audio-visual advertising for local and international television[1] and official documents are only some of the many texts and practices in which the visual image of the XO laptop—representing not just the material artifact but the whole policy—becomes available and recurrent to society at large. To better illustrate this, I will draw on the Plan Ceibal website and the Plan Ceibal en Inglés TV spot. Both represent mediatized scales of the policy to which the lay citizen has access.

Image 5.1 shows Plan Ceibal's official website in 2016. Like most official websites, this page blends advertising and institutional discourse, information and publicity, to achieve two main purposes: informing and persuading citizens of the importance of the policy. The main page of the website design includes an icon that depicts the XO laptop. The icon is personified to interact with the website user. "Coco"—the name assigned to the icon—is an XO laptop that helps users (any user, not exclusively students) navigate the website and can also be used for consultations and questions. In the *Help* section, Coco—the XO laptop—invites the user to ask questions on how to use the site, among other things by stating: *¿Quieres que te ayude?* (*Would you like me to help you?*).

In this manner, Coco—a personified representation of the XO laptop—serves as a cohesive icon within the website (helping users navigate,

5 Technology and EFL across Policy Scales   109

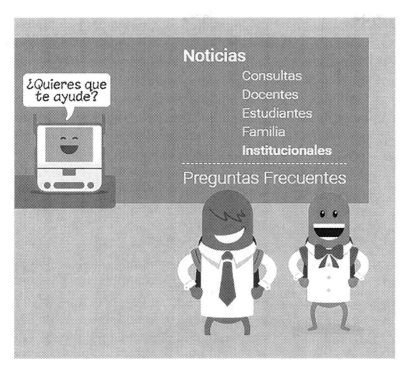

Image 5.1 XO laptop "Coco" in Plan Ceibal's website reproduced with permission by Plan Ceibal

find information, make questions, etc.). But at the same time it works intertextually and interdiscursively as a cohesive icon connecting the website and other texts, discourses and practices made by the policy, given the great visibility of the XO in society at large. A similar representation of the XO laptop can be found in merchandise, TV spots, banners, stickers and even in other material objects used in public spaces to share information about the policy.

Another example of the social visibility of Plan Ceibal laptops is their recurrent visual representation in Ceibal en Inglés advertising campaign in 2013. Interestingly, this was the first time in the history of the country in which a foreign language taught in public education was advertised on national television, making the policy also present—in a different genre—for the local audience. In this case, since public education in Uruguay is free of any charge what is "sold" in the advertisement is not a product to be bought, but rather consensus with the left-wing government and its actions in local education (in particular, the action of expanding EFL to primary public education).

Transcripts 5.1 TV spot script in Spanish and the English translation

Voice over: La educación pública está llevando la enseñanza del inglés a todas las escuelas del Uruguay [another voice: YES]. Para lograrlo cuanto antes, Educación Primaria y Plan Ceibal están trabajando juntos. Crearon salas de videoconferencia para que maestros y alumnos trabajen con profesores de inglés [EFL Remote teacher: Hello, Claudia! Hello, Children!] [Students: Hello, teacher!] que no están allí físicamente. Más de 700 escuelas tienen ya su sala de videoconferencia [song plays along] (Screen reads: "El inglés es muy importante. Alentá a tus hijos". Plan Ceibal").
[Voice over: Public education is taking the teaching of English as a Foreign Language to all schools in Uruguay [another voice: *YES!*]. To achieve this goal as soon as possible, Primary Education and Plan Ceibal are working together. They have created video-conference rooms so that teachers and students work with EFL teachers [EFL Remote teacher: *Hello, Claudia! Hello, Children!*] [Students: *Hello, teacher!*] who are not there physically. More than 700 schools already have their video-conference room [song plays along] (Screen reads: "EFL is very important. Encourage your children. Plan Ceibal")]

Throughout the spot, two main scenarios are depicted: schools and homes. These scenarios represent the far-reaching aim of the policy (bridging home and school practices), which in turn tells the policy apart from previous right-wing policies, as I will discuss below.

In the TV spot school classrooms are depicted with the Plan Ceibal technology artifacts (XO laptops, tele-conference screen), which show the changes that took place in the classroom ecology of public education. Likewise-as Image 5.2 shows—children's homes and schools are also depicted with the artifact as the roof of each house. Schools and houses look all the same, pointing to the democratization and universalization goals of the policy. Such discursive strategy in which universalization and democratization are instantiated by erasing off differences can be understood in the context of other traditional school policies. For instance, in Uruguay all primary school children who attend public school have to wear the same white school tunic and a dark blue bowtie. In doing this, their own clothes do not need to get dirty and, at the same

5 Technology and EFL across Policy Scales 111

time, it is thought they will all "look the same" and therefore will not be judged based on clothing.

In many shots throughout the TV spot these houses and schools show XO laptops depicted as roofs, visually representing the importance of XO laptops in bridging out-of-school and in-school technology practices and opportunities. This can work intertextually for the local audience, creating particular political and ideological meanings by separating Plan Ceibal from previous attempts by right-wing governments. As mentioned in Chap. 4, in the 90s the local right-wing government first started a policy to equip some public schools with computer labs and desktops. Such policy was not made universal and had a very small reach compared to Plan Ceibal. However, in more recent political campaigns some right-wing politicians claimed this attempt in the 90s was the inspiration for left-wing Plan Ceibal, discursively attempting to deprive the left from one of its most iconic social policies while in office. In this context, the fact that the TV spot represents XO laptops in homes and not only in schools can be read as a way of setting Plan Ceibal apart from previous right-wing policy attempts to incorporate technology in education by—somewhat implicitly—foregrounding discontinuity in policy-making.

Image 5.2 XO laptops (see roofs) in "Ceibal en Inglés" local TV spot (0:07) reproduced with permission by Plan Ceibal

These two examples from the larger ethnographic data are merely illustrative of the visibility and iconic value of XO laptops as artifacts that become signifiers for many different meanings at different scales. Despite such differences, the recurrent use of this icon can be thought to serve various purposes. On the one hand, these visual representations circulate across various social spaces creating a sense of cohesion among Plan Ceibal discourse (official and institutional documentation, advertisements, etc.) in a similar way that logos help to achieve cohesion in any advertising campaign (Cook 2001; Goddard 1998). On the other hand it can also be argued that these representations also serve the purpose of creating affective bonds with the audience, as the term "bondicon" (Martin 2008) suggests. As a bondicon, the visual representation of XO laptops across policy discourses attempts to underscore the role technology plays within the policy in achieving the main purposes of universalization and democratization of education and, at the same time, it associates such positive affect with the left-wing initiatives. The most obvious example of this, perhaps, is the TV spot in which school children's schools and homes (which provide a sense of positive affect) are literally next to Plan Ceibal's XO laptops (as the roof of each child's school and home) while other visual elements surrounding Ceibal technology (such as the national flag and the coat of arms) set an affective and nationalistic tone for the policy. Thus, these visual representations of the actual XO artifact become the "trademark" of the policy. Iconically, these visuals represent the actual XO laptop artifacts. Symbolically, they point to the goals of the policy: to democratize and universalize access to technology and to EFL in education and in society at large.

Anecdotally, through ethnographic fieldwork I learned that this emphasis the TV spot lays on positive affect and on the nationalistic tone of the policy is the result of previous TV spot sketches that were unsuccessful and did not air. For instance, at some point one agency involved in the advertising of Plan Ceibal sketched a TV spot which showed the Uruguayan map and then British flags started to appear all over the map, as a means to represent the expansion of EFL in Ceibal policy (universalization). Given the obvious imperialist and colonialist meanings that could be associated with such visual representation, it was decided that a different story would be told, which in the end resulted in the TV spot discussed in this section. In terms of scales, it is interesting to note how a failed attempt at designing particular meanings at one scale might have had an effect on the resulting meanings, which in this case foreground national values and identities. It is also interesting to note that such meanings are the result of the intertextual contestation to previous social practices—such as designing the spot—which are not available to the audience but certainly impacts semiotic processes.

EFL in Official Policy Discourse: Foregrounding and Backgrounding Technology

Looking into official documentation is certainly not enough to capture the complexity of policy design, implementation and enactment. Neither is it enough to explore the meanings that a policy makes and how they circulate. However, analyzing official documentation is an important task in this type of research because—from the point of view of policy-making—the meanings official texts make are expected to circulate and endure across time and space scales (Hult 2015), dictating—or at least attempting to shape—the implementation and enactment processes. In other words, official texts will foreground the desired paths of the policy and will attempt to background the undesired paths and meanings. However, how these meanings will actually circulate depends on their recontextualization (Johnson 2013) across scales.

Since its inception, Plan Ceibal's official discourse has associated the XO laptops with universalization and democratization policies. For instance, when discussing the introduction and use of XO laptops in public education, official policy discourse underscored the democratic aim of technology in Uruguayan education and linked this with the agenda of the left-wing government. This points to the wider aims of Ceibal Policy, which focus on the expansion (universalization policy) of technology access as a means to achieve social/educational equity (democratization policy). To illustrate this point, I will draw on the Executive Summary by Plan Ceibal (the first executive summary written which circulated in society at large). This document was written in 2009. The target audience is specialized (central government, institutions involved in Plan Ceibal, school administrators, etc.). The document is 32 pages long and was simultaneously published in Spanish and English, as most Plan Ceibal official documents are. It circulated in institutional spaces, although it is also available online.

I chose this document to illustrate my point because it is the one official texts in which the aims and goals of the policy are discussed in more detail.

Excerpt 5.1 Excerpt of the First National Monitoring and Evaluation Report on Plan Ceibal, Executive Summary (2009, 5)

Section 01: Objectives

Plan Ceibal's objectives focus on **the increase of social equity through the implementation of measures to universalize access and use of *new* technologies**[2] (particularly computers and the Internet) in Uruguay, initially through public primary school and, in a second stage, expanding the Plan to lower high school and private education. According to the Plan objectives (www.Ceibal.edu.uy and www.ceibal.org.uy) and to Presidential Decrees 18/April/2007 and 15/December/2008, **to provide primary and high school students with an Information Technology tool that allows connectivity through public *education***, will allow students and their families to access, appropriate and produce knowledge and get involved in new ideas, aiming at generating possible impacts on:

- Other members of the family who will be able, through the student, to access IT global services, regardless of geographic location or social condition
- The way in which citizens relate to information and knowledge, thus widening access to new and better services and job opportunities
- The increase in the number of original contributions and in innovation in different parts of the country as a result of the massive ICT use
- Improvements on teaching and learning processes, an increase in children's and teacher's motivation to acquire knowledge and the effective incorporation of IT literacy
---

A look at this text—as well as other official documents pertaining to the wider Plan Ceibal policy—reveals that it underscores the role of technology—and in particular the role of XO laptops as an icon of the policy—in democratizing access to information, learning opportunities and bridging the digital gap across the country. In the previous excerpt, lexico-grammatical choices show how *technology* and *democratization* (using words such as *equality, universalize* and *divide*) are connected in such a way that the introduction of the former is ideologically assumed (Fairclough 1989) as the trigger of democratization by causing structural social changes. As an example, let us see the following thread of lexical cohesion from Excerpt 5.1.

increase of ***social equity*** *» to* ***universalize access*** *and use of new technologies » to provide primary and high school students with an Information Technology tool » allow students and their families* ***to access*** *»* ***appropriate and produce***

knowledge » *access IT global services, regardless of geographic location or social condition* » ***widening access*** *to new and better services and job opportunities* »*increase in the number of original contributions.*

The notion that universalization of access to technology—through the XO laptops offered by Plan Ceibal policy—is a means to achieve educational democratization and equity has been present in official documentation from its inception allowing it to operate across a broad time/space scale in official discourse. Such democratization foregrounds public education, since private education is assumed to be one of the factors or symptoms of inequality.

However, when it comes to the narrower EFL policy of Ceibal en Inglés, the role of technology is somewhat different. Actually, as the TV spot transcripts (Excerpt 5.1) showed, EFL becomes the actual goal and technology is relegated to a means to achieve this goal.

To illustrate this, let us consider the Ceibal en Inglés Methodology Statement (2014) which—like the Executive Summary—discusses the goals of the policy in detail. This is a nine-page text dealing with the main goals and detailing the implementation process of the EFL policy. The target audience is specialized (central government, school administrators, EFL teachers, etc.). The document was produced within the context of Plan Ceibal as well as the previous text, even though new stakeholders were at stake since Ceibal en Inglés worked together with the British Council. The document was published simultaneously in Spanish and English. To date, it is one of the few official documents available for Ceibal en Inglés, and it circulated in official/institutional domains as well as on the web.

Excerpt 5.2 English Ceibal Policy Statement (2014, 4)

Ceibal en Inglés is an educational program **designed for teaching English to Uruguayan primary school children** and their teachers in fourth, fifth and sixth grades. For the program, **a new pedagogical model has been developed which consists of a blend of face-to-face and remote team teaching and adopts an innovative use of telepresence technology which allows for remote teaching in real time without losing the benefits of communicative language teaching methodology.** The program has been designed to tackle a problem in Uruguayan primary education: the lack of teachers of English. It is also based on a strength in Uruguayan education: the commitment of classroom teachers and their belief that learning English may become a most useful tool for the future of their students (…)

The addition of EFL to the wider policy discourse has an effect on the way in which technology is recontextualized from the broader Plan Ceibal. If compared to the summary, in the Ceibal en Inglés text technology is backgrounded or even downgraded: EFL becomes underscored as the democratizing and universalizing aspects of the policy, and Plan Ceibal technology becomes the means to reach them.

EFL is represented as the one element that needs to be universalized and democratized within the country, implicitly drawing on previous arguments education policy-makers had made about the privilege middle and upper class students have had in the past: foreign language teaching was not universal in public primary schools, but had always been part of private schools (CPLEP 2008). In fact, for a long time one of the most attractive features of private education highlighted in TV spots, school websites and other promotional discourses was access to foreign languages and, in particular, to English. EFL was—and to a great extent still is—perceived as a commodity (Cameron 2012) of high value in education and, for such purpose, EFL is a signifier of belonging to certain socio-economic groups.

Later in the document, the fact that technology is further problematized and backgrounded (as being a means, but not the goal of universalization and democratization) becomes apparent.

Excerpt 5.3 English Ceibal Policy Statement (2014, 4)

> **Technology imposes certain specific conditions.** The remote teacher **may not** walk around the classroom to see students' work, or speak personally to them; the remote teacher and the children **cannot typically** see each other's full body, this has to be taken into account when doing certain activities or representations which include movement; the frontal grouping of the class (i.e. with the teacher standing at the front and all students looking toward her) **is hard to change**. It also has positive consequences or potentially beneficial consequences. Integration of digital material is far more consistent and systematic in video-conference lessons (it does not depend on additional equipment, it is an integral part of the proposal). All materials can be maximized in size on the screen, this offers valuable teaching strategies.

Lexico-grammatical choices associated with technology make more negative meanings about the use of technology in the language program (see extracts in bold). However, this is representative of the first stages of implementation of Ceibal en Inglés but not necessarily of what happens at present. Interviews with stakeholders and fieldwork in the Ceibal en Inglés workplace indicate that during the first steps of the Plan Ceibal en Inglés policy it was met with some fear as to how this innovative policy would work out during the implementation (Brovetto 2011). Face-to-face teaching and the printed textbook were perceived as the default options for teaching and learning and thus the introduction of new technology such as the video-conference screen for remote teaching was seen as a potential deficit in teaching and learning practices. At present, however, Ceibal en Inglés is slowly starting to foreground the role of technology in the language program (with a view to potentially conceptualizing technology as more than a means to teach and spread the target language). For instance, a 2015–2016 study by Plan Ceibal en Inglés and other stakeholders set out to analyze remote teaching and classroom practices to explore the use of technology and learning outcomes (*vid* Marconi et al. 2018). It would appear that in the official Plan Ceibal en Inglés policy the status of technology is slowly transitioning from *means* to something else (potentially a *goal*, but still second to EFL). This points to the present stage of implementation of the policy and to the ways goals become reformulated as the policy spreads throughout the country across time and space. Based on the ethnographic fieldwork, this also seems to point to the ways in which stakeholders are changing how they orient to technology and to their use/adoption in education as the policy expands and the potential of new technology artifacts are further explored.

Technology and EFL: A Look at Policy *Bright Spots*

So far in this chapter I have focused on the meanings that are made about the policy (and in particular about technology and EFL) in different scales outside of classrooms, such as official documentation and advertisements. These scales foreground public education and the left-wing government's desire to universalize and democratize access to technology and/or EFL, depending on what is foregrounded for a particular audience. The remaining chapters of the book will look into a blind spot of the policy (i.e. a private school classroom) to explore what meanings are made in a classroom which is not the center of attention of official discourse but which also enacts the policy. In this section, however, I will briefly discuss what the situation seems to be in policy bright spots: public school classrooms. To do this, I will draw on the ethnographic data I collected during 2015 and 2016. In this period I visited several public schools and reviewed around 100 classroom videos in the Plan Ceibal en Inglés data bank. I also had access to the standardized lesson plans of the British Council and interviewed classroom and remote teachers, as well as other policy stakeholders in Plan Ceibal, schools and the Ministry of Culture and Education. In addition, I visited several private schools and interviewed teachers and school administrators, and I also was—for an 18-month period—an external consultant for a Plan Ceibal en Inglés research project.

It should be noted that my aim here is not to compare public school classrooms to private school classrooms or to suggest that my observations are generalizable. This lack of interest in comparing sites resides in a theoretical and a practical reason. Theoretically, I have delineated what a socio-semiotic approach has to offer to policy research and to learning research. This approach shares with ethnographies the idea that meaning-making is situated and context-bound. Each context of sign making, interpretation or circulation is—in theory and in practice—unique. Of course there might be more or less similar features when comparing contexts, but they are by definition different and the elements that constitute each context might operate differently. Along these lines, in this book I am not interested in comparing ways of enacting the policy in private and public schools or bright and blind spots. Instead, I am interested in exploring what a particular enactment throughout a school year (in Fleetwood School) can tell us about the policy, and about learning and how such findings can potentially migrate to other scenarios inside and outside the policy. A more practical argument against comparison is that my data from public and private schools were collected in very different ways and for different purposes. My access to public schools depended on the stakeholders' intention to take me to schools and—for practical and bureaucratic reasons—I did not have permission to record or videotape lessons myself. My main aim in attending public school was to get to know more about policy implementation and enactment and to have more robust data to contextualize the study. Despite these differences, considering both types of data is fundamental to understand how the policy operates across different scales and environments, since considering both types of data is highly informative of the many ways in which the policy constantly becomes recontextualized. At the same time, considering these data is important to better situate the bigger picture of the policy under investigation.

Having access to many sites in which the policy becomes recontextualized for the purposes of implementation and enactment allowed me to find some general trends in Ceibal en Inglés policy implementation, which of course derive from a main difference: unlike private education, its implementation in public education is highly regulated. For instance, in public education lesson plans, the units of classroom work and classroom activities and tasks are designed for teachers. Also, classroom materials (songs, videos, etc.) are offered to them, and EFL *mentors*[3] by Plan Ceibal supervise the enactment of lessons and the coordination between the remote teacher and the classroom teacher, among other things. Also, students' performance is assessed—nation-wide—via an EFL adaptive test,[4] as mentioned in Chap. 4. This test is completed with the XO laptops, but it only seeks to measure language ability, following a traditional ideology of learning for which it is demonstrated only linguistically. Most of the test design uses closed practice and closed questions, such as multiple choices, true or false, and so on.

The enactment in private education is very different, if compared to public schools and also if different private schools are compared. I call private school classrooms policy blind spots because these are not the focus of attention of the policy and therefore they do not face many restrictions. In fact, private schools do not even have access to standardized lesson plans or to the EFL program. They only have access to the actual XO artifacts (see Chap. 4).

In practical terms, this means that both the implementation of Plan Ceibal technology and how the EFL lesson is designed and enacted mainly depends on the school dynamics, whereas in public schools there are many curriculum elements (lesson plans, mentors, video-conference screen, remote and classroom teacher coordination) that make up an apparatus that operates to support—and also to standardize—implementation and enactment. There is a unified set of expectations for policy enactment in public schools, whereas expectations for private education depend on each school since the government does not have any particular expectation for them. This makes sense if put against what democratization and universalization means in official Plan Ceibal discourse and in the left-wing ideology, which foregrounds the need for public school children to access technology and EFL as a means to bridge educational, social and cultural gaps in Uruguayan society.

This main difference between bright and blind spots is one of the many doors to exploring the different ways in which the EFL classroom can be constructed within Plan Ceibal. Even though each classroom represents an ecology of its own (van Lier 2004a, b), policy scales posit some top-down restrictions on EFL classrooms. In public classrooms, for instance, interactions and practices are shaped and regulated by standardized lesson plans and scripts, material distribution and mandated nation-wide assessment tests. To some extent, this shapes how technology artifacts are used and for what purposes. For instance, the lesson design and script that teachers receive every week already indicate what materials are to be used, for what purposes, how they ought to be used and how the lesson should unfold in time. On the contrary, in private schools adopting Plan Ceibal technology implementation allows for a higher degree of situated agency (by school administrators, teachers and students) since goals and expectations need to be set by each school. This—in principle—allows for more creativity in use while it requires teachers to design their own lesson plans, assessment tests, and so on, and to negotiate the role technology will play in the EFL classroom, while of course it requires more time to plan and design lessons.

In this particular scenario, some of the questions I had in mind during the ethnographic fieldwork were the following: *What is the role of EFL and technology in these lessons? How do the discourses of universalization and democratization become recontextualized in classroom practices? Do they draw on Plan Ceibal's foregrounding of technology or do they draw on Plan Ceibal en Inglés backgrounding of technology and foregrounding of EFL?* The fieldwork indicates that in public schools EFL becomes an aim in itself and technology becomes somewhat relegated to a *means* to

5 Technology and EFL across Policy Scales

achieve this goal, as official Ceibal en Inglés policy documents dictate. For instance, Ceibal en Inglés lesson plans and actual enactment have EFL goals which pertain to the learning of lexical items, grammatical structures and phonic features, among others, but they do not have any goals as for how to interact and use technology. In fact, lesson plans generally do not even expect students to use technology artifacts such as the XO laptops but rather to witness how the remote teacher uses it to deliver the lesson. Democratization and universalization are then interpreted as having access to EFL lessons and technology is the means to achieve such goal regardless of whether students use it or not in the classroom.

The use of technology with the remote teacher mostly relies on the video-conference screen, which actually makes it possible to have the lesson. This means that in most of the in-class activities with the remote teachers, students do not use the XO laptops, but instead are exposed to EFL lessons by means of technology artifacts (video-conference screen, microphones, speakers and video-conference) which are most often controlled by the remote teacher from the teaching point. XO laptops are sometimes used—but not so often—when the video-conference is not present: the classroom teacher can sometimes review previous lessons by the remote teacher (as expected in a few lesson plans) and this might require the use of XO laptops. Interestingly, since the classroom teacher might have some, little or even no-ability in English, the use of the XO is seen as a means to support the teacher by providing guided practice or drills.

However, in remote lessons, which are delivered by the remote teacher, there is a wide range of activities, software and other resources used to teach, but there are mostly handled by the remote teacher and not by students. As a consequence, learning to use these artifacts—and developing digital literacy—is not associated with the goal of the Ceibal en Inglés policy. In this respect, while the ecology of the classroom (remote teacher, tele-conference screen, etc.) is quite innovative, the actual classroom practices can be said to be traditional in that EFL goals mainly entail the introduction and practice of vocabulary and grammar through structured practice. In fact, these practices reflect a traditional ideology of learning and a traditional ideology of EFL, as discussed in Chap. 3. As was stated earlier, however, supervisors and other stakeholders are starting to envision the potential of eventually incorporating technology as another one of the goals of the EFL lesson. This, in turn, might impact classroom practices.

Some of the Plan Ceibal en Inglés stakeholders I interviewed indicated that one of the reasons they were being cautious about technology is because of the way lessons were designed. The one weekly lesson delivered by the remote teacher (EFL-speaker) focuses on what constitutes—for the policy—the *legitimate learning*, which entails the introduction and practice of linguistic points. Therefore, technology artifacts do not become foregrounded but are just a means for *curricular learning* to take place. On the other hand, the other two lessons taught by the classroom teacher (non-EFL expert) are mainly used for *reviewing* and *recycling* and therefore allow for more technology artifacts to be used by students, such as the XO to work with the CREA2 platform, among others. Actually, the official document that provides guidelines and suggestions for classroom teachers underscores the benefits of using the CREA2 and other platforms in class (Plan Ceibal en Inglés Handbook 2013) so as to favor the use of XO laptops in these lessons, but not necessarily in the lessons taught by remote teachers. At this point of implementation, the extent to which technology artifacts—other than the video-conference screen—are used mostly depend on the enactment, and their use is not an aim in itself, but a means to practice what has been *officially learned* in the remote teaching lesson.

The prototypical enactment of a Plan Ceibal en Inglés lesson implies similar routines every week in terms of the roles the remote teacher and students are officially assigned in relation with the technology artifacts. The remote teacher (located in a teaching point outside of the school) video-conferences with the students (located in an equipped room at the school)[5] to deliver the EFL lesson. While technology affordances allow for either party to make adjustments (to the speakers, screen, directionality of camera, etc.), whatever is shared on the screen is controlled by the remote teacher.

The way in which this technology is used can vary substantially. For instance, during one of my visits the unit of classroom work *Clothes* was being enacted based on the standardized weekly lesson plan delivered to both the remote and the classroom teacher. At different points of the 45-minute lesson, the remote teacher shared content on the screen in order to, for instance, introduce a new task (*Let's play a game* read on the video-conference screen), to explain the objectives and delivery of the whole unit of classroom work (at another point *Objectives. What are you wearing?* reads on the screen), or even to complete a classroom task (a matching exercise requiring students to match pictures of different garments with their appropriate name in English). However, while students performed the matching orally, it was the remote teacher who controlled the technology to actually do the matching by moving the mouse and clicking on the clothes. In this manner, some technology affordances (pointer, cursor, mouse arrow) which are shown on the screen can then be used as signs of engagement (Bezemer and Kress 2016) produced by the shaping-agent (i.e. the RT) based on the modal affordances of the artifact. However, in such instances students themselves did not make their own signs with technology but instead they were supposed to attend to technology in the EFL lesson.

Unlike remote teachers—who are in charge of the teaching of content and the unfolding of the full lesson and what it implies in terms of technology—the role of classroom teachers is more varied in the enactment. While some classroom teachers sit and observe the lesson, others participate in the enactment by regulating or helping regulate students' behavior, by "acting" as students and performing tasks to learn together with their students, or even by co-teaching with the remote teacher. A detailed account of these roles is far beyond the scope of this chapter, but a closer look into these can be found in Frade (2018). For the purposes of this chapter, suffice it to say that most of the technology is used by the remote teacher and not by classroom teachers or students, and that most of the teaching is expected to depend on the remote teacher.

This brief illustration gives us an idea of how students experience technology in this policy by *witnessing* (i.e. by demonstration) while they perform tasks to learn the target language. Along the same lines, it should also be noted that Ceibal en Inglés nation-wide assessment focuses on testing language components and skills (*grammar, vocabulary, listening comprehension*[6]) but to date there are no items measuring the extent to which students are able to use the XO laptops or other Ceibal technology artifacts to make meanings in the classroom. Students use the XO laptops to complete the test, but they only use the artifact as a replacement of paper-based tests. In this respect, the artifact has a similar function in the assessment as a means to "transfer" meanings, not focusing on the affordances of this medium to construct particular types of meanings. This also contributes to foregrounding EFL—and more implicitly some particular ideologies of learning—as the main objective of Ceibal en Inglés and relegating technology to a means to do so.

In the next section, I will describe some of the meanings attached to XO laptops and EFL at Fleetwood School, one of many policy blind spots. I will mostly draw on ethnographic data from individual and group interviews with students. I will not present data from classroom interaction and work because these will be the focus of the remaining chapters, which will adopt a more micro-analytical stance to exploring scales and meanings in policy enactment.

Technology and EFL: Fleetwood School as a Policy *Blind Spot*

As explained in Chap. 4, Fleetwood School offers students two *learning streams*: the bilingual and the regular one. Students attending the regular stream pay a lower fee, stay in school for four to five hours a day and have EFL lessons three times a week, while students attending the bilingual stream stay longer and have EFL lessons every day. This seems to have an effect on the ways in which students and teachers represent XO laptops in particular and, more generally speaking, new technology and its use in EFL classrooms. School administrators, teachers and parents share some expectations for each stream. This, in turn, creates particular meanings about EFL, about what being bilingual is and about the role of the new artifact in teaching and learning experiences, as shall be studied in the next chapter.

Several of the interviews I conducted with students and teachers show a recurrent pattern. Students attending the regular stream are positioned—by others and by themselves-as Spanish monolinguals because they do not have as much EFL class work and as many class hours as those attending the bilingual stream. They also identify themselves as not being bilingual because they do not perform certain school activities, such as sitting for international EFL exams, planning a trip to London during Summer break in third-year high school, among others. This traditional ideology of bilingualism that relates the amount of exposure to the language with the degree of bilingualism the student possesses is still quite dominant in Uruguayan education and permeates EFL classroom discourse and practices (Canale 2014). It is precisely within this ideology that English overtly appears as a commodity reproducing differences of social power and access, but quite different from the way this difference appears in public education.

As noted earlier in the chapter, Plan Ceibal official discourse orients to EFL as a commodity that has for a long time been the almost exclusive possession of middle and upper classes who pay for private primary education. In this context, Plan Ceibal en Inglés seeks to eradicate this difference. In accessing EFL in public schools, English might no longer be a signifier of belonging to certain socio-economic groups in Uruguayan society. In a private school like Fleetwood, however, the situation is quite different. Students with more exposure to the language, more opportunities to travel to the countries in which the language is used and more EFL certificates are valued as being *more bilingual* than those who have not had such access and therefore the former are considered to have more opportunities to succeed in, for instance, the job market. Here it is not a matter of access/no-access to English, but instead *how much* access you have to it and what school practices legitimate your "status" as a speaker and as a student.

This distinction does not only pertain to access to EFL, but instead to how students see themselves, the lessons they attend and even the access to XO laptops and technology. While students in the regular stream of Fleetwood School are positioned as non-bilinguals or monolinguals, those attending the bilingual stream, who are positioned by themselves and by others as Spanish-English bilinguals, complain about the dynamics of their own classes. They mostly complain about not using the XO laptops—or any other technology artifact—and position students in the regular stream as being "lucky" for having not only "easy" lessons (due to their *lack of EFL knowledge*, as they put it), but also for their regular use of XO laptops and other technology artifacts. Teachers in the bilingual stream argue they do not use such technology, because students need to work toward international examinations and so there is no time for using the XO laptop. The following excerpt from a group interview with five students on the bilingual stream illustrates my point.

Extract 5.1 Interview with third-year high school students (6/17/2015)

G: And so, what do you like doing outside of school?
S39: Mmm video games.
G: Oh, videogames… do you video-game in English?
S12: Yes (inaudible).
G: So, tell me any videogame you play that is in English.
S39: Mmm. The, the legend of Zelda.
G: Oh, ok. Not sure I know it. Good.
S31: Yes, me too. And I play in English because it's an online… so you play with other people and they speak English so… I play in English. Some games are not local locally served, so now, now we play, we can play some in Spanish.
G: So now there are some in Spanish.
S39: But still it's faster if you play in the English group.
G: So you're all in the bilingual stream, right?
S34: Well, not me. I was but this year now I changed to the normal, the regular one.
G: And what was your impression when you changed?
S34: **That it is harder. The bilingual is harder.**
G: Why?
S39: **Because the level is higher.**
S34: **Yes, the exercises are harder, what you have to do is harder. It's for bilingual students, you know?**
S313: And you have to prepare exams. International exams.
G: And what do the others do?
S34: **But they** [students in the regular stream] **have a different level. They cannot talk too much in English or understand everything. It's different. They are not bilingual, but they do some things in English, of course. But that's why we go to London, to England in third [year]…and they don't.**
G: So what do they do?
S33: (inaudible) In… **in a way it's better for them.** We all do, I mean all we do is exam practice now. **We do mocks from the books. We don't do other things. They do other things. Have more fun. They use the computers.**
G: You don't use the XO laptops much in the English class?
S34: No. Never.
S31: No, we don't use them. We practice for the exam because we need to pass it. In the bilingual stream we take international exams.
G: Did you use it in previous years?
S34: No.
S31: Not too much. We also prepared other exams. Like PET or KET. Now we are preparing First.

There is a whole set of school practices that contributes to the positioning of these students as bilinguals: learning-to-the-test experiences, longer hours of work, not using some curriculum artifacts (such as the XO laptops) while legitimating the use of others (textbooks for exam preparation) and even traveling to England.

However, while students attending the regular stream are positioned as non-bilinguals, their classes are perceived as more fun due to the use of technology artifacts (in particular the XO laptop). The XO laptop comes to be a signifier of innovative EFL lessons, even though they do not represent—according to most students—any benefit for educational and curricular EFL purposes, as shown in the next excerpt of an interview with a student attending the bilingual stream (in the same year as the previous students).

Extract 5.2 Interview with S17, first-year high school student in the bilingual stream (11/6/2015)

G: And so, what do you do in the EFL class?
S17: Uh?
G: In the English class, what do you usually do?
S17: We… we learn vocabulary, grammar, do listenings, we practice [for] the exam.
G: What exam?
S17: I will take FCE [First Certificate Examination] this year.
G: Is it similar to what your classmates on the regular stream do, more or less?
S17: Mmm…no.
G: Why?
S17: They… **they do not speak English so much. They do more easy things.**
G: And they don't do exam preparation, right?
S17: Yes, but they… **they… it's better for them. They go out, eh, they do other things. They don't have exams. They go to the computers, they use Ceibalitas** [XO laptops].
G: Do you use computers too?
S17: At home, yes. Here, no.
G: And they do… I mean your classmates on the regular stream.
S17: Yes, the Ceibalitas [XO laptops] and the computer room. And…yes. They, yes.
G: Would you like to use the laptops in the English class, then?
S17: Eh, yes. We use it in Math, in drawing class, in geography sometimes [subjects taught in Spanish]. Not in the English class. I like use the laptops. Using the laptops.
G: **Do you think they have an advantage in learning English with those laptops?**
S17: **Mmm, no. Because we learn more. We do difficult exercises. We travel to England. We know more English but are…they have fun more funny in the class.**

Extract 5.2 also shows the mismatch students in the bilingual stream perceive between their use of technology at home and in the school. However, traditional (and exam-based) classroom practices come to be signifiers of bilingualism, and even when they claim to "envy" students on the regular stream for using XO laptops, they represent these students as monolinguals, drawing on a "deficit" or traditional ideology which assumes *the more exposure, the better* in terms of achieving proficiency in the target language. As reported by the focal teacher Vera—who teaches in both the regular and the bilingual stream (see Extract 5.3), this distinction of bilingual/non-bilingual students and the notion that XO laptops play a different role in EFL classes whether they are designed for regular or bilingual stream students are in consonance with school discourses and expectations.

Extract 5.3 Interview with Vera (7/13/2015)

G: So, is it different, I mean the extent to which XO laptops are used in the bilingual and the regular stream?

V: Oh, yes. Yes, it is different. We…**the teachers, we agree that for the bilingual stream they need a lot of practice for the exam. A lot of practice. They need to know and master the test,** you know? **In the regular stream they can do more things. I can include laptops, I can take them anywhere outside of the school. Well, they do not use English that much because remember they are not bilingual. Right? But in the class you can teach in better ways because you can include technology and not only the textbook. They get bored with the textbook sometimes.**

G: Do you like that, I mean, incorporating technology?

V: **Yes. I think. I think it is very important nowadays. For their future. They will learn some English and they will learn how to use the computers. They need to know how to use the computers. And even better if they know how to use the computers in English. That's very important.** I know in the bilingual stream they have to learn to take the test, it's not the same as learning English for pleasure, but, you know, we need to make sure they pass the test because parents pay a lot of money and the school wants that the bilingual students take international exams.

G: And why is that so?

V: Because they are bilingual. So they have to … they need to have a certificate that proves they have attended a bilingual school and that they can speak and write in English fluently. But I would love to do other things with them, like using laptops like I use with first graders. But I can't.

Even when the teacher seems to draw on the same deficit ideology to define bilingualism, she does see a benefit in introducing XO laptops in the foreign language classroom. As shall be seen in the next chapters, the flexibility—typical of the blind spots I visited—she sees in the regular stream EFL lessons, allows her not only to introduce XO laptops in the lesson, but also to blend the focus of the EFL curriculum—from EFL learning (vocabulary items, grammar structures, etc.)—with digital literacy goals. She does not find such flexibility in the bilingual classes, as well as classroom and remote teachers do not seem to generally find such flexibility in public education or policy bright spots. For Vera, such flexibility for regular EFL lessons provides a space for teacher's agency in deciding what EFL is in a classroom in which technology artifacts are employed and how new technology should be incorporated in the official EFL curriculum (even when the EFL official curriculum does not foresee the use of technology since it was published before Plan Ceibal was officially launched) (see Chap. 4).

At Fleetwood, this difference in teacher agency and flexibility between the regular and the bilingual stream also translates to wider school practices. For instance, students attending the bilingual stream are tested on their EFL proficiency by standardized international tests (designed, administered and graded by international agencies), while the test used to assess EFL students in the regular stream is generally designed by each teacher or agreed upon among school teachers. For these reasons, there seem to be two main meanings attached to learning English at Fleetwood: on the one hand learning English means *getting the certificate* (legitimation of knowledge by institutions), while on the other hand learning English means *learning to use the language to learn about other things* (including technology), which represents a way of conceptualizing content-based instruction model. This particular meaning attached to English (*learning to use the language to learn about other things*) will be the focus of Chap. 7.

Needless to say, the meanings about XO laptops which circulate in Fleetwood are different from those which circulate in other private schools, even in schools who opt out Plan Ceibal and do not use XO laptops or any other Ceibal technology. A recurrent pattern seems to emerge in schools of the upper class metropolitan area. In these schools, administrators and principals claimed they did not opt in Plan Ceibal because their students already have access to better and more advanced technology in the school and at home. In some cases, other issues seem to be at stake as well, such as the association of XO laptops with a social outreach plan. For some, the fact that the main goal of Plan Ceibal is to democratize and universalize access of technology (and also EFL) within the country implies focusing on the working class and mostly the underprivileged. While they did not necessarily manifest disagreement with the policy, they pointed to the fact that XO laptops for them are signifiers of socio-economic groups with very different interests, needs and expectations from their own.

Conclusions

Meanings are context-bound, they move in unpredictable ways across time and space, and they also become recontextualized as they travel across scales. This chapter showed this by describing some of the ways in which some policy key terms (such as EFL and technology) are represented across several policy scales. The aim was not to provide an exhaustive analysis of the policy at various scales, but to draw on larger ethnographic data to make a theoretical point about the instability of meaning and how this can contribute to several positionings to the policy within and across scales. In this respect, the policy (Plan Ceibal) and its key terms (EFL, technology) come to be signifiers of very different things as they continuously become recontextualized.

While XO laptops are highly visible for society at large—metonymically representing the whole policy—particular scales and different stakeholders make particular meanings about them. In official documentation, XO laptops and Plan Ceibal technology in general are foregrounded as the goal of democratization and universalization. However, Ceibal en Inglés documents recontextualize this by backgrounding technology to a means and foregrounding EFL as the policy goal.

This multiplicity of meanings does not only pertain to policy design and implementation, but also to enactment. Learning goals and instruments are recontextualized in different scales. Public school classrooms—as policy *bright spots*—tend to draw on traditional ideologies of learning and of EFL to foreground EFL learning goals (language/grammar based).

Such bright spots will use Plan Ceibal technology to achieve these EFL goals, through video-conference sessions. Technology, then, is mostly seen as a means (or even as a "problematic" means in official documentation) to achieve the goal of spreading EFL in primary schools. Democratization and universalization are about EFL, and technology is a means to achieve such goal.

Private school classrooms—as policy *blind spots*—such as Fleetwood School have more agency in making decisions about what technology to use, how to use it or for what purposes. Therefore, there are potentially more diverse ways in which the EFL school subject can be constructed through classroom practice and work. This is the case because public EFL classrooms need to follow standardized day-by-day (scripted) lessons as well as to use standardized classroom materials. Also, because they have the supervising figure of *mentors* who on a regular basis attend schools and talk to RTs and CTs to make sure coordination between both is taking place. All these regulations, of course, shape—albeit not entirely—how EFL is constructed as a school subject.[7]

Technology and EFL may make different meanings to different stakeholders even within the same scale. As for Fleetwood School, for instance, it has been noted that the use of XO laptops differentiates "bilingual" from "non-bilingual" EFL students. Along these lines, bilingualism is characterized by the non-use of technology, together with many other school rituals such as: standardized tests, traveling abroad, exam preparation and practice, and so on. Many factors in the school and classroom environment—such as Vera's perceived greater agency in enacting the EFL curriculum in the regular stream—also contribute to the use of XO laptops, which allows Vera to blend technology and EFL goals: while traditional EFL goals (learning vocabulary and grammar structures) are maintained in her enactment—as dictated by the National EFL curriculum-, she also adds a digital literacy aspect to her class and attempts to find ways in which both goals can co-exist. As will be noted in the following chapters, the ways in which these goals are "blended" characterize the way in which the school subject EFL is constructed in her class, pointing to both the stage of implementation of technology in EFL lessons and her own conception of how technology should be incorporated into the EFL classroom.

While in official Plan Ceibal documents and policy design there is a focus on democratization and universalization of technology and EFL, being a private school—with less policy restrictions and constraints—discourses of democratization do not become entextualized in Fleetwood because such democratization of access is not required or is not a valid reason for the introduction of technology. The implied discourse is one of social distinction through the status provided by English as a language of power associated with local elites. For instance, since its inception Fleetwood has had a computer lab for students to use technology in any subject, and most students own desktops and/or laptops at home. The complex curricular scenario of the school, however, creates particular meanings about XO laptops. Students are institutionally positioned as bilingual or non-bilingual based on the stream (their parents) chose for them (or were able to afford). XO laptops, albeit associated with *having fun in class*, become associated with non-bilingual classes (who have the time to *not learn to the test*) and thus XO use becomes a signifier of *not being bilingual, not having enough knowledge of the target language*. In this respect, the artifact has a dual meaning as a signifier of lower status, but also as a resource for more engaging learning experiences.

To sum up, the discussion presented in this chapter is indicative of the many ways in which meanings can be made and re-made within a policy to foreground the social, the economic, the technological or even the linguistic depending on the scale at hand. It also shows how meanings about a policy are constructed and reconstructed in different ways across time and space scales, pointing to the fractal nature of scales (Blommaert et al. 2015). This fractality is in a way mirrored by the vast meaning-making potential of two signifiers which are key to the policy: (XO) technology and EFL. As key elements, what these terms mean, how they mean and how social actors position toward them gives us an idea of how social reality and the policy are continually constructed and reconstructed.

Notes

1. See, for instance: https://www.youtube.com/watch?v=S-2lJdutHAw (Last accessed: 4/8/2015).
2. Throughout the chapter italics are mine.

3. Within Plan Ceibal en Inglés implementation, mentors are Plan Ceibal hired staff who—among other things—are in charge of ensuring the coordination between the classroom and the remote teacher. They might also assist teachers or oversee the weekly lesson enactment.
4. Prueba Adaptativa: http://ingles.ceibal.edu.uy/wp-content/uploads/2015/08/Evaluacion-adaptativa-Ingl%2D%2Ds-2014_Resumen-Ejecutivo1.pdf (Last accessed: 10/02/2017) (ANEP 2014, 2016; Plan Ceibal/Departamento de Segundas Lenguas y Lenguas Extranjeras 2014).
5. This means students have lessons with the remote teacher in a room different from the room they use with the classroom teacher. In my observations, I learned equipped rooms vary depending on the school (schools may equip one classroom, older computer lab rooms, an indoors school yard or even the school kitchen depending on their availability). Private education classrooms, however, do not face this equipping issue because they do not buy the video conference equipment, but the actual XO laptops.
6. At present there is also a new proposal to work on oral skills as well.
7. By this I do not intent to say there is no room for teacher agency. On the contrary, during my visits to public schools and to Plan Ceibal teaching points I saw teachers who also added extra materials to their lessons or adapted tasks and exercises for their own purposes. However, it is true that such standardized materials and practices normalize the school subject EFL, limiting the degree of teacher agency.

References

ANEP: Administración Nacional de Educación Pública Consejo de Educación Inicial y Primaria Plan Ceibal, VV.AA. (2014). Prueba Adaptativa. Retrieved October 2, 2017, from http://ingles.ceibal.edu.uy/wp-content/uploads/2015/08/Evaluacion-adaptativa-Ingl%2D%2Ds-2014_Resumen-Ejecutivo1.pdf

ANEP: Administración Nacional de Educación Pública, Plan Ceibal, VV. AA. (2016). Prueba Adaptativa. Retrieved February 17, 2017, from http://www.ceibal.edu.uy/Documents/Presentaci%C3%B3n%20Prueba%20Adaptativa%20Ingl%C3%A9s.pdf

Angenot, M. (1977). Présupposé, topos, idéolog idéologème. *Études Françaises, 13*(1/2), 11–34. https://doi.org/10.7202/036642ar

Angenot, M. (2010). *El discurso social. Los límites históricos de lo pensable y lo decible*. Buenos Aires: Siglo XXI.

Bezemer, J., & Kress, G. (2016). *Multimodality, Learning and Communication. A Social Semiotic Framework*. London and New York: Routledge.
Blommaert, J. (2007). Sociolinguistic Scales. *Intercultural Pragmatics, 4*(1), 1–19. https://doi.org/10.1515/IP.2007.001
Blommaert, J., Westinen, E., & Leppänen, S. (2015). Further Notes on Sociolinguistic Scales. *Intercultural Pragmatics, 12*(1), 119–127. https://doi.org/10.1515/ip-2015-0005
British Council. Plan Ceibal Lesson Plans (samples) (for circulation among RTs and CTs) (unpublished).
Brovetto, C. (2011). Alcances y limitaciones del uso de tecnologías para la enseñanza de inglés en educación primaria. In L. Behares (Ed.), *V encuentro internacional de investigadores en políticas lingüísticas* (pp. 37–41). Montevideo: Asociación de Universidades Grupo Montevideo.
Cameron, D. (2012). The Commodification of Language: English as a Global Commodity. In T. Nevalainen & E. C. Traugott (Eds.), *The Oxford Handbook of the History of English* (pp. 352–361). New York: Oxford University Press.
Canale, G. (2014). *Adquisición de la fonología. El inglés como lengua extranjera en estudiantes montevideanos*. Montevideo: Comisión Sectorial de Investigación Científica de la Universidad de la República.
Cook, G. (2001). *The Discourse of Advertising*. London and New York: Routledge.
CPLEP: Comisión de Políticas Lingüísticas en la Educación Pública. (2008). *Documentos de la Comisión de Políticas Lingüísticas en la Educación Pública*. Montevideo: Administración Nacional de Educación Pública.
Fairclough, N. (1989). *Language and Power*. New York: Longman.
Frade, V. (2018). (Des)construcción de la identidad docente. Estudio de caso de enseñanza de inglés por videoconferencia en Uruguay. *Linguagem & Ensino, 21*, 121–146.
Gadamer, H. G. (2002). *Verdad y método II*. Salamanca: Sígueme.
Goddard, A. (1998). *The Language of Advertising*. London and New York: Routledge.
Hult, F. M. (2015). Making Policy Connections across Scales Using Nexus Analysis. In F. M. Hult & D. Cassels Johnson (Eds.), *Research Methods in Language Policy: A Practical Guide* (pp. 217–231). Malden: Wiley.
Johnson, D. C. (2013). *Language Policy*. New York: Palgrave Macmillan.
Kress, G. (2011). 'Partnership in Research': Multimodality and Ethnography. *Qualitative Research, 11*(3), 239–260. https://doi.org/10.1177/1468794111399836
Kress, G. (2015). Designing Meaning. Social Semiotic Multimodality Seen in Relation to Ethnographic Research. In S. Bollig, M. S. Honig, S. Neumann, & C. Seele (Eds.), *MultiPluriTrans in Educational Ethnography. Approaching*

the Multimodality, Plurality and Translocality of Educational Realities (pp. 213–233). Verlag: Transcript.

Kristeva, J. 1986. *The Kristeva Reader* (T. Moi, Ed.). New York: Columbia University Press

Lemke, J. (1995). *Textual Politics. Discourse and Social Dynamics.* London and Bristol: Taylor & Francis.

Lemke, J. (2000). Across the Scales of Time: Artifacts, Activities, and Meanings in Ecosocial Systems. *Mind, Culture, and Activity, 7*(4), 273–290. https://doi.org/10.1207/S15327884MCA0704_03

Marconi, C., Brovetto, C., Perera, M., & y Méndez, I. (2018). *Enseñanza de Inglés a través de videoconferencia: Estudio sobre calidad, características y prácticas docentes, interacciones en el aula y aprendizajes.* Montevideo: Plan Ceibal.

Martin, J. R. (2008). Intermodal Reconciliation: Mates in Arms. In L. Unsworth (Ed.), *New Literacies and the English Curriculum. Multimodal Perspectives* (pp. 112–148). London: Curriculum.

Mortimer, K. S., & Wortham, S. (2015). Analyzing Language Policy and Social Identification across Heterogeneous Scales. *Annual Review of Applied Linguistics, 35*, 160–172. https://doi.org/10.1017/S0267190514000269

Plan Ceibal. Ceibal en Inglés Handbook. (2013). Montevideo, Uruguay.

Plan Ceibal. Ceibal en Inglés Methodology Statement. (2014). Montevideo, Uruguay.

Plan Ceibal/Departamento de Segundas Lenguas y Lenguas Extranjeras. (2014). *Evaluación Adaptativa de Inglés en el Sistema Educativo Uruguayo.* Montevideo, Uruguay: Administración Nacional de Educación Pública.

Plan Ceibal. Executive Summary. (2009). Montevideo, Uruguay.

Plan Ceibal Website. Retrieved from October 2, 2017, from http://www.ceibal.edu.uy/

van Lier, L. (2004a). The Semiotics and Ecology of Language Learning. Perception, Voice, Identity and Democracy. *Utbildning & Demokrati, 13*(3), 79–103.

van Lier, L. (2004b). *The Ecology and Semiotics of Language Learning. A Sociocultural Perspective.* New York: Kluwer Academic Publishers.

Williams, R. (1983). *Keywords. A Vocabulary of Culture and Society.* New York: Oxford University Press.

Wodak, R., & Fairclough, N. (2010). Recontextualizing European Higher Education Policies: The Case of Austria and Romania. *Critical Discourse Studies, 7*(1), 19–40. https://doi.org/10.1080/17405900903453922

Wortham, S. (2006). *Learning Identity. The Joint Emergence of Social Identification and Academic Learning.* Cambridge: Cambridge University Press.

6

Laptops and Textbooks as Curriculum Artifacts: Audience, Authorization and Ideologies in the Classroom

The previous chapter looked into several policy-making scales and how these operate in particular ways triggering situated meanings about policy key terms. It also discussed how the meanings made in the context of such policies circulate not only across classroom events, school practices and official policy-making but, in a broader sense, across society at large. In this context, the meanings made and re-made across policy scales do not pertain only to the interpretation of the policy itself (what it seeks to do, how it seeks to do it, who is involved in this and how) or to the interpretation of participants' roles and statuses (policymakers, teachers, students, parents and other stakeholders). On the contrary, the meanings that are made to circulate across policy scales also pertain to and permeate material objects such as curriculum artifacts themselves. This, in particular, is relevant when attempting to explore an education policy from a socio-semiotic approach, since not only human participants are engaged in meaning-making, but also the objects that inhabit the environment, such as the curriculum artifacts used for pursing policy aims, as is the case of the XO laptops within Plan Ceibal in Uruguay.

For theory development, the assumption that artifacts also play a key role in semiosis and in policy recontextualization allows us to think of policy implementation and enactment and learning in much more complex ways: a policy not only attempts to design a space for learning—*how* and *what* is legitimated as such—but it also attempts to ensure that meanings will be made and will circulate in particular ways across scales. However, situated agency, as discussed in earlier chapters, shows that this is not always the case. For policy research, the assumption that artifacts play a key role in meaning-making processes opens up a space for different ways of understanding the materiality of the classroom, as well as the materiality of policy scales implicated in a particular environment. Conceiving the classroom, sign-makers and artifacts in socio-semiotic terms (see Chap. 3), we can draw on several data collection tools and engage in different types of analyses to explore the many different ways in which a policy is constructed and reconstructed across scales, as well as how learning becomes implicated in such multi-scalar practices and processes.

This chapter explores some of the ways in which curriculum artifacts interact with each other and with humans in the classroom.[1] My focus is on two artifacts that are used throughout the school year to offer cohesion to teaching and learning practices: the (XO) laptop and the EFL printed textbook. In exploring this, my aim is to investigate the meanings of XO laptops and EFL textbooks—as material artifacts—with a focus on the classroom environment. In particular, I draw attention to two interrelated aspects: (1) the teacher's agency in selecting which artifact learners will use for completing a particular task and—at the same time—how this selection is dictated by the requirements and expectations of two legitimating audiences inside and outside of the classroom (students and EFL supervisors, respectively), and (2) the teacher's use of (multimodal) regulatory discourse to sign-post which artifact is authorized for a particular task and how this establishes some division of labor between the laptop and the textbook.

Both points raised will help us better characterize the two ideologies of learning described in Chap. 2. The first ideology of learning foregrounds the foreign language as *the* legitimate resource for making meanings in the classroom and the second one foregrounds the multimodal nature of communication, positing language as *one* of the many resources available to students for making meanings and learning.

As the analysis[2] will show, the teacher and the deployment of certain artifacts shape classroom experiences and practices, creating particular meanings of EFL and learning through organizing and framing the lesson. For this reason, understanding the degree to which the teacher has agency in certain policy scales—such as the actual classroom—is paramount to understanding how and why she designs spaces for learning, which often implicitly defines learning in particular ways. Chapter 7 will focus on learners' agency in appropriating artifacts and transforming available signs to represent and communicate to others. Taken separately, each of these chapters foregrounds different types of situated agency based on the roles of each participant (teacher, students). However, taken together these two chapters demonstrate that agency across scales is far more complicated than the mere addition of teachers' and students' agency in learning. In other words, the decision to explore the teacher's and students' agencies in two different chapters is for the sake of argumentation and clarity. However, theoretically speaking the situatedness of meaning-making processes requires us to think of agency as something that becomes articulated in different ways at different scales in a particular environment.

The Textbook and the Laptop as Curriculum Artifacts within the Policy

The use of textbooks or laptops in schools and classrooms does not just imply a change in the media (printed page v. screen page) authorized for learning. On the contrary, the use of laptops as curriculum artifacts responds to broader changes in the resources and affordances provided to learners, which ultimately impact meaning-making processes. This is because different artifacts provide different organizations of textual material within the medium (printed or screen page) as well as different possibilities for multimodal ensembles (Bezemer and Kress 2015, 2016). These, in turn, provide particular resources for interacting with the artifact and learning. When this is thought in terms of a classroom and school environment, it becomes evident that legitimating the use of certain artifacts throughout the school year authorizes certain artifacts for learning, and such artifacts become more salient to parents, students, and other stakeholders. Also, throughout classroom practice and interaction with the artifact, particular routes of interaction are also legitimated and even routinized.

To illustrate this, let us consider some of the differences between the two curriculum artifacts under investigation. Because of their explicit pedagogical orientation, printed textbooks tend to guide semiosis in explicit ways and attempt to socialize students (Curdt-Christiansen 2017) perhaps in more implicit ways. This is not only done by the selection of information and "facts" or by authorizing some types of meanings and representations (van Dijk 1981; Weninger and Kiss 2013), but also by presenting and structuring activities and tasks in a particular manner which represents the ways in which designers assume students should interact with the artifact for "appropriate learning". Learners and teachers have some degree of agency in classroom practices and can contest such expectations (Luke et al. 1989). However, the ways in which this artifact is usually designed and framed in school practices contributes to establishing particular types of interactions with the artifact and to legitimate particular pedagogies and ideologies of learning, which may coincide to a greater or lesser degree to that of the teacher or the students. For their part, laptops offer a more open semiosis (Jewitt 2004, 2006) since they allow for more—and structurally less guided—ways of interacting with them (for instance, searching, selecting, evaluating and even creating texts), different readings paths, more dense hypermodal and hypertextual connections (Lemke 2002) and even more possibilities for "playing around" with affordances and re-shaping the traditional notions of audience and author (Rymes 2012).

EFL classrooms in Uruguay have traditionally been characterized by the widespread use of (printed) textbooks,[3] as has been the case in most parts of the world (Gray 2002). Language textbooks foreground verbal language as *the* authorized resource for meaning-making processes in the classroom. Notions such as *monomodal literacy culture* (Kress 1997) and *traditional view of learning* (Kress 2013) account for this monomodal tradition which has permeated (still) governing views of foreign language teaching (Kress 2000) and—in a more general sense—applied linguistics (Kress 2015) and additional language studies, as addressed in Chap. 3.

The implementation of Plan Ceibal policy has started to change the learning environment by introducing XO laptops and other technology artifacts, which provide particular affordances and reshape the authorized ways of making meanings as well as the authorized curriculum artifacts. Potentially, this change can bring about a shift in local ideologies of learning and on the role of affordances (other than verbal language) for meaning-making processes in the classroom. However, such change is—to my mind—yet to be seen. For instance, most of my visits to schools and conversations with stakeholders provide evidence that even though XO laptops are becoming more frequent and less marked curriculum artifacts for classroom interaction and work, the ideologies of learning underlying assessment design still rely heavily on monomodal ideologies. In most cases, tests that only seek to measure linguistic achievement (mostly by mechanical practice and drillings) are designed in XO laptops. The reason for this—it could be argued—is that while using the laptops for assessment is a signifier of progress and universalization of access to the Uruguayan society which foregrounds Plan Ceibal as a successful policy, the promotion of still dominant monomodal practices and assessment secures some continuity in the educational environment and also complies with traditional notions of power in education.

Regardless of this, it is fair to say that at present the landscape of curriculum artifacts in local EFL classrooms is transitioning and is quite complex. On the one hand, this complexity is connected to the fact that most of the official documentation and syllabuses for EFL instruction were designed before the introduction of XO laptops (ANEP 2008; CES 2006). This announces a potential conflict: curricular design, syllabi and other official discourses were conceived before the plan to introduce XO laptops and before making Plan Ceibal official. On the other hand, the complexity of EFL classrooms is also due to the different degrees of regulation or non-regulation the policy has had, which impacts on which are the mandated and available curriculum artifacts in particular classroom environments. For instance, for EFL primary-level classes in public education there is no mandated textbook, so Plan Ceibal classrooms mainly make use of video-conference screen and students' XO laptops, with the particular division of labor between the remote and the classroom teacher, as explained in

Chap. 4. EFL high school classes in public education, however, make use of a mandated EFL textbook (which by the time of data collection was *Uruguay in Focus*[4]). They also make use of video-conference screens and XO laptops for "conversation lesson" purposes. However, not all schools have been fully equipped yet, so some schools still do not use video-conference technology and, for those reasons, they follow a different EFL syllabus. Private schools have always been less restricted: they can choose to use any material (although some EFL textbooks are recommended) and they can also make use of XO laptops if they have opted in Plan Ceibal. Eventually, they can also use any other technology artifact available at their own cost.

These diverse classroom scenarios within the same policy not only show a stage of implementation of the policy, but also point to the many ways in which the school subject EFL can be constructed with regards to what artifacts are mandated, available or chosen for curriculum enactment. Such a situation, however, might not be strange or unknown to teachers across the world, who are used to such complex and diverse teaching and learning scenarios.

In the remaining of this chapter, I will study how a particular combination of artifacts (XO laptop and printed textbook) cohabit a specific classroom environment and how the teacher (Vera) frames their use. The aim is not to provide generalizable findings or to discuss the need to use one or the other artifact for particular purposes. Grounded in data analysis, my intention is to show—in policy enactment—the teacher's situated—and to some extent restricted—agency in designing particular spaces for students to interact with artifacts in the classroom, at the same time that such designs provide us with an insight of what Vera considers learning to be about. In framing these artifacts in the classroom, I will show how Vera sign-posts which meaning-making processes will be authorized and to what uses artifacts can/should be put in the classroom. Framing the use of these artifacts, in turn, contributes to characterizing which type of artifact-learner interaction will be regarded as "good learning" or at least "authorized learning" in the classroom. I shall return to this later in the chapter.

Constructing the Audience(s) of the Lesson: Authorizing Textbook and Laptop Use

A look at the enactment of all five units of classroom work throughout the school year (see Appendix) points to an interesting fact about the use of XO laptops and the EFL textbook in Vera's classroom. For the first units of the academic year, the EFL textbook was always more regularly used in the first lessons while the XO laptops were more often used by the middle and end of each unit of classroom work. Also, as the academic year unfolded, the XO laptops were used more often and the EFL textbook was used less systematically.

This recurrent pattern responds to Vera's own conception of curriculum artifacts use and learning objectives. Vera's agency in designing and enacting the EFL-regular stream lessons allowed her to introduce more technology-based tasks and projects than for bilingual stream lessons (as discussed in the previous chapter). Each unit was project-based and the final project always consisted of an XO laptop-made end-of-unit text, which represented an aspect of the main topic of the unit and related it to learners' own lives. As reported by Vera, this allowed her to teach EFL—in the traditional sense—while at the same time she was able to teach students how to use XO laptops and the software and tools available in a socially meaningful way.

With this in mind, it makes sense that the EFL textbook was mostly used at the beginning of the unit as an authorized artifact to introduce the content and vocabulary at hand, while the XO laptops were used by the middle and end of the unit, when they first explored the software and tools and then designed and presented their own texts to the whole class.

A deeper look into the data also shows that this division of labor between the mandated EFL textbook and the XO laptops responded to Vera's construction of two different audiences for her class, each of which had particular expectations and requirements. Vera acknowledges that the incorporation of technology is important for EFL students to learn digital literacy for the twenty-first century. She finds it important to allow students to become social agents who can act on the world around them. On the other hand, Vera also claims that EFL state supervisors (*inspectores*)[5] expect teachers to use the mandated textbook with a certain frequency and therefore she needs to make sure that—to some extent—that requirement is met. She is aware of how this could/should be translated into school documentation: while her teacher's book (see previous footnote) highlights the monomodal (linguistic) goals of each unit (vocabulary and grammar structures learned by students), her enactment of the lesson focuses on the use of XO laptops for digital literacy goals which underscore multimodal texts and students' agency in deciding how and what texts to design. Ultimately, the two audiences for Vera's lessons respond to the co-existence of traditional and alternative ideologies of learning, pedagogy and education, or the transition from the agency of teaching to the agency of learning (Kress 2013).[6] This is illustrated by the mismatch between her teaching records (for the school and EFL supervisors) and her actual enactment of the lesson. For instance, for *My Family* unit of classroom work, her records indicate that the focus is on the linguistic goals—mostly vocabulary and grammar—and on the verbal skills required for learners to successfully complete their work (for instance, present tense, possessive adjectives, object pronouns, etc.). According to the records, these linguistic goals are to be achieved mainly by filling out exercises, drilling and controlled and semi-controlled practice, all of which point to a traditional construction of the school subject EFL.

Interestingly, while there is no mention of the XO laptop in these records, the mandated EFL textbook is mentioned under the label "classroom material" (actually, it is the only classroom material mentioned). If this is checked against the actual enactment of the lesson (see Appendix), the focus on XO laptop use becomes evident. The recontextualization (Bernstein 2000) of one practice into the next (i.e. from lesson design to enactment) implies a change in focus. Vera's agency does not only lie in the incorporation of XO laptops and the combination of EFL goals and digital technology goals, but also in the way she addresses each audience (learners and supervisors) and how the EFL lesson is presented to them. In other words, recontextualization always implies a change of social context (Kress 2015) and in this particular case the construction of an audience outside of the classroom (supervisors) and the construction of an

6 Laptops and Textbooks as Curriculum Artifacts: Audience...

audience inside of the classroom (learners) make evident how the classroom environment is part of a larger—and much more complicated—institutional and national education system.

In general, the textbook tasks selected by the teacher focus on language drilling and controlled practice. These tasks are short and to be completed within the lesson. Interestingly, although the textbook offers some basic end-of-unit projects (e.g. *writing a postcard to a friend using photographs you have taken, writing a tourist guide for those who visit your neighborhood*, etc.), Vera does not make use of these. Instead, she leaves project-based instruction for the use of the laptop, increasing substantially the degree of difficulty in the projects and final outcome (texts).

Her design of projects for which the laptop must be used impacts learner-artifact interaction as well, as Image 6.1 shows.

The use of the laptop requires students to interact with the artifact in different ways. On this occasion (see Image 6.1) students are walking around the school block and documenting what they see and hear for the eventual making of a 3D map of the block. For such purpose, one student is drawing their walking direction on her notebook, while another one is recording sounds with the laptop and the third one is taking photographs

Image 6.1 Students' division of labor for laptop use (Unit 5, Day 10)

with the laptop. This task is prototypical of the laptop use in Vera's classroom in that it required students to work in collaboration and divide tasks and to explore on their own. It is also prototypical in that it required students to work on their laptops at different moments in different lessons, thus achieving curricular cohesion within the unit at hand.

As can be noted from the example above, Vera orients the use of each artifact to each of her classroom audiences: one projected to wider scales outside of the classroom (parents, EFL supervisors) and another one inside of the classroom (the actual students). Other classroom practices also respond to these dual audience requirements for artifact use and interaction. For instance, assessment entails two types of classroom events: the final text students make with the XO laptops by the end of each unit (which will be analyzed in the next chapter) is considered a test and Vera assigns grades to students based on this assignment and based on their ability to explain the decisions they made while designing it. However, she also designs a traditional EFL final test—which is kept with other school files—for which students need to sit by the end of the academic year.

In contrast to the texts made by students with the XO laptops, this final test designed by Vera focuses on mechanical practice (filling out blanks, matching sentences, completing dialogues) and writing. From our previous discussion on the concept of recognition, we could ask what it is that she can recognize of students' meaning-making processes with each of these instruments. My tentative response to this will be provided in the next chapter.

For the sake of the current chapter, suffice it to say that in Vera's more traditional test students' expected production seeks to demonstrate their "EFL competency" focusing on the monomodal ability to communicate using written language resources. This meets the expectations and regulations set by EFL supervisors and contrasts with the final texts students make with their XO laptops, which are also used for assigning grades to students. In this way, the construction of two audiences for Vera's class does not only pertain to the ways in which official and school documents are filled out, but also to everyday classroom practices involving students' meaning-making and the assessment of their learning. For formal assessment, however, Vera finds it easier to design tests to measure

6 Laptops and Textbooks as Curriculum Artifacts: Audience…

language achievement and she finds it harder to come up with guidelines for assessing the multimodal work of students, as discussed in more detail in the following chapter.

During one of my interviews with her, Vera addressed this topic and her orientation to each audience.

Extract 6.1 Interview with Vera (7/23/2015)

G: And so, how do you design lessons? I mean, in general.
V: Well, you know. It takes some time to design each unit. I've used this and other units before, but I always change something. It's always like designing a new one. The students are also different every year, so I have to have a new one. Always.
G: And what do you consider for the design?
V: Well, yes. You know, I always want them [students] to use the computers [XO laptops] so I… I make sure the unit has to do with things and technology. Something for them to use the computers and learn vocabulary but also learn to do something with the computers using that vocabulary.
G: Oh, I see.
V: And of course you also need to use the book. Parents buy the books and inspectors [state EFL supervisors] want us to use the book. So I use the book as well, but parts of the book, not all. I find the things, I mean, the exercises I like about the book and the other parts I don't use.
G: So how do you know what parts you choose? Tell me about that.
V: Things I know students may like, or things that are useful for recycling, revising, or sometimes things that I can connect to the exercises with the computers.

Aware of administrative requirements and of parents'[7] expectations, Vera agrees to use some units and sections of the EFL textbook, which she sees as *a* (not *the*) legitimate curriculum artifact. However, her focus is mostly on the use of XO laptops and to achieve this she blends monomodal (linguistic) goals (present in the official syllabus and on the textbook) with digital literacy goals, which she introduces to her class during the enactment of the lesson. Then, while the curriculum—and traditional pedagogy—legitimates the textbook, the enactment legitimates XO laptops.

The way in which Vera addresses both audiences is actually well received by other EFL teachers I interviewed at the school. Teachers her own age—and even younger teachers with less experience—look up to her work because even though she has been teaching long before Plan

Ceibal was set up, Vera was willing to introduce technology into her classroom and to look for innovative ways of using it for EFL purposes. However, more traditional practices still cohabit her classroom, such as formal written tests, as expected by other stakeholders, and in these practices there seems to be no room for the XO laptops or other new technology artifacts.

Framing the Use of Curriculum Artifacts: Teacher Regulative Discourse and the Demarcation of Artifact Functions

In the previous section I briefly characterized how a teacher might address different audiences while at the same time designing and enacting the class. Addressing such audiences, as was shown above, has an impact on curriculum in terms of classroom interaction with curriculum artifacts, among other things. In this section, I will look into how the teacher frames classroom tasks in order to design particular spaces for learning in the EFL lesson by regulating—at the same time—behavior and content. Behavior here does not only refer to human behavior (what students must or mustn't do) but also to human-artifact interaction (when and how an artifact should be used or how students should interact with the artifact). Such regulation is also a signifier of successful learning: particular ways of acting and interacting with an artifact can be positively or negatively rewarded based on what the task at hand is and what Vera's expectations for learning are.

Following the work of Bernstein, Christie (2002) discusses the concepts of regulative and instructional register. For Christie, classroom genres are based upon the interrelatedness of both notions. On the one hand, (first order) regulative register refers to a set of lexico-grammatical choices pertaining to and showing regulation of classroom behavior, activities, and so on. On the other hand, (second order) instructional register refers to a set of lexico-grammatical choices pertaining to and constructing the content being taught. Such characterization is useful to understand teachers' agency in interaction and enactment and in designing particular learning environments, as discussed in Chap. 3 when I addressed issues of agency and the Sydney School.

The notions of regulative and instructional discourse can be expanded to also account for non-verbal choices and resources to better represent the multimodal nature of semiosis and the many *pedagogic modalities* (Rose 2014, 2018) involved in classroom discourse. Regulative and instructional meanings are made in the classroom by means of several resources other than just verbal language (writing and speech). Gesture, gaze and posture are some of the many resources that can contribute to the regulation of classroom events as well as to the content and tasks at hand, as we shall see next.

Oftentimes in Vera's classroom—and more often for the first units of classroom work—when a task required the use of the XO laptop, she used highly regulative discourse to frame how and when this artifact should be used. Boundaries between the use of the XO laptop and the textbook are interactively constructed even when both artifacts may be physically present at the same time and space. On most occasions, even when textbooks and laptops may be physically together in the space of the classroom, they are "alone" when it comes to a particular classroom activity, that is to say, either one is generally used, but not both for the same task or activity, and students do not get to decide which artifact is to be used.

Let us take an example from unit 1 (*My family*), day 2. This was one of the few occasions on which both artifacts were physically present in the classroom environment, since later on the XO laptop became part of everyday tasks and the textbook was not used any more throughout the unit. On this day, Vera had brought the XO laptops from the computer lab room where they are kept and given one to each student.

After working with students on the description of some famous families (with pictures on the whiteboard), Vera asked them to look for other families online and to make comparisons between their own families, the family they had chosen and the families they had already worked with in class. However, the presence of both artifacts on students' desks did not imply the joint use of artifacts to fulfill the same task. Regulative discourse by the teacher interactively set tasks boundaries, establishing when one artifact should be used and how it should be used.

Extract 6.2 Regulatory discourse for laptop use (Unit 1, Day 2)

Time	Participant/s action (gesture, hand, body, gaze)	Verbal interaction
32:07	V walks along classroom	V: (to the whole class) Ok, so now turn on the laptops, las prenden, ¿ta? *[turn them on, right?]* And look for information about the famous family ¿Qué van a usar entonces para buscar la familia? *[What are you going to use to look up the family?]* (at different points, students turn on their XO laptops)
32:19	S2 raises hand V looks at S2	S2: Internet
32:26	V points at S2's XO laptop	V: Sí, las ceibalitas [laptops] para buscar en Internet lo que sea. *[Yes, the laptops to look up whatever on the Internet]*
		S4: ¿Tenemos que escribir la información en inglés, teacher? No me acuerdo algunos nombres de la familia. *[Do we need to write the information in English, teacher? I don't remember some of the names of family members]*
32:49	V looks at S4	V: If you can't remember a word about family and family members what can you do? ¿Qué pueden hacer si no se acuerdan de algo? *[What can you do if you don't remember something?]*
32:58	S4 raises hand V looks at S4 and nods	S4: ¿Buscamos en internet? *[We look it up on the Internet?]*
33:06	Points at textbook on S4's desk	V: No, no. Van al libro, que ahí ya está todo el vocabulario que vimos. ¿Estamos? Se fijan en el libro y ahí repasan el vocabulario que se tendrían que acordar. *[No, no. You go to the book because there is all the vocabulary we saw. Ok? You check the book and there you review the vocabulary you should remember]*

To explore how this type of interaction serves both purposes of classroom regulation and setting boundaries for artifact use and interaction, I will focus on the experiential and interpersonal meta-functions or, in other words, on how experience is represented and how interpersonal relations are constructed in this brief classroom event, respectively. For such purposes, I draw on speech function and negotiation sequence analysis (Martin and Rose 2007). Speech function pertains to the interpersonal metafunction and describes exchange in interaction, whether in terms of question, offer, statement or command. This allows us to analyze how social identities are constructed and reconstructed in discourse and how participants position themselves and others. Negotiation sequences, on the other hand, allow participants to take up different roles in interaction and to signal them through particular interactive moves. For instance, a participant can present themselves as the one performing an action (A1) or expecting somebody to perform an action (A2). They can also present themselves as owning information (K1) or requesting information to others (K2). Needless to say, in interaction these moves can be realized by several resources (not only by written or oral language) and other moves can be incorporated to add layers of complexity to negotiation. For instance, a participant can offer feedback (F) to a previous move or delay (d) what a previous move poses as the preferred next move.

Speech function and negotiation sequence analysis show how interpersonal meanings are made in this interaction, establishing teacher's, students' and even artifacts' identities with regards to the task at hand.

Extract 6.3 Speech function and negotiation sequences

Participant	Clause / Action	Speech function	Negotiation / Sequence
V	Ok, so now turn on the laptops	Command	
V	las prenden, ¿ta? *[turn them on, right?]*	Command	A2
V	(and) look for information about the famous family	Command	
V	¿Qué van a usar entonces para buscar la familia? *[What are you going to use to look up the family?]*	Question	K2
Ss	(students turn on their XO laptops)		A1
S2	Internet	Answer	K1
V	Sí, las ceibalitas [laptops] para buscar en internet lo que sea *[Yes, the laptops to look up whatever on the Internet]*	Statement	K2F

(continued)

Extract 6.3 (continued)

Participant	Clause / Action	Speech function	Negotiation / Sequence
S4	¿Tenemos que escribir la información en inglés, teacher? *[Do we need to write the information in English, teacher?]*	Question	K2
S4	No me acuerdo algunos nombres de la familia *[I don't remember some of the names of family members]*	Question (expanded)	
V	If you can't remember a word about family and family members, what can you do?	Question	dK1 (delayed)
V	¿Qué pueden hacer si no se acuerdan de algo? *[What can you do if you don't remember something?]*	Question	
S4	¿Buscamos en internet? *[We look it up on the Internet?]*	Answer (modalized)	K1 / K2[a]
V	No, no. Van al libro, que ahí ya está todo el vocabulario que vimos. *[No, no. You go to the book because there is all the vocabulary we saw]*	Answer Command	K1
V	¿Estamos? *[Ok?]*	Question	
V	se fijan en el libro *[You check the book]*	Command	
V	(y) ahí repasan el vocabulario que se tendrían que acordar. *[and there you review the vocabulary you should remember]*	Command	

[a]"¿Buscamos en Internet?" modalizes the force of the statement (the answer to Vera's question) by presenting it in the form of a question

Most of Vera's moves imply a command through which she explicitly regulates how the activity shall be performed (*Ok, so now turn on the laptops*) or a pedagogical question through which she checks whether students understand how to use the XO laptops (*If you can't remember a word about family and family members, what can you do?*). Students, on the other hand, mainly answer her questions or ask questions about the regulation of the activity (*¿Tenemos que escribir la información en inglés, teacher?*). The asymmetry in the interaction becomes apparent through these patterns, and also through students' actions. For instance, aware of Vera's interactive evaluation of their understanding of the task, S4 raises her hand (awaiting Vera to bring her into the interaction) and modulates her answer by presenting it as a question (by means of intonation), which mitigates the force of the assertion (*V: ¿Qué pueden hacer si no se acuerdan de algo? S4: ¿Buscamos en Internet?*). Through verbal and kinesthetic modes, then, students' and teacher's identity are interactively negotiated in order to make sense of the current task and of classroom expectations. This is also evidenced in the negotiation sequence. Most of the times, Vera is positioned as the one participant requiring action or information (A2, K2). This makes students either perform an action (such as turning on the laptops at 32:07) or answer a question about the regulation of the activity (*V: ¿Qué van a usar entonces para buscar la familia? S2: Internet*). Asymmetry in interaction is also evidenced here, since Vera can also delay moves (see dK1) or extend them by follow-up (see K2F), which construes Vera as having more possibilities not only to regulate the activity, but also to regulate the interaction through which the activity is introduced and explained. Concomitantly, artifact-learner interaction is also regulated, as shown in the excerpt. This brief illustration shows how—drawing on several semiotic resources—the teacher can create particular interpersonal relations with students and with the artifact so as to shape and regulate the activity. By doing this, she can also authorize particular ways of interacting with the artifact in future classroom events.

Let us now turn to the analysis of experiential meanings. To do this, I will draw on transitivity analysis (Halliday 2014). I will focus on the analysis of main clauses, for which I will explore the representation of processes and participants. Processes are nuclear elements in representational structures which construct the events, states, and so on participants engage in. They can be material ("doing"), mental ("sensing"), verbal ("saying"), relational ("being" or "becoming"), behavioral ("behaving") and existential ("being").[8] I will also analyze participants and their roles in these events/states. For instance, in material processes participants can be "actors" if they "do" something in the physical world, "goals" if they are the result of what is "done" or "scope" if they are an entity affected by the "doing", among others. In mental processes participants can be "sensers" if they do the "sensing" or "phenomena" if they are "sensed". In verbal processes they can be "sayers" if they communicate, or they can be "verbiage" (what is said) or "addressees" (to whom something is said). In relational processes they can be "carriers" when they are the entity being described or they can be "attribute" when they describe the entity, among others. A thorough description of these labels can be found in Halliday (2014).

Extract 6.4 Experiential meanings

Participant	Main Clause	Process type	Participants' roles
V	Ok, so now **turn on** the laptops	Material	Actor: students Goal: laptops
V	las **prenden**, ¿ta? [***turn** them **on**, right?*]	Material	Actor: students Goal: las (laptops)
V	(and) **look for** information about the famous family	Material	Actor: students Scope: information about the famous family
V	¿Qué **van a usar** entonces para buscar la familia? [*What **are** you going to use to look up the family?*]	Material	Actor: Students Scope: qué
S2	Internet	Material	Actor: (implicit "us"), students Scope: Internet
V	Sí, las ceibalitas [laptops] para buscar en internet lo que sea [*Yes, the laptops to look up whatever on the Internet*]	Material	Actor: (implicit, students) Scope: las ceibalitas
S4	**Tenemos que escribir** la información en inglés, teacher? [*Do we need to write the information in English, teacher?*]	Material	Actor: us (students) Goal: la información

(*continued*)

6 Laptops and Textbooks as Curriculum Artifacts: Audience...

Extract 6.4 (continued)

Participant	Main Clause	Process type	Participants' roles
S4	No **me acuerdo** algunos nombres de la familia [*I **don't remember** some of the names of the family members*]	Mental	Senser: "I" (student) Phenomenon: algunos nombres de la familia
V	If you can't remember a word about family and family members, what **can** you **do**?	Material	Actor: you (student/s) Goal: do
V	¿Qué **pueden hacer** si no se acuerdan de algo? [*What **can** you **do** if you don't remember something?*]	Material	Actor: you (student/s)
S4	¿**Buscamos** en internet? [*We look it up on the Internet?*]	Material	Actor: (us) students
V	No, no. **Van** al libro, que ahí ya está todo el vocabulario que vimos. ¿Estamos?[b] [*No, no. You **go to** the book because there is all the vocabulary we saw, ok?*]	Material	Actor: ustedes (students) Scope: el libro
V	**se fijan** en el libro [*You **check** the book*]	Material	Actor: you (students) Scope: el libro
V	(y) ahí **repasan** el vocabulario que se tendrían que acordar. [*and there you **review** the vocabulary you should remember*]	Material	Actor: ustedes (students) Scope: el vocabulario

[a] "¿Estamos?" (literal translation: *Are we?*) pertains to the interpersonal level operating somewhat in a similar way as an "ok?" backchannel question in English. For this reasons, it is not included in the analysis of material process

The previous extract shows the coding of experiential meanings through the analysis of participants and process types in main clauses. The analysis of experiential meanings helps us to understand the ways in which students' and teacher's authorized behaviors are negotiated interactively, such as in what language to perform the activity, what artifact to use and when and how to use it.

As can be noted, experientially the regulative discourse is mainly constructed though the use of material processes where students are expected to be the actors. Most of the processes involved are material and point to the regulation of the task at hand and how the artifact must be used to successfully complete it (*turn on, look for, van a usar [going to use], tenemos que escribir [have to write]*). Through these processes, students are represented as actors, whether they are positioned by Vera (*las prenden, van a usar, se fijan, repasan* [*turn them on, going to use, check, review*]) or by themselves (*tenemos que escribir, buscamos*) [*have to write, look up*]; in the latter case this contributes to the self-representation of students as a single class identity: "we, students". These actors are expected to follow certain patterns or routines to successfully perform a task.

There is only one mental process (*no me acuerdo*) [*I don't remember*], which helps to construct individual experience, and for which only S4 is represented as the actor. This reinforces the idea that through material processes, which regulate the ways in which the laptop should be used, Vera represents all students as having the same goals within the task. On the other hand, most of the times the scope or goal of material processes are the XO laptops or any of its affordances (for instance, the Internet).

These meanings are not only conveyed verbally, but through other modal resources as well. For instance, the fact that Vera represents all students as a single audience to which the same requirements and rules apply is conveyed kinesthetically by the way she moves across the room to signal that all students are the audience (see Extract 6.2, 32:07). The way she establishes eye-contact with a particular student when a command is directed to them (see Extract 6.2, 32:49) also helps to interactively construct the audience and to help students notice and engage in a particular aspect of the environment (Bezemer and Kress 2016). She even uses pointing to bring the artifact (XO laptop) into the discourse (see Extract 6.2, 32:19–32:26), or what Rose (2014, 17) has referred to as *sourcing*. The introduction of the XO laptop into the classroom task is first anticipated by Vera: *¿Qué van a usar entonces para buscar la familia?* [*What are you going to use to look up the family?*] However, as students' answer (*Internet*) is not the one expected by Vera, she makes use of pointing to bring the XO laptop into the discourse, turning it into a new participant of the classroom event.

In contrast to the framing of XO laptop use, for which Vera deploys more regulative discourse through her speech and actions, textbook use generally does not require much framing to regulate behavior and explain task mechanics. The following transcript—which also belongs to day 2 of unit 1 "My family"—illustrates my point.

As for experiential meanings (see Extract 6.6), it can be noted that most processes are material and involve students as actors who would perform actions with the XO laptops (as either scopes or goals). These actions are mandated interpersonally through commands. However, a

6 Laptops and Textbooks as Curriculum Artifacts: Audience... 157

Extract 6.5 Regulatory discourse for textbook use

Time	Participant/s action (gesture, hand, body, gaze)	Verbal interaction
18:02	V browses the textbook V looks at students Ss open the textbooks and browse them	V: (to the whole class) Bueno… ahora vayan al libro, now we'll do exercise 6 to fill the gaps with "our, your or their", ¿Se acuerdan? Este es el ejercicio 6, que está después del family tree. [*Ok, now go to the book, now we'll do exercise 6 to fill the gaps with "our, your or their", do you remember? This is exercise 6, after the family tree*]
18:15	Ss get to work on the exercise	(choral response): Yes. Sí. [*Yes*]

mental process interpersonally represented through a question (*¿se acuerdan?*) [*do you remember?*] serves the purpose of organizing classroom behavior and structuring the task. A relational process (*este es el ejercicio 6, que está después del family tree*) [*this is exercise 6, after the family tree*] also helps to regulate behavior and frames the task by making activities within the unit (and within the textbook page) overtly cohesive for students.

Negotiation sequences (see Extract 6.7) also show that—either by verbal or kinesthetic resources—students are positioned as the ones who are requested to perform actions (A1) or have information to share (K1), or actually information about the task dynamics they need to demonstrate they master before attempting to do it.

Extract 6.6 Experiential meanings

Participant	Clause	Process type	Participants' roles
V	Bueno… ahora **vayan** al libro [*Ok… now go to the book*]	Material	Actor: (you, students) Scope: el libro
V	now we'll **do** exercise 6 to fill the gaps with "our, your or their" [*now we'll do exercise 6 to fill the gaps with "our, your or their"*]	Material	Actor: we (V and Ss) Goal: exercise 6
V	¿Se **acuerdan**? [*Do you remember?*]	Mental	Senser: se (students) Phenomenon: (implicit, about "there is" and "there are")
V	Este **es** el ejercicio 6, que está después del family tree. [*This is exercise 6, after the family tree*]	Relational	Identifier: Este Identified: el ejercicio 6

Extract 6.7 Interpersonal meanings

Participant	Clause / Action	Speech function	Negotiation / Sequence
V	Bueno… ahora vayan al libro, now we'll do exercise 6 to fill the gaps with "our, your or their" [*Ok, no go to the book, now we'll do exercise 6 to fill the gaps with "our, your or their"*]	Command	A2
Ss	(Ss open their textbooks)		A1
V	¿Se acuerdan? [*do you remember?*]	Question	K2
V	Este es el ejercicio 6, que está después del family tree. [*This is exercise 6, after the family tree*]	Statement	K2F
Ss	Sí [*Yes*]	Answer	K1
Ss	(Ss get to work on the exercise)		A1

The very nature of the interaction also requires Vera to regulate students' behavior before the textbook task is completed, by commands (*vayan al libro*) [*go to the book*], by questions that regulate how to go about the task (*¿se acuerdan?*) [*do you remember?*], by relating the current task with previous tasks (*Este es el ejercicio 6, que está después del family tree*) [*This is exercise 6, after the family tree*] and by mirroring actions (such as browsing the textbook herself). However, unlike the previous example in which regulation pointed to how the XO laptop should be used and for what purposes, the use of the textbook does not seem to require many interactive moves to frame the task: locating the task spatially (in relation to previous exercises on the previous page) seems to be enough for framing the task.

There might be several reasons for this. It may happen because of the pedagogical design of the artifact at hand. Within the textbook page, each activity is framed to signal boundaries with other activities (for instance, "activity 6" which is after the family tree) and within the page activities are also organized in the order they are expected to be completed; each activity also offers a brief task description students can read on their own. Also, because the textbook as a curriculum artifact has a long tradition of use in foreign language classrooms (Blyth 2009) and in formal education in general, students are more familiar with it—in EFL as well as in other classes—and aware of the uses to which it is generally put, as well as the fact that the textbook tends to present students with similar exercises across units. In this respect, the very design of the textbook favors the repetition of certain routines across classroom events as the expected interaction path with the artifact. To this, we could also add that students are also less familiar with the dynamics of XO laptops in the class since they are kept in the school computer lab room and are only brought into the classroom for particular activities (i.e. when the teacher brings them or asks a student to do so). We could also add that in her framing of how curriculum artifacts should be used, Vera manipulates the textbook with her own hands, while the same is not true for the laptop. Since XO screens are small—and she does not have an overhead projector for her own classroom—she does not take a laptop and show students how they will use them. Instead, she hands out laptops and makes rounds across the room while she explains what needs to be done, or even sits next to some students to explore the software with them. This also implies a change in attention and engagement (Bezemer and Kress 2016): whereas when using the textbook students get to see Vera perform the actions on the textbook and are expected to look at her, when they use the laptop they are mostly expected to listen to her while they themselves perform actions on the artifact. In later conversations with the teacher, she made another point: laptops can distract students because of the many possibilities of interaction, so tasks need to be well-framed. Also, she felt that with the textbook she could always model and scaffold more throughout the exercise (because all students were doing the same thing at the same time) and she could provide "right or wrong" answers. For the laptop, however, this was not the case: exploration could take students in different directions and she did not have pre-established "right or wrong" answers for the types of tasks for which laptops were used. Whatever the reasons may be, it is evident that through regulative discourse Vera does not only establish the differences between using one artifact or the other, but also sets boundaries as for how and when to use each.

In fact, within the same unit of classroom work, a particular task or activity may authorize the use of one or the other, but not the use of either. As Extract 6.2 showed, while the XO laptop should be used for looking up information about famous families online, they could not be used for looking up vocabulary they have already addressed in class.[9] The textbook was the authorized artifact for such purpose. This also points to the two audiences for Vera's EFL class: while the XO laptop is used for digital literacy practices such as learning how to look up information online, the textbook is used for linguistic goals such as reviewing vocabulary items which pertain to the unit. Artifact boundaries, then, do not only pertain to how to use them, but also to what goals demand the use of one or the other in the classroom.

Another example from unit 5 (*My neighborhood*) shows how these boundaries between the two artifacts continue to be operative by the end of the academic year, even when the textbook is not used so frequently. On day 4 of this unit, students also had both textbooks and XO laptops available on their desks, as also happened in our first example of unit 1. Right before the event, students had been working on naming and describing places in a neighborhood, including shops and stores and had also worked on giving directions and locating places on a map. By the time of this event, students had just gone over the use of prepositions to describe where places and people are located on a map of the school block Vera drew on the board. As soon as the oral activity was completed, Vera asked students to do a task which required using a 2D map represented in the textbook.

Extract 6.8 Framing textbook and laptop use

Time	Participant/s action (gesture, hand, body, gaze)	Verbal interaction
10:22	V takes textbook from her desk and opens it All students but one open textbooks	V: Eh, people… now page twenty-four from the book.
10:26	V shows textbook to S5 and points to the task	V: S5, do you have the book?
10:32	S5 looks down Some Ss laugh V points to the textbook	S3: No trajo el libro pensando que (inaudible) [*He didn't bring the book thinking that* (inaudible)] V: Ok. I have this one. I can give you this one.

(*continued*)

Extract 6.8 (continued)

Time	Participant/s action (gesture, hand, body, gaze)	Verbal interaction
10:46	V writes "p. 24" on the board Points to a map on the page	V: Ok, and here you have… What do we have here?
10:59	V points to the map	S3: Department store Choral response: Map V: Very good. A map. This is something that you will have to do. Eh? One person in the group is going to do this.
11:03	V looks at students	S6: What? V: A map. In each group one of you will have to draw a map and the other record with the laptop for the final project. Right? But you are not using laptops now. Let's go to the book.
11:18	V points to the task on the textbook	V: But now, there is and there are. Fill the gaps using there is and there are, ok?
11:25	Ss read instructions on the textbook	V: Lean las instrucciones en un minuto y díganme si entienden qué tienen que hacer, ok? [*Take a minute and read the instructions and tell me if you understand what you have to do, ok?*]
11: 59	V sits on her chair Ss read	V: Any questions? Choral response: No V: So now do the task

As shown above, the regulation of discourse patterns operates in a similar way to the previous examples from unit 1. However, they are realized in a slightly different way. To begin with, even though the interaction for framing the use of the textbook seems longer than the previous one, there is an embedding of turns about the eventual use of XO laptops (see bolded section of the previous extract).

Extract 6.9 Experiential meanings

Participant	Clause	Process type	Participants' roles
V	Eh, people… now page twenty-four from the book. S5, do you **have** the book?	Relational	Possessor: S5 Possession: the book
S3	No **trajo** el libro pensando que (inaudible) [*He **didn't bring** the book thinking that* (inaudible)]	Material	Actor: S5 Goal: el libro
V	Ok. I **have** this one.	Relational	Possessor: I (Vera) Possession: this one (book)
V	I **can give** you this one.	Material	Actor: I (Vera) Scope: this one (book)
V	Ok, and here you **have**…	Existential	Existent: (the map, implicit) Scope: Internet
V	What do we **have** here?	Existential	Existent: What / Department store / map
S3	Department store	Existential	
Ss	Map	Existential	
V	Good. A map. This **is** something that you will have to do. Eh?	Relational	Identifier: This Identified: something that you will have to do
V	One person in the group **is going to do** this.	Material	Actor: One person in the group (student) Goal: this
S6	What?		Goal (previous process)
V	A map.		Goal: map (previous process)
	In each group one of you **will have to draw** a map.	Material	Actor: one of you (students) Goal: a map
V	(and) the other **record** with the laptop for the final project	Material	Actor: the other (student) Goal (implicit)
V	Right?		
V	But you **are not using** laptops now.	Material	Actor: You (students) Scope: laptops
V	Let's **go** to the book.	Material	Actor: us (Vera and students) Scope: the book

(*continued*)

6 Laptops and Textbooks as Curriculum Artifacts: Audience...

Extract 6.9 (continued)

Participant	Clause	Process type	Participants' roles
V	But now, there is and there are. **Fill** the gaps using there is and there are, ok?	Material	Actor: (You, students) Goal: the gaps
V	**Lean** las instrucciones en un minuto [*Take a minute and **read** the instructions*]	Material	Actor: you Scope: las instrucciones
V	(y) **díganme** si entienden qué tienen que hacer, ok? [*(and) **tell me** if you understand what you have to do*]	Verbal	Sayer: (you, students) Target: si entienden qué tienen que hacer Receiver: I (me)
V:	Any questions?	Existential	Existent: questions
Ss:	No		
V:	So now **do** the task	Material	Actor: (you, students) Goal: the task

Like the previous examples, experiential meanings (see Extract 6.9) show that there are many material processes for which students are positioned as actors and which require regulations on artifact use (*not using, go to, fill, lean*). Unlike the previous examples of experiential meanings for framing artifact use, however, more relational and experiential meanings are created to represent the relationship between classroom participants and artifacts (who brought the textbook to the lesson and who did not).

As for interpersonal meanings (see Extract 6.10), speech functions and negotiation sequence also point to the asymmetry in the interaction and how the identities and roles of teacher and students are negotiated while framing the use of the textbook.

Extract 6.10 Interpersonal meanings

Participant	Clause / Action	Speech function	Negotiation Sequence
V	(takes textbook from her desk and opens it) Eh, people… now page twenty-four from the book.	Command	A2
Ss	(All students but one open their textbooks)		A1
V	(shows textbook to S5 and points to the task) S5, do you have the book?	Question	K2

(*continued*)

Extract 6.10   (continued)

Participant	Clause / Action	Speech function	Negotiation Sequence
S5	(Looks down)	Answer	
Ss	(Laugh)	Answer	K1d
S3	No trajo el libro pensando que (inaudible) [*He didn't bring the book thinking that* (inaudible)]	Answer	K1
V	(Points to the textbook) Ok. I have this one. I can give you this one.	Statement	K1
V	V writes "p. 24" on the board (Points to a map on the page) Ok, and here you have…	Statement	K2
V	What do we have here? (Points to the map)	Question	
S3	Department store	Answer	K1
Ss	Map	Answer	K1
V	Very good. A map.	Statement	
V	This is something that you will have to do	Statement	K2f
V	Eh? One person in the group is going to do this. Looks at students	Statement	
S6	What?	Question	K2
V	A map.	Answer	K1
V	In each group one of you will have to draw a map and the other record with the laptop for the final project. Right?	Answer (expansion)	K1f
	Let's go to the book.	Command	
V	(Points to the task on the textbook) But now, there is and there are. Fill the gaps using there is and there are, ok?	Command	A2
V	Lean las instrucciones en un minuto y díganme si entienden qué tienen que hacer, ok? [*Take a minute and read the instructions and tell me if you understand what you have to do, ok?*]	Command	
SS	(Read instructions on the textbook)		A1
V	Any questions?	Question	K2
Ss	No	Answer	K1
V	So now do the task	Command	A2

On most of the occasions Vera deploys commands and statements, which construct her authority as the one in charge of dictating how to go about the task at hand with the artifact (*now page 24 from the book, fill the gaps using there is and there are*) and also the future task with the XO laptop (*this is something that you will have to do, one person in the group is going to do this*). The type of questions she asks also helps to regulate artifact use and task requirements (*Do you have the book? What do we have here?*). This is also reinforced by her sequences which more often position her as demanding an action (A2) from students or asking information (K2) which refers to their understanding of the task.

Through the use of verb tense and deixis, boundaries between textbook and XO laptop use are also drawn in the EFL lesson while temporal scales are constructed. While the "now" of the classroom requires the use of the textbook and task regulation that applies to the textbook, the future is used to refer to the eventual use of the laptop: (***This is** something that you **will have to do**, one person in the group **is going to do this**, but **now** there is and there are. **Fill** the gaps using there is and there are*). Gestures, such as Vera's pointing to the textbook (see Extract 6.8, 11:18) are also spatial deictics which serve a two-fold purpose: on the one hand, they draw students' attention to the current activity; on the other hand, they sign-post the artifact at hand required for such activity, marking boundaries with future activities which will require other artifacts and to which other classroom regulations will apply. In this respect, artifact boundaries are not only demarcated in terms of spatial scales, but also temporal ones.

Finally, the data also suggest that artifact framing is also signaled by the use of space in the classroom. For both units, there seems to be a recurrent pattern in the way Vera orients to the artifacts and to the students in the classroom space while framing the use of each of these artifacts.

Image 6.2 shows a recurrent trend in Vera's framing of artifact use. In general, when introducing tasks that will require the use of the textbook, she positions herself at the front of the classroom, behind her desk. In this respect, she creates a space for the teacher, and a space for students, who are on their chairs. Her framing of the textbook also implies manipulating the actual artifact (as Image 6.2 shows) and it may occasionally imply pointing to the actual placement of the task at hand within the textbook page. Each student, then, proceeds to do the task on their textbook without division of labor with other students to complete the exercise.

On the other hand, the use of the laptop seems to require a different type of positioning within the classroom space (see Image 6.2). Generally, Vera will walk around the classroom while introducing the task and

Image 6.2 Vera's orientation to students and to each artifact while framing their use (Unit 5, Day 4)

framing how the laptop will be used during task completion. At points—as the image shows—she will even sit next to a student (or a group of students) and start to explore the artifact with them. In these instances, she makes use of most of the classroom space without establishing spatial boundaries between teacher and students. This is also reinforced by the fact that she will even sit together with them to explore the artifact. There is no *teacher demonstration* but, instead, *collaborative exploration*. Tasks, at the same time, may require students to work together and so they may divide labor for task completion (as will be shown in the next chapter). These differences also respond to other differences examined throughout this chapter, such as the fact that textbook tasks are shorter and more mechanical, while laptop tasks require collaboration, joint work and may extend over several lessons to achieve curricular cohesion.

To sum up, the events analyzed in this section exemplify how Vera can regulate students' behavior in the classroom, and also their understanding of the artifacts at hand, by establishing rules for when and how to interact with each artifact in the EFL lesson. In the first event, for instance, the laptop is framed as a legitimate artifact for looking up information, but not to look up vocabulary items which are in the textbook, which is authorized for more traditional ways of "learning EFL". Along the same lines, the last classroom event analyzed showed that even though both artifacts may not be physically present, Vera may explain how both are or will be used for different tasks within the unit *My neighborhood*. This brings a sense of unit cohesion to students (as pedagogical connections between tasks or activities are made available), but at the same time it frames boundaries between artifacts. Through lexico-grammatical choices (for instance, present tense vs. future tense), gestures (pointing to the artifact), or the distribution of space to mark—or not—boundaries between the space of students and the space of the teacher, Vera is able to demarcate such differences while at the same ensuring students understand how future tasks will unfold so that the division of labor between artifacts is maintained throughout the school year.

The XO laptop, in particular, is represented as an artifact that can be used for purposes which are not served by the textbook, imposing certain restrictions. For instance, the laptop will not be used for linguistic purposes or to review content that was learned with the textbook. Ethnographic data from all five units of classroom work support this. In general, Vera plans for students to use the textbook or their own notebooks to look up information and vocabulary, and then the XO laptop is used for those purposes only when the information or vocabulary are not present in the units of the textbook they have already addressed in class, or the textbook is not present in the physical space of the classroom.

Conclusions

While the previous chapter explored the various situated meanings that can be made as a policy moves across scales in society at large (inside and outside of classrooms and schools), this chapter discussed how situated meanings about the policy do not only pertain to human participants but also to material artifacts or, in this case, curriculum artifacts as the laptop and the textbook in Plan Ceibal policy. A closer examination of classroom interaction and work with both artifacts showed the various ways in which these artifacts—in interaction with humans and the sedimental history of the classroom—authorize particular ideologies of learning, dividing semiotic labor for completing classroom tasks in ways which may not necessarily be predicted or expected by the policy. It also showed that teacher's agency—foregrounded throughout the analysis—plays a key role in shaping spaces for learning by authorizing particular ways of interacting with an artifact, by using the classroom space in a particular manner or even by positioning participants in particular ways depending on which artifact will be used to "learn" during an activity in the EFL classroom.

In the case under investigation the teacher frames curriculum artifact use for particular classroom activities. This framing points to a particular division of labor between the textbook and the XO laptop in the EFL classroom, which in turn draw on the semiotic residue of what printed textbooks and laptops have come to mean or index in classrooms historically. Such division of labor between both artifacts contributes to shaping classroom experiences and constructing the school subject EFL.

The textbook is authorized in the classroom—and legitimated through school practices and traditional views of this artifact in education—for "learning EFL". This corresponds to a traditional ideology of learning which has implications for both pedagogy and curriculum: (i) the teacher and the artifact represent "authorities" in the classroom, (ii) learning focuses on language, (iii) language is a set of lexico-grammatical items and rules to be learned through practice and drilling.

As for *i*, the tasks Vera selects from the textbook and even the way she herself interacts with the textbook and with students while framing its use (through demonstration and manipulation of the actual textbook to explain tasks) points to this traditional ideology of learning: she "shows" students what to do and how to do it and she sets boundaries between the space of the teacher and the space of students within the classroom. As for *ii*, the very design of the EFL textbook foregrounds language and Vera does not make changes for the textbook to fit her digital literacy goal. As for *iii*, the tasks students do with the textbook require them to memorize and then remember vocabulary items, verb tenses and inflection and to use them for controlled practice purposes. Far from being a condition of a textbook (which has the potential to draw on either ideology of learning) associating the textbook with more traditional EFL teaching and learning goals seems to show the semiotic sediment of what textbooks are traditionally considered to be for in education.

On the other hand, the use of XO laptops in Vera's classroom responds to an alternative ideology of learning, with implications in terms of curriculum and pedagogy. Within this ideology of learning: (i) the teacher may guide or even work together with students to explore the artifact, (ii) learning happens in collaboration and exploration of artifacts and affordances, (iii) language is one of many—authorized—resources deployed to make meanings in the classroom. As for *i*, the analysis suggested that the teacher erased boundaries between the space of the teacher and the space of the students when framing laptop use, and even sat together with them to explore the artifact, without taking a clear or traditional authoritative stance (even though still regulating behavior through discourse). As for *ii*, most tasks involving laptop use require—at some point—students' collaboration and division of tasks to get the project/final text done. As for *iii*, the making of final texts with laptops—as will be analyzed in the following chapter—shows that written and oral language are not seen as the only legitimate semiotic resources for making meaning in the EFL classroom. Again, this characterization of the artifact seems to draw on semiotic sediment of new technology as innovative, creative and alternative in education. What is more important—from the perspective of how EFL is constructed—the division of labor between artifacts is most times maintained in the classroom, which means that throughout the school year each artifact is legitimated for particular tasks and purposes for which the other is not.

These two co-existing ideologies of learning are also recurrent in many other classrooms at present and are in consonance with the many audiences that overlap in any classroom. Oftentimes teachers need to address many audiences with particular requirements. In the case under investigation, Vera designs a more traditional EFL lesson plan for supervisors in order to meet the requirements set by the official EFL curriculum, who also expect the textbook to be used. However, when it comes to her own enactment, she introduces project-based instruction tasks with the use of XO laptops to cater for what she considers to be the actual needs of students to be inserted in the twenty-first century. Both audiences play such an important role in the EFL classroom that even Vera's tests for assessing students and assigning grades respond to both.

Along these lines, through classroom interaction and work, the textbook as artifact comes to encapsulate a traditional ideology of learning for which language is *the* legitimate resource for making meaning and for which tasks such as drilling and controlled practice are core elements in the (official) curriculum. On the other hand, the laptop as artifact comes to encapsulate an alternative ideology of learning for which language is *one* of the many resources for making meaning and for which other resources are also incorporated in the curriculum to cater for the multimodal nature of communication. Despite this, both ideologies of learning cohabit the classroom without much resistance or contestation by participants, partly due to the fact that each artifact is used for different tasks at different moments of classroom enactment.

At this point, it is important to note that I do not claim each artifact (in terms of design or materiality) encapsulates an ideology of learning per se. Instead, I claim that through classroom interaction and work—and in the interactive negotiation between design and use—each artifact *comes to* encapsulate a particular ideology of learning, which shapes how participants interact with it and what learning means in the classroom.

From a socio-semiotic perspective, this points to the situated agency of the teacher and, at the same time, to the unstable nature of meaning: what a traditional EFL lesson entails does not conflict with an alternative view of EFL even within the same classroom environment. It also points to the ways in which situated agency is restricted by wider historical and cultural scales. Complementarily, from the perspective of language policy, this sheds light on the agency of stakeholders in deconstructing and reconstructing the policy, as the teacher does in attending to a dual audience for her class. Also, it points to the meanings of EFL that can be produced at this particular time of implementation in which teachers—such as EFL Uruguayan instructors—begin to introduce XO digital practices into their lessons while at the same time they need to comply with traditional regulations and expectations which do not contemplate the use of such artifact in the classroom. Finally, it shows that the classroom is situated in a larger and multi-scalar environment and the decisions and meanings made at one scale affect—and are affected by—other scales.

As for the more general discussion of curriculum artifacts in the classroom, such as the (printed) textbook and the laptop, the analysis points to the various complex factors that shape and reshape the *which, what, how* and *when* of student-artifact interaction in the classroom environment. Looking into actual human-artifact interactions—and the wider environment in which they take place—is needed to better account for both the situatedness of meaning-making processes and the restrictions imposed to such processes. To understand these dynamics, we cannot only look at one scale, such as policy design, curricular mandates, classroom enactment, students' actual work with the artifact, students' performance in assessment or tasks, and so on. We actually need to look at the ongoing tensions that take place across scales, and that give way to such scales, such as: the situated agency and the restrictions individuals find in the environment, macro and micro aspects of the policy, the creative aspect of a particular classroom and the cultural sediment of previous classrooms, artifact design and artifact use, among many others.

Notes

1. An earlier draft of this chapter was presented at the Fellowship Colloquium of the *Georg Eckert Institut* (*Leibniz-Institut für internationale Schulbuchforschung*) in Braunschweig, Germany. I am most thankful to the audience for their insights and to the GEI researchers and staff for their support during my research stay.

2. A preliminary analysis of some of the classroom events explored here appears in Canale (2018).
3. In 2016, there was an attempt to incorporate digital EFL textbooks, but it did not succeed, for reasons which do not pertain to the medium itself, but to political and economic debates around purchasing licenses for such textbooks.
4. Uruguay in Focus is the local adaptation of an internationally published ELT textbook. Actually, it was adapted from an already existing adaptation of the book in Argentina (De Oliveira Lucas et al. 2018) to introduce local culture and issues to students.
5. EFL state supervisors are in charge of designing EFL official curricula for public schools and for private school classrooms which do not follow a "bilingual stream". They are also in charge of selecting EFL textbooks. Supervisors may enter a classroom to oversee EFL teacher's skills and to check whether they are following the mandated EFL syllabus and to go over the teacher's book to check what type of activities are designed for the classroom. However, these supervisors more often do this for public school classrooms than for private school classrooms.
6. As has been noted by Kalantzis et al. (2010) and Kress (2013), the incorporation and actual use of new technology in the classroom on its own does not eradicate older fashions and teaching practices, which tend to co-exist due to teaching styles, preferences, lack of policy support, and so on.
7. At first sight, the fact that the teacher assumes parents demand the use of the textbook seems counter-intuitive since within the policy there is more expectation for laptop use. However, my conversations and interviews with the teacher revealed two important aspects: the fact that parents pay for textbooks (while they are not charged for the laptops) and also the fact that being a working-middle-class school, most students at Fleetwood have digital technologies at home. Also, parents' interest in students using the textbook point to the still dominant traditional ideology of learning which mostly focuses on language practice and legitimates the textbook as the learning artifact *par excellence*.
8. Throughout the chapter, verbal data analysis focuses on main clauses. Ellipsis of process -if part of the main clause- is also analyzed.
9. In this sense, XO laptop use in this environment seems to operate in a different way from other 1:1 contexts, for which researchers have found that the most extensive use of laptops pertains to the search of information, vocabulary and other areas of human-artifact distributed

memory, and which has even been characterized as one of the most frequent laptop-student practice in some Plan Ceibal settings (Gabbiani 2010; Kachinovsky et al. 2013).

References

ANEP: Administración Nacional de Educación Pública. (2008). Teaching Programs (Planes de Estudio). Retrieved February 11, 2017, from http://ipa.cfe.edu.uy/index.php/estudiantes/plan-de-estudios

Bernstein, B. (2000). *Pedagogy, Symbolic Control and Identity: Theory, Research, Critique*. London: Taylor & Francis.

Bezemer, J., & Kress, G. (2015). The Textbook in a Changing Multimodal Landscape. In N. M. Klug & H. Stöckl (Eds.), *Language in Multimodal Contexts* (pp. 21–28). New York: De Gruyter.

Bezemer, J., & Kress, G. (2016). *Multimodality, Learning and Communication. A Social Semiotic Framework*. London and New York: Routledge.

Blyth, C. (2009). From Textbook to Online Materials: The Changing Ecology of Foreign Language Publishing in an Era of ICT. In M. Evans (Ed.), *Foreign Language Learning with Digital Technologies* (pp. 174–202). London and New York: Continuum.

Canale, G. (2018). La construcción de la clase de inglés como lengua extranjera a través de dos artefactos curriculares. *Linguagem & Ensino, 21*, 97–119.

CES, ANEP: Consejo de Educación Secundaria, Administración Nacional de Educación Pública. (2006). Programa de 1er año de secundaria. Montevideo, Uruguay.

Christie, F. (2002). *Classroom Discourse Analysis. A Functional Perspective*. London and New York: Continuum.

Curdt-Christiansen, X. L. (2017). Language Socialization through Textbooks. In P. A. Duff & S. May (Eds.), *Language Socialization. Encyclopedia of Language and Education* (pp. 195–210). Cham: Springer.

De Oliveira Lucas, P., Díaz Maggioli, G., & López-Barrios, M. (2018). Teaching Materials and Their Importance in ELT: Some Perspectives from the Mercosur Region. In J. I. Liontas (Ed.), *The TESOL Encyclopedia of English Language Teaching*. Hoboken, NJ: Wiley-Blackwell.

Gabbiani, G. (2010). Interacción entre pares y realización de tareas en edad escolar. Actas de las III Jornadas de Investigación y II de Extensión de la Facultad de Humanidades y Ciencias de la Educación. n/p.

Gray, J. (2002). The Global Coursebook in English Language Teaching. In D. Block & D. Cameron (Eds.), *Globalization and Language Teaching* (pp. 151–167). London and New York: Routledge.

Halliday, M. A. K. (2014). *Introduction to Functional Grammar*. London and New York: Routledge.

Jewitt, C. (2004). Multimodality and New Communication Technologies. In P. Levine & R. Scollon (Eds.), *Discourse & Technology. Multimodal Discourse Analysis* (pp. 184–195). Washington, DC: Georgetown University Press.

Jewitt, C. (2006). *Technology, Literacy and Learning. A Multimodal Approach*. London and New York: Routledge.

Kachinovsky, A., Martínez, S., Gabbiani, B., Gutiérrez, R., Rodríguez Rava, B., Ulriksen, M., & Achard, P. (2013). Impacto de Plan Ceibal en el funcionamiento cognitivo y lingüístico de los niños. In A. Rivoir (Ed.), *Plan Ceibal e Inclusión Social. Perspectivas Interdisciplinaria* (pp. 99–151). Montevideo: Plan Ceibal y Universidad de la República.

Kalantzis, M., Cope, B., & Cloonan, A. (2010). A Multiliteracies Perspective on the New Literacies. In E. A. Baker (Ed.), *The New Literacies. Multiple Perspectives on Research and Practice* (pp. 61–87). New York and London: Guilford.

Kress, G. (1997). *Before Writing. Re-thinking the Paths to Literacy*. London and New York: Routledge.

Kress, G. (2000). Multimodality: Challenges to Thinking about Language. *TESOL Quarterly, 34*(2), 337–340. https://doi.org/10.2307/3587959

Kress, G. (2013). Recognizing Learning. A Perspective from a Social Semiotic Theory of Multimodality. In I. de Saint-Georges & J. J. Weber (Eds.), *Multilingualism and Multimodality. Current Challenges for Educational Studies* (pp. 120–140). Rotterdam: Sense.

Kress, G. (2015). Semiotic Work. Applied Linguistics and a Social Semiotic Account of Multimodality. *AILA Review, 28*, 49–71. https://doi.org/10.1075/aila.28.03kre

Lemke, J. (2002). Travels in Hypermodality. *Visual Communication, 1*(1), 299–325. https://doi.org/10.1177/147035720200100303

Luke, C., de Castell, S., & Luke, A. (1989). Beyond Criticism: The Authority of the School Textbook. In S. de Castell, A. Luke, & C. Luke (Eds.), *Language Authority and Criticism. Readings on the School Textbook* (pp. 245–260). London and New York: Falmer.

Martin, J. R., & Rose, D. (2007). *Working with Discourse*. London and New York: Continuum.

Rose, D. (2014). Analysing Pedagogic Discourse: An Approach from Genre and Register. *Functional Linguistics, 1*(11), 1–32. https://doi.org/10.1186/s40554-014-0011-4

Rose, D. (2018). Pedagogic Register Analysis: Mapping Choices in Teaching and Learning. *Functional Linguistics, 5*(3), 1–33. https://doi.org/10.1186/s40554-018-0053-0

Rymes, B. (2012). Recontextualizing YouTube: From Macro-Micro to Mass-Mediated Communicative Repertoires. *Anthropology & Education, 43*(2), 214–227. https://doi.org/10.1111/j.1548-1492.2012.01170.x

van Dijk, T. (1981). Discourse Studies and Education. *Applied Linguistics, 2*(1), 1–26. https://doi.org/10.1093/applin/II.1.1

Weninger, C., & Kiss, T. (2013). Culture in English as a Foreign Language (EFL) Textbooks: A Semiotic Approach. *TESOL Quarterly, 47*(4), 694–716. https://doi.org/10.1002/tesq.87

7

Learners as Sign-makers: Technology, Learning and Assessment

The previous chapter investigated how through classroom interaction, work and semiotic sediment, each curriculum artifact (the XO laptop and the EFL textbook) comes to encapsulate a particular ideology of learning: a traditional ideology for which the target language is the learning goal *par excellence*, and an alternative ideology which underscores the multiplicity of modal resources students deploy in communication and learning. In particular, the chapter looked at the role of the teacher in designing spaces for learning in which students could interact with each artifact. This interaction—as well as the learning goals associated with it—was regulated by the teacher's multimodal discourse: through speech, gesture, gaze and the use of classroom space, among others, Vera was able to demarcate boundaries in the use of each artifact, providing a particular division of labor for the EFL lesson. Focusing on the teacher foregrounds her situated agency in the enactment of the policy, which entails a recontextualization of meanings made at larger institutional scales (see Chap. 5). However, agency is distributed among participants and artifacts in the environment of the classroom. Attending to the learners' situated agency in interacting and making meanings with curricular artifacts offers a

© The Author(s) 2019
G. Canale, *Technology, Multimodality and Learning*, Palgrave Studies in Educational Media, https://doi.org/10.1007/978-3-030-21795-2_7

unique path to recognizing the learner as a legitimate sign-maker and to recognizing as much of their learning as possible.

This chapter explores how the XO laptops—as technology artifacts—and students' interactions with them contribute to shaping the school subject EFL.[1] The focus is on how—within the alternative ideology of learning and the space for learning Vera designs through her framing of tasks and classroom work—learners become agentive makers of (multimodal) signs with technology artifacts. The analysis focuses on sign-making processes, the resulting signs students make, and how these circulate inside and/or outside of the classroom environment. In particular, the chapter investigates learners' agency by drawing attention to (i) how software affordances and limitations are collaboratively explored and evaluated in human-artifact interaction, (ii) students' appropriation, transformation and design of (multimodal) signs and (iii) how such multimodal signs come to evidence learning in the classroom or, in other words, how such signs become recognized. The chapter also reflects on the theoretical and pedagogical implications of recognition for stakeholders such as researchers, policy-makers, teachers and learners themselves.

Learners as Sign-makers: Engagement, Learning and Recognition

Chapter 3 drew on socio-semiotic literature to define learning as the transformation of signs and to point to the fact that such process occurs in all communicative events, regardless of whether transformation is legitimated as "learning" in the environment in which it takes place and by the social actors implicated. This is, in fact, what happens in many classrooms: a lot of the semiotic work done by learners may pass unnoticed (Bezemer and Kress 2016). The need for teaching and—above all—assessment practices and tools to *recognize* such semiotic work is on a par with the demands of education in the twenty-first century and, concomitantly, with the goals posited by an alternative ideology of learning.

Recognition, as discussed earlier in the book, can start by looking into students' signs of engagement and how these may be indicative of signs of learning over time (Bezemer and Kress 2016). In a formal environment or a Route B type of learning, in which a shaping agent is in many ways "in control of" learning, what will count as learning and what types of signs will be regarded as signs of learning affect the ways in which identities are enacted—through pedagogy and curriculum, and also the ways in which the school subject is constructed. For instance, within the traditional ideology of learning, the target language and controlled practice are considered the legitimate route to learning. Other modes of communication, alternative tasks and activities and alternative types of classroom interaction and practices are not recognized, even though they are part and parcel of meaning-making processes.

For this reason, a *culture of recognition* (Kress and Selander 2012) or a *generosity of recognition* (Bezemer and Kress 2016) is required to underscore the semiotic work by students in formal settings, or to make "what is currently unnoticeable noticeable" (p. 5). For this purpose, throughout the analysis the chapter considers two interrelated aspects which account for the agentive nature of learning: (1) sign-makers' interest and criteriality (introduced in Chap. 3), and (2) the resourcefulness (Mavers 2007) and availability of modes for making meanings in the classroom.

The remaining of this chapter will focus on how students interact with artifacts to explore affordances and limitations, how they make (multimodal) signs in the classrooms by drawing on the target language and on many other semiotic resources, and how the teacher assesses students' semiotic work. Unlike the previous chapter, the present chapter will focus on learners' agency as sign-makers. The first part of the analysis explores the enactment of the first unit of classroom work (*My family*) and the second explores the final unit of classroom work (*My neighborhood*) so as to be able to show how laptops-students interaction and meaning-making processes unfold throughout the school year in different time/space scales.

The Enactment of *My family* Classroom Unit

During the enactment of unit 1 (*My Family*, see Appendix), Vera asked students to pick one of three free software tools (*Impress*, *Draw* and *PiTiVi*)[2] and to explore it with their laptops so that they could sketch their final project task: a digital text representing their own family to show to Vera and to the other students. This was, for Vera, an alternative way to make students know more about each other and share aspects of their family structure and life. The final project needed to meet two requirements: (1) to make use of visual and verbal resources, (2) to be somewhat different from the original family tree of the textbook (see Extract 7.1). These requirements sought to make students reflect on alternative ways of representing their family by not using speech or writing exclusively and by not "copying" the available sign shown in the textbook. These aspects foreground the multimodal and transformative nature of meaning-making, respectively.

Extract 7.1 Interview with Vera (7/25/2015)

G: And so, what is the aim of this unit?
V: Teaching them about family members, vocabulary and family relations. They are beginner students, they are not bilingual and they need a lot of exposure to the language and also to use the language. I also want them to use the laptops, to learn how to use them. I want them to be able to do useful things in English.
G: Useful things? Like… what things?
V: Like writing texts, planning texts, explaining how and why they write texts. Combining images and written texts. They need to know those things. They need to be able to explain why they do things and how they do things. That is important for learning English (EFL) or any other subject.
G: And what do you expect to see in the final projects?
V: Well, I expect them to be able to make visual and written texts. To show their family and to be creative. They can take the family tree as a model, but I don't want them to copy and paste. It's a good opportunity for them to learn how to use the *Ceibalitas* [XO laptops]
G: And how do you assess this? I mean, what do you look for?
V: Well, they are beginners. It's ok if they have language mistakes. I want them to be able to use the software in a creative way and to be able to explain how and why they made the final texts the way they did. Of course they need to show they have learned some of the vocabulary related to family and family members, but I don't worry if they make language mistakes in English.

At the beginning of unit 1, students worked with a family tree of the textbook. Given that students claimed they had never seen a family tree before, Vera first explained to them how to "read" or interpret a family tree, as she announced the final project.

7 Learners as Sign-makers: Technology, Learning and Assessment

Extract 7.2 Vera's explanation of how to interpret a family tree (Unit 1, Day 1)

V: Ok, so this is a family tree, right? What is a family tree? Un árbol genealógico... ¿Qué es? ¿No saben qué es un árbol genealógico? *(A famliy tree... What is it? Don't you know what a family tree is?)*
S3: Yo no *(I don't)*
S7: No teacher, no sé. No sabemos. *(No, teacher. I don't know. We don't know)*
V: Ok, a family tree, right? A family tree is a tree that shows your family members and relations, ok? So look at the picture. How do you read this tree?
S2: De arriba para abajo *(Top-down)*
V: Ok, and what does it mean? ¿Quiénes son? *(Who are they)* (pointing to each name in the picture) Who are they?
S3: Ah, los famil... *(Oh, the family memb...)*
V: In English!
S3: Eh, los familiares. *(The family members)*
V: Ok, and how are they organized?
S3: Big, small. Eh, el más grande arriba y los hijos abajo, y los más chicos más abajo *(The oldest one above and the little ones below)*
V: Good. And who are these? (pointing to the names in the picture). Remember before, in the beginning of the year we introduced him. Who is he?
S4: Ah el (personaje) del libro. *(Oh, the textbook character)*
V: Ok, he is the main character. Remember we described him? His age, his height, his clothes, his nationality. Where is he from?
S7: Canada.
V: Ok, so now we are talking about his family, ok? But we are looking at his family in a family tree, so we know who is who.

Vera set the tone of the project and made students focus not only on the verbal resources required by the official EFL curriculum (such as family vocabulary) but mostly on visual and graphic representations of family relations and how these have an impact on the audience, making students aware that there are also ways of "reading" or interpreting visual and graphic elements in signs and that written language is embedded in wider ensembles of semiotic resources.

With a view to also attending to EFL goals, throughout the unit she introduced students to technology-related vocabulary in English so that they could name objects, actions and processes (such as *download, upload, click on*, etc.). She introduced these with mechanical exercises such as filling out blanks or choosing the appropriate word to complete a sentence.

Interestingly, she designed these tasks drawing on a traditional ideology of learning, as evidenced in the mechanical nature of the exercises. These tasks were designed to support or scaffold language learning and eventually to support learning to make signs with the artifact. Later in the unit, these tasks would be combined with alternative tasks that would go way beyond mechanical and language practice. This parallel unfolding of the lesson, attending to more traditional and alternative goals at the same time, evinces the discussion of the division of labor between artifacts and how both in the environment of this particular EFL class came to encapsulate particular ideologies of learning attending to the two audiences at hand, as discussed in Chap. 6, and in turn associated with particular types of tasks and work.

After addressing aspects of both EFL and technology use, students were ready to explore the software tools. The following section will address data of a pair of students who worked together and who—in the eyes of Vera—got to very different results in terms of learning. Their interaction shows the role of different participants (teacher, students, artifacts) and their agency in this particular meaning-making scenario.

Distributing Agency: Students-Laptop Interaction

On day 5, students were allotted some class time to explore any one of the three different programs Vera suggested for the final project. As in other opportunities in which the XO laptop was used in the EFL classroom, two or three students sat around one laptop to use it collaboratively. Below is an excerpt of S3 and S4 interacting with the *Impress* software, while the teacher was making rounds to assist each group.

7 Learners as Sign-makers: Technology, Learning and Assessment

Extract 7.3 S3 and S4 exploring the Impress software with a picture of the Simpsons family (Unit 1, Day 5)

Time	Participant/s action (gesture, hand, body, gaze)	Verbal interaction	Artifact action
2:00	S4 points to "zoom" icon on the screen	S4: *Achicá la imagen, sabés achicarla? Ahí!* [Make the image smaller, do you know how to? There you go!]	Zooms out image to center of screen
2:05	S4 points to picture and laughs	S4: *Ahora está muy chica. Nadie la ve. A ver, poné la flecha en la punta de la foto y agrandala un poco, se tiene que poder* [Now it's too small. No one can see it. Let's see...place the arrow on the corner and make it a bit bigger, there must be a way]	Places arrow on image and expands it
2:23	V comes close to the group	V: *If there's something you cannot do with the software, write it on your handout*	Arrow expanding the picture
2:30	V looks at screen	V: *The image looks good. Now see if you can write with this software. If you can't, write "no" in your handout*	Still image
2:43	S3 clicking on different icons and then scrolling down the page	S4: *Ah no entiendo este programa* [I don't understand this program] S3: *Yo tampoco* [Me neither] S4: *Vamos a ver si se puede escribir* [Let's see if we can type]	Page scrolling down
3:08	V uses hand and fingers to show that most of the page is blank	S4: *No sabemos usar esto.* [We don't know how to use this] V: *Ok, from what I see you know you can use pictures.* S4: *Yes* V: *This shows the whole page... you have the picture, now can you write in the rest of the page? Does it let you write? Try that.*	
3:35	S3 clicks on several icons (to find out how to incorporate texts)	S3 (whispers): *fotos, imágenes, formato* [pictures, images, format] S5: *Herramientas* [Tools]	Displaying tools
3:51	V comes to group, offers assistance and points to the icon they need to insert text	V: *¿Pudieron?* [Were you able to do it?] S4: No (laughs) V: Ok, it should be on "insertar" ["insert"] You click on... right?	

(*continued*)

Extract 7.3 (continued)

4:01	V points to the "T" on the screen and then to the square	V: Ah no, ya me acuerdo [*Oh, I remember now*] The T there means "Texto" [*"Text"*], see? Now you can write. So what do you do?	Displays square on screen for typing text
4:15	S3 writes "The Simpsons"	S4: Dale, pone. Hace clic [*Ok, do it. Click on it*] V: Hace click? Cómo? [*Click, how?*] S4: Eh, sí. [*Yes*] Click icon. V: ¿Solo click era? [*Was it just "click"?*] S4: Click on there V: Good (to the whole class) Chicos, todos usen el vocabulario que vimos, ¿sí? Si no cómo van a usar las Ceibalitas en inglés? [*Everybody use the vocabulary we learned, right? Otherwise you won't be able to use the laptops in English*] (S4 types) No me gusta esta letra. Es la que sale, pero no me gusta. [*I don't like this font. It's the one that's here, but I don't like it*] V: A ver, ¿cómo la cambiás? [*So, how can you change it?*] S4: Ah no sé cómo. No sé... la dejó así? La dejo así. [*Oh, I don't know how. I leave it like this? I leave it like this*] V: Bueno... entonces la letra hay que ver cómo cambiarla. ¿Saben grabarse con las ceibalitas? [*Ok...so you'll need to see how to change fonts. Can you record yourself with the laptop?*] (Ss: Yes) Prueben grabarse ahora a ver qué programas les deja usar video y sonido [*Try to record yourself to see what programs allows for video and sound*]	Underlines "The Simpsons" in red. Displays dictionary options in Spanish S4 takes notebook and goes over notes Mouse cursor moves around the page Mouse cursor moves around the page

(*continued*)

7 Learners as Sign-makers: Technology, Learning and Assessment

Extract 7.3 (continued)

4:27	S4 clicks on camera and starts recording	S4: *Salimos?* [*Are we on the shot?*] S3: *Bueno... dale* [*Ok, now*] *(laughs)* S4: *Dale* [*Now*] Both: *1, 2, 3 (laugh)* S4: *Hello my name is S4* S3: *Hello my name is S3*	Laptop camera shows. Both students appear on screen and record themselves
4:38	Students save the video file	S4: *Lo guardamos, pero borralo después* [*Let's save it, but then delete it*]	Screen shows options for saving document
4:46	Students click on several icons to see how to incorporate the video next to the Simpsons image	S4: *No sé hacerlo* [*I don't know know*] S3: *¿Cómo se hace? S5, cómo se hace?* [*How do you do it? S5, how do you do it?*] S5: (comes in to help them) *Ahora apretá ahí y arrástralo hasta donde lo que querés. Ya está. No sé si quedó guardado.* [*Now click there and take it wherever you want. Done. I'm not sure if it's saved*] S4: *Ok, igual ya está... poner video se puede.* [*Ok, it's ready anyways. Videos can be added*]	Square drags across the screen moving the video.

Throughout the interaction, S3 and S4 become engaged in exploring several *Impress* affordances as well as they become aware of the potential impact of using some tools to manipulate image, sound, layout, and so on (Extract 7.3). As the transcript shows, this is not achieved by S3 and S4 in isolation, but in collaboration with Vera, the artifact itself, and other students (such as S5, see 4:46). The activity is completed thanks to the distribution of tasks and roles among human and non-human participants. The interaction requires participants to attend to what each task entails and to what extent a participant has agency in the execution of a particular action. In this manner, agency is distributed, and affordances and limitations (of participants, the artifact and the environment) are continually assessed. To better illustrate my point, I will briefly mention some of the main characteristics of the various types of interactions that take place and the participants involved.

(a) *Students interacting with Vera.* Vera shapes the context of learning by signposting what will be considered as "good interaction" with the artifact (see Chap. 6) which, in turn, signposts what she will consider evidence of learning. In doing this, she enacts her institutional agency—at least at the scales of the classroom and the activity at hand—by playing two main regulative roles in the interaction. The first one is that of shaping students' engagement with the artifact and the second is to regulate the use of the target language while students perform the task. Both roles are achieved multimodally through speech, gestures, gaze, and so on.

As for the first role, she orients students toward exploring software affordances and limitations,[3] as can be noted in 2:23–2:30 and in 3:08 and 4:15 of the previous extract. Both speech and gaze (see, for instance, 2:30) are used for her to become a participant in the interaction and to evaluate students' performance. Through gaze, for example, she draws students' attention to the image on the XO laptop screen to signpost their work will be evaluated. Through speech (*The image looks good. Now see if you can write with this software. If you can't, write "no" in your handout*) she provides a positive evaluation of students' engagement with the artifact.

On some occasions when students seem to fail to explore an affordance, she either assists students on the spot or delays the exploration of the affordance. For instance, after inserting the image, S3 and S4's attempt to explore how to insert text seems to go wrong at first, since the image size changes again and becomes too small when they attempt to do so. Through gesture (3:08) she orients students' attention to this (for them to use the zoom tool) and then verbally guides students through the different steps (4:15). However, when students find it difficult to explore other features (such as changing fonts) Vera delays this (4:15), which is kept unexplored during the interaction. It seems that some of the features of the software (inserting text, inserting image, etc.) seem to be considered more "relevant" or necessary at the moment, while others (such as changing font type) are left for students to explore later on.

Perhaps a less visible role Vera plays in this interaction is that of regulating the use of EFL vocabulary while performing the task. While focusing on non-verbal resources (image, sound, layout, etc.), linguistic goals are somewhat present and some expectations need to be met (especially with regards to the vocabulary she introduced for exploring the artifact).

7 Learners as Sign-makers: Technology, Learning and Assessment

However, this role is less frequent in the data; in general while exploring software or using the laptops her focus is on students' understanding of what can be done with the XOs and not on the target language. In this extract, however, she does focus on language as well. For instance, in 4:15 her question *¿Solo 'click' era?* [Was it just "click"?] is directed for students to use the preposition *on* in *click on*, a collocation they had reviewed in previous lessons. Despite her focus on the vocabulary that students use in their interaction with the artifact, it is interesting to note that Vera does not provide corrective or other types of feedback on the aptness of the EFL language used for their final project. Her final assessment of the task focuses on students' demonstration of their ability to use the software (digital literacy goals) and is not so strictly tied to whether they can draw on expected EFL vocabulary and grammar. The latter becomes relevant mostly when students are using the EFL textbook (for controlled or semi-controlled practice), as explained in Chap. 6.

(b) *Students interacting with the XO laptop*. Non-human participants also play a key role in this interaction since their actions draw students' attention and engagement in particular directions and to some extent shaped students' use of their affordances. For instance, while students promptly demonstrated they were able to insert images and manipulate size with the software, inserting written texts into it seemed to complicate matters further for them (see 4:01) since this required them to consider how inserting text would impact other modal resources, such as design or images by making them move across the slide. The interrelatedness of textual elements that belong to different modes within the page becomes evident to students as their attempt to insert written text ends up making the image size go smaller again. This episode makes Vera regulate students' interaction with the artifact a little more so that they can go over every step they need to take for written texts to be appropriately inserted next to the image. For this purpose, the artifact plays an important role in shaping students' attention, engagement and course of action. In 4:15, for instance, the directionality of open tabs (from left to right and also up and down) tells students which steps need to be taken first. Also, the blue background for the tab where the mouse arrow is placed draws students' attention to the current step being taken at the same time it shows what steps have been taken previously. This affordance of the artifact favors a particular division of labor in which memory is shared between the user and the artifact to keep track of what steps have been taken and in what order, shaping future interactions.

Along these lines, the artifact also plays an important role in shaping stages for sign design. After their attempts to introduce text next to the image, students learned that the order in which elements of different modal resources are inserted into the page does have an effect on the way the text is arranged. In this respect, the default template of *Impress* caters for the insertion of text, but not of image (see Image 7.1). As a result, if S3 and S4 had attempted to insert text first, they probably would not have encountered the same problems in the following stages. However, the previous insertion of image had changed the layout of the default template, thus making it harder to introduce text after image had been inserted.

Neither S3 and S4 nor Vera explored other built-in *Impress* templates; instead they used the default template, which can be considered the *unmarked option* (Djonov and van Leeuwen 2013; Zhao et al. 2014) or the option more readily available to the artifact user. In this manner, the very artifact and its affordances imposed a template to students, making their labor harder when attempting to work around such template.

(c) *Students interacting with human and non-human participants.* Overall, students' interaction with human and non-human participants

Image 7.1 Default template for *Open Office's Impress* (reads: "Click to add title" and below reads "Click to add text")

while exploring the *Impress* program allows them to evaluate what can be done with this tool so that they can weigh up affordances and limitations for the design of their own final sign. Let us take the example of the Simpsons' family image again to show this. For this image, S3 and S4 discuss textual meanings and organization within the online page (2:00–2:05) while they explore how to use the zoom tool. In doing this, they negotiate the design of interpersonal meanings, such as which picture size is the best option for the audience to actually see the image (since the image was "too big" first and then became "too small" for the audience to see). In this process, Vera acts as the shaping agent judging size adequacy: "*The image looks good*" (2:30), which allows students to assume their performance on using the zoom was successful and so they can move on to explore other tools.

Next, they start to explore how to insert text into the online page (2:43–4:15). With Vera's assistance, they navigate the toolbar options to actually insert text into the page (3:35). Students become familiar with different modal resources, how they can be arranged within the page and why design needs to consider the interaction between these resources.

As can be noted from the discussion of the above interaction, exploring laptops and their affordances allowed students to reflect on several aspects which pertain to the complex layers of design and meaning-making processes with technology. Exploring such technology requires users to make negotiations with the artifact about what resources can be used and for what purposes and how the temporal unfolding of actions has an effect on the interconnectedness of elements (i.e. how the order in which actions are taken has an effect on the organization of elements), taking into account both artifact design and own interest in artifact use.

Such students-artifact interactions to use *Open Office* software allow them to reflect mostly on the design of textual and interpersonal meanings. Particular aspects of representation or ideational meanings—such as what and how elements are included or excluded from the representation—are not underscored in this type of interaction, mainly because the task at hand was designed for them to explore the tools without focusing on the actual final project of their preference. It might also be the case because in this stage of design students were more focused on learning how to use the software rather than on making decisions as for what to represent and how to do it (they actually did not have the actual pictures they were going to use yet).

The following stage (i.e. final project design) shows two main differences with this first interaction with the artifact. On the one hand, it focuses on ideational meanings, as shall be discussed in the next section. On the other hand, students get to use the target language more systematically. In exploring software, the role of the target language becomes obscured: Spanish is mostly used during the introduction and reflections around technology use do not revolve around the verbal mode, but other modes instead. However, students will get to use the target language both when designing the final project and when presenting orally before the whole class.

Learners' Criteriality, Agency and Signs of Learning

Investigating signs (as meanings that have already been made) is important to understand how agency works in sign-making and how students are able to demonstrate such agency. However, it is also important to consider the very process of design to better understand semiosis. Although it is fair to say we cannot access all of the meaning-making that revolves around designing and sketching, it is necessary to consider how such processes involve different scales and social practices that give way to the constant recontextualization of meaning. One of the main advantages of adopting a socio-semiotic and ethnographic approach to meaning-making is the possibility to focus on both the resulting signs—as is generally done in socio-semiotic research—and on the temporal and spatial processes of negotiating such signs, as advocated by ethnographic research (Dicks et al. 2011). For this reason, the chapter considers both students' semiotic processes of designing and sketching and the resulting final sign.

After interacting with the laptops to explore potential tools to make their final signs, Vera asked students to jot down both the features they thought they had mastered and the problems they had encountered while interacting with it. She gave each student a sheet to fill out in which they needed to answer the following questions: *What things can I do now with this program? (e.g. I can upload pictures, I can use audio, etc.), What things*

7 Learners as Sign-makers: Technology, Learning and Assessment   191

can't I do with this program? Why? What do I need to bring next class (images, audio, etc.) to work on my text? This served as an activity for reflection on the software at hand which would come in handy when students engaged in actually making their own family tree.

Due to time constraints, students were asked to also use the programs at home so that they could further explore them. On the remaining days of the unit, students started to design their final project both in the classroom and at home, while the final text was to be made at home. Vera requested students to design their final text on paper so that they could visualize what it would look like—and because it was "faster"—and to think of the elements (images, recordings, etc.) they would need for the actual making of the final project. The final project would be assessed by Vera during a two-minute oral presentation before the whole class so as to make meaning-making processes available to others (Images 7.2 and 7.3).

The different modal resources available for each stage—the design and the actual making of the final project—offered students particular affordances and restrictions, and the transition from designing to actually making required a transduction of meanings (Bezemer and Kress 2016). This

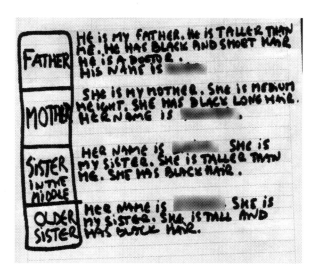

Image 7.2 S4's design on paper

She is my mother, she is medium height. She has black hair. Her name is

Her name is   She is my sister. She is tall. She has black hair

Her name is   . She is my sister, she is taller than me. She has black hair

He is my father, he is taller than me. He has black and short hair.
He is a doctor.
His name is

Image 7.3 S4's final project (*Impress*)

is to say, there are transformations in terms of the modal resources employed in the design and in the final project. For the design, only paper and pencils were available to students (and not the actual laptops), so they needed to draw on their previous interaction with the artifact—or go back

7 Learners as Sign-makers: Technology, Learning and Assessment

to their notes—and anticipate what their family tree would look like. In this manner, two different scales in meaning-making were connected.

As Image 7.2 shows, S4 used written language to describe family members (on the right side) and to name or "translate into verbal language" what the pictures would depict in the final text (on the left side). In this case, verbal language is used for meta-semiotic purposes (Silverstein and Urban 1996; Urban 2006): to explain what an image will actually "do" in the representation. For instance, the family member labels (*mother, father*, etc.) indicate that images will be used for the purposes of denoting conceptual processes (focusing on who participants *are*) and not narrative process, which would present "unfolding actions and events" (Kress and van Leeuwen 2006, 79).

In terms of representation, S4's design and final family tree respond to the structure of a conceptual process. S4 decided to use the *Impress* software to represent her family by means of a complex sign that—like the original family tree of the textbook—represents a classificational conceptual process (Kress and van Leeuwen 2006, 79), that is to say, a structure "representing participants in terms of their more generalized and more or less stable and timeless essence, in terms of class, or structure or meaning". This can be noted in the visuals S4 used which—like family trees in general—provide little or no background and lack contextual details. The focus then is on *showing* who they are and not on the particular actions or events they might have been engaged in when the picture was taken. The lack of details or background, then, helps to construe a *conceptual feel* (Machin 2004, 320) in the representation, as does S4's choice of close-up and medium shot images.[4] As for her own exclusion from visual representation, S4 was aware of the impact of inclusion and exclusion decisions on the final sign. During my interview with her, she stated she did not include herself because her classmates and Vera already knew her, and therefore it was not necessary—or criterial—to focus on herself. She also said that the text already showed her family member's relation with her in the *mother, father*, and so on labels, and so in order not to be redundant or bore her classmates she had decided to exclude herself (visually) from the text.

As for layout, let us focus on the interrelated systems of informational value, salience and framing (Kress and van Leeuwen 2006; Roderick 2016), which contribute to the meaning of the composition of elements.

Roughly speaking, informational value refers to the relative significance of elements in terms of their placement within the space (left/right, center/margin, up/down). The overall distribution gives the audience an idea of relative relevance of each element within the sign/text (Roderick 2016). Salience refers to the prominence of elements within the text/sign and can be achieved in different ways (color, font, size, etc.). Finally, framing refers to the ways (and the degrees) in which elements within the text/sign are presented as being connected or disconnected, which gives the audience an idea of whether each element should be interpreted as isolated or connected to any other element within the text/sign. All three elements together, then, allow us to better understand compositional meanings.

As can be noted, in her design S4 decided to have all images on the left side and all written descriptions on the right. Even though the organization of family members did change from design to the final text (for instance, the father is presented at the top of the page in the design, but then presented at the bottom of the page in the final text), the image/written text patterns of organization remained untouched.

S4 chose a different organization from the one in the family trees they had worked with in class. While in the family tree arrows and placement of images within the page (*up-down*, *left-right*) indicate certain hierarchy in terms of the relation of one member of the family to others, in S4's representation "hierarchy" is indicated verbally and not graphically or compositionally. Writing is used to explain the relationship between the members of the family, taking a *subjective* orientation to the conceptual structure (as evinced by the use of possessive determiners: *my mother*, *my sister*, *my brother*, etc.). This also shows a difference with the original family tree; one could argue the family tree takes an *objective* orientation to family representation (no particular member of the family is taken as a point of departure). However, in S4's representation she opts to show family kinship through her own eyes (*my mother*, *my father*, etc.). While in the design process S4 seems to follow an image space-organization pattern to indicate kinship (for instance, parents are placed in the upper part of the page and siblings are below), the final sign does not make use of this pattern. When I asked S4 about this during an interview, she mentioned the fact that she had placed the pictures on the page as she found them and so since she found her father's picture last, then she placed it below all the others. I also asked her if she thought this change had an effect on her actual final text to which

7 Learners as Sign-makers: Technology, Learning and Assessment

she responded the information was conveyed in the same way anyways. In this respect, S4 takes each image and its corresponding written text as a full and complete meaningful sign, and does not consider how individual/local signs operate together to construct a complex multimodal sign.

Given that the writing is used to express kinship, then a hierarchical organization of pictures to show kinship was not criterial to S4. However, this seems to be due to the student's heavy reliance on the *unmarked option* or *built-in template*. S4 mentioned she did not use arrows or lines—as the original family tree did—because it was "too complicated" to insert an arrow, change its size and then place it on the right place within the page. In fact, she mentioned she had learned to erase off the built-in elements of the template (see Image 7.1) in order to leave the whole page blank.

The use of different font size and bolded fonts in the final project sign could indicate S4 attempted to make some elements more salient than others for textual or ideational purposes. However, during my interview with her she mentioned the fact that her use of different font sizes and bolded font did not attempt to convey any particular meaning for her other than the fact that she wanted to show Vera that she had learned how to use those. S4 had encountered some problems changing font type and Vera requested she explored that feature later. In this respect, salience—through font type and bold-becomes a meta-sign through which S4 signposts the teacher what she herself considers *evidence of learning*, even when that *learning* does not seem to match the requirements of the task at hand. This clearly illustrates that student's agency does not pertain to how the sign is made—in terms of representation or compositionality—but also to for what purposes the sign is made interpersonally and how a sign in itself is intended to shape interpretation by the shaping agent or teacher. In this manner, the use of salience to indicate S4's own learning indicates her understanding of Vera as the real audience of her text, as well as the judge of her performance using the XO laptop.

To sum up, at first glance it could seem that most of the decisions S4 made were based on either time constraints or her own familiarity with the software. However, the very design and placement of elements within the page seems to indicate a transformation of signs, which can be taken as "more valuable" evidence of learning, since she showed agency in choosing a particular layout and organization to represent her family, to make choices as for whether intermodal reinforcement was needed or not (e.g. not needing to organize pictures in terms of kinship but instead to *label* family members verbally), to choose an "easy" layout that would not require her to use elements she was not familiar with (such as how to insert arrows or other symbols) and even to choose an *orientation* in representation. However, practical restrictions also led her not to explore two of the main affordances of the *Impress* software, which tell this apart from other tools: the slideshow and animation. This led Vera to consider S4's as one of the least successful projects.

Extract 7.4 Interview with Vera (8/3/2015)

G: So when you say she [S4] learned less than the others, what do you mean?
V: Well, I mean… she learned but not as much as the others. She didn't know how to use some of the things. You know?
G: For instance?
V: Well, she didn't know how to include pictures, change things…size. She couldn't change the type of letter, the font, for writing and that is something even *Word* has. And she didn't use slideshow or animation. That is basic *PowerPoint* or *Impress*.
G: But in her final project she does use different fonts, right?
V: Yes, but without any meaning. I asked her because I couldn't find anything in the fonts she used…she said she was trying to use different fonts, that's it. I mean, she did ok, I think she's learning to use the Ceibalitas [XO laptops] and that is ok, but she needs to keep on working.
G: And who would you say learned the most?
V: Mmm, S5. But he always does. S3… and S8 maybe.
(…)
G: Why?
V: Well, she [S3] changed the family tree. Do you remember the lines she used?
G: Yes
V: It means she learned exactly what the family tree is and what you can do with it. She also used the slideshow, font color, size, and more things, and not like S4 because she [S3] used it with a purpose, S8 too.
G: And wh…
V: And S5…I mean… he is like an XO expert [laughs] he knows so much about computers and he is into computers. He always used everything he learns in school and also at his home. He even helps classmates understand the programs in the computers.
(…) S8 normally does not do so good but I think he did very well this time. His project was really good and he used several things like the animated ah… and the slideshow, which are the main things to use in this program.
G: So, overall, are you happy with the results from all final projects?
V: Yes, I am. I mean, things can always be better, improve, but I think they all did it. Some did better, but at least all did a good job.

7 Learners as Sign-makers: Technology, Learning and Assessment

As Extract 7.4 shows, Vera regards different types of signs of learning in particular ways. For her, some signs of learning demonstrate legitimate learning (i.e. those which are made to communicate something to the audience, that is to say to other students) while the status of other signs of learning is less apparent (i.e. those which rather than communicating and representing experience to others are made to explicitly demonstrate or guide semiosis to her by indicating what should be regarded as a sign of learning. A sign might not be regarded as a sign of learning if it addresses her directly as the shaping agent. A meta-sign makes power relations explicit while at the same time it attempts to contest them by signposting to what aspects Vera should orient to in her assessment and by changing the apparent roles of the shaping agent and the sign-maker. The identities of both sign-maker (student) and judge (teacher) are overtly signposted, and this particular aspect is what Vera seems to oppose. Also, what Vera considers to be more important in using the software is highly shaped by the design of the software. In terms of design, *Impress* as well as *PowerPoint* is mostly used for animated presentations and then that seems to be what Vera mostly focuses on in her evaluation of students' performance. Actually, this is one of the arguments she uses to assess S3's final project as one of the most successful ones (since S3 included animation and slideshow to represent her family, as will be discussed in the next section).

Let us now turn to the design and final text by S3 (Images 7.4 and 7.5).

As for ideational meanings, it can be noted that S3's different use of the design sheet translated into the final project. Unlike S4, she decided to incorporate more affordances, such as the slideshow and the animation tools. For that purpose, her design sheet was divided into squares, each of which would come to represent a different slide. Like S4, she mostly made use of writing resources and layout to design what the final text would look like. Writing was also used meta-semiotically to organize the final text: slide four presents the sketch of what closely resembles a family tree classificational process and in slide 5 she explains in written language how this would work as a slideshow: "Y van apareciendo de a poco las personas" (*And the (images of) people start to appear*). Unlike S4, who focused on each unit of text (image and written language) as full and

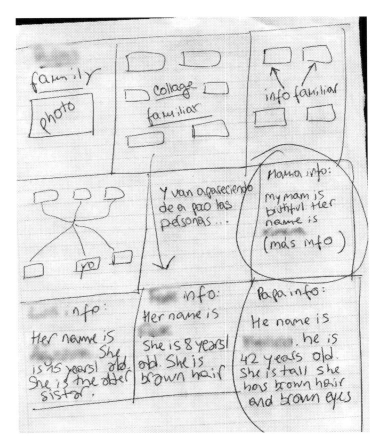

Image 7.4 S3's text design

meaningful entities, S3's design plans for the slideshow functionality to provide global cohesion to the text within and across slides. This was also evident when she orally presented the text before the class, since she was able to control how and when each element appeared on the screen, achieving coordination between her speech and the slideshow.

As well as S4, she also made changes from her design to her actual final project: she deleted some slides and simplified some of the visual and verbal content. According to her, this was due to the fact that she thought it was going to be too difficult for her to explain so much in English and

7 Learners as Sign-makers: Technology, Learning and Assessment   199

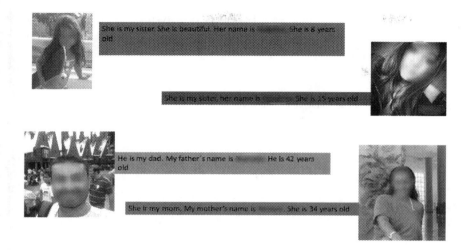

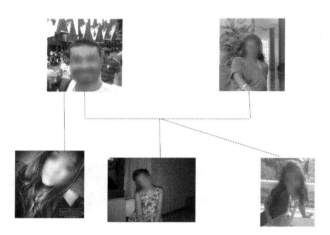

Image 7.5 S3's final animated text. Slide 2 (above) and slide 3 (below)

that it would also be too long (considering the 2 minutes allotted to each oral presentation). S3 was also aware of other restrictions, such as time constraints for the presentation and the need to make the text meet these demands. She was also able to visualize her own family tree as a text she would have to use for other purposes rather than just for the sake of making it, that is, she would have to show it to other students rather than just completing an individual classroom task. Unlike S4 whose choices were based on assuming Vera as the audience of her text, S3 assumed the whole class as the audience and the oral presentation as the context.

Extract 7.5 Interview with S3 (8/2/2016)

G: Y entonces... (*and so*) ¿por qué sacaste esto? (*why did you delete this?*)
S3: Al final porque era mucho... era mucho para inglés (*In the end, because it was too much...to much in English*)
G: Ok, so you deleted some. ¿Y cómo sabías qué dejar y qué poner? (*And how did you know what to include and what to exclude?*)
S3: Eh... quería dejar lo más importante para que mis compañeros supieran quiénes son mi familia. Los members y esas cosas. No da mucho el tiempo y era en inglés, así que puse lo más importante para que supieran más de mi familia (*I wanted to keep the most important things so that my classmates would get to know who my family is. The members and that stuff. It is only a short time and it was in English, so I included the most important things so that they knew more about my family*)

Her representation of the family also points to a classificational process, which focuses on who the represented participants are rather than on their actions. As well as in S3's final project, this is evinced in the lack of background details in the images, the tendency to use decontextualized images and the medium and close-up shots of the images selected.

However, the use of the slideshow tool contributes to S4's ability to represent the family in different ways. The final slideshow contains three slides (the first one not included here because it only contains her family last name). The second and third slides (see Image 7.5) represent her family in different ways. In slide two, family members are represented visually and verbally. Hierarchy or family kinship is expressed verbally and so no visual hierarchical organization is used. Slide three, however, makes use of visual and graphic resources. Family kinship is expressed in the visual hierarchy of organization since no verbal language is used to express this.

As for the elements of layout, information value plays an important role in organizing elements within the text. Each picture of a family

7 Learners as Sign-makers: Technology, Learning and Assessment

member is next to a short written description about that person. Unlike S3, S4 opted to place some images on the right and others on the left. When asked about this choice, she said it was due to image size. During the interaction with the artifact they had learned to zoom in and out (a change of size that accommodates to the sign-maker), but not to shrink or expand images (a change of size that affects the resulting sign and accommodates to the audience),[5] so the only way for her to incorporate her pictures into the screen page in an appropriate size was to make them fit in their original size. However, in order to be able to design her own layout, S3 opted to choose the "blank" slide on the *Impress* software and not to use the default built-in template as S4 did. Although this evinces the fact that S3 did not master some features (such as expanding images), the fact that she found a way around it also shows her awareness of an audience for whom picture size needs to be catered for.

Salience seems to play a different role, if compared to S3. In order for written texts to be clearly distinct from one another, S4 made use of several affordances. Background color (different in each written text box) helps to frame and identify each text box (which would not be salient on the white background). However, using background color also forced her to consider different font color (black for the green background and white for all the rest). This choice, for S3, was based on audience awareness: she knew when presenting her final text to the class (with a data projector) there was a chance her classmates would not be able to read the written texts unless she changed font color (see Extract 7.5). Her use of the slideshow feature also allowed her to better present the texts to her audience and to achieve cohesion within the slide: she could make each element appear (i.e. the image and its corresponding written description), so that the audience would not be confused as for which written text belongs to an image.

Slide three made use of the same images of family members to also represent them—visually and graphically—as a classificational process and, in fact, as a more traditional family tree. S3 included a picture of herself so that she would also be in the representation-while in the previous slide S3 was present through possessive determiners (*my mother, my sister, my father*). Slide 3 shows a more *objective* orientation to the family representation than slide 2, since there is no particular member of the family taken as a point of departure.

While presenting her final text to her classmates, Vera asked a question to S3 about this family tree representation, which made a sign of learning explicit and available to the whole class. At the time, S3 had both her slides and the original family tree representation for The Simspsons family (which they had used in class).

Extract 7.6 Vera and S3 during S3's oral presentation of her family tree (Unit 5, Day 12)

V: (points to both S3's slide and the Simpsons' family tree on the board) So, do you see, ¿ves diferencias con el de Los Simpsons? *(Do you see any difference with The Simspsons?)*
S3: Eh?
V: De la manera en que lo hiciste vos y la manera en que está hecho el de Los Simpsons? *(The way you did it and the way the Simpsons one is done?)*
S3: Yes, This family eh tiene grand… grandparents *(it shows grandparents)*
V: Grandparents? ¿Abuelos? *(Grandparents?)*
S3: Yes, grandparents. El mío no tiene abuelos (*Mine doesn't show grandparents*)
V: But the lines are also different, right? En los dos árboles… son distintas ¿Se te corrió una línea? *(In the two family trees [lines] are different. A line just moved?)*
S3: Ah, this. No, esta la hice así porque es mi hermanastra, la hija de mi padre, pero no de mi madre. *(No, I did it like this because she's my stepsister, she's my father's daughter but not my mother's)*

It is interesting to note that the way S3 represents her family through this conceptual process demonstrates her appropriation of the original family tree sign. An available sign of learning for this is the way in which she used different types of lines to represent to different kinds of kinship. While S3 herself and one of her sisters are linked to both their parents by lines, which are connected to their parents' images, the third sister is connected by a line that originates in the image of the father only (see Image 7.5). While Vera first orients to this as a potential formatting problem (i.e. that S3 had not found a way to connect that line to the other lines), S3 demonstrates agency over the representation and also over the layout and organization of a family tree diagram. While the family trees they had seen with Vera represented *traditional families*, S3 found a way to represent the fact that one of her sisters was in fact her stepsister.

During an interview with her, I asked S3 if she thought slide two and three represented her family in different ways given that she did not use the term "stepsister" in slide two. Interestingly, she said the only reason why she had done so was because she did not know the word for stepsister in English. As a result, she had just decided to represent it visually, even if slides two and three did not match completely in terms of family representation.

From the point of view of meaning-making, what is interesting about this is that S3 transforms previously available signs (the family tree in the textbook and the Simpsons' family tree) into a new sign of her own to fulfill her communicative purpose as sign-maker and to underscore aspects she considers *criterial* in the representation of her family (i.e. to make a distinction between *blood sister* and *stepsister*). To describe her own family, then, she decides to include some elements and exclude others. For instance, her stepsister is included and her stepsister's mother is excluded. In accounting for such decisions, she demonstrates appropriation of the sign and also understanding of the impact of these exclusion and inclusion criteria on the actual representation. During our interview she mentioned, for instance, that her family tree would have another connecting line if her stepsister's mother had been included, but that she had decided not to do so on purpose because she was not family to her. In this way, her explanation makes evident her understanding that the selection of particular semiotic elements does have an impact on the representation and also on the audience's understanding of it.

Some Final Remarks about the Enactment of *"My Family"* Classroom Unit

Through interaction with human and non-human participants, students came to explore affordances and limitations in the *Impress* software and to negotiate between artifact design and artifact use based on what Vera expects from them as signs of learning.

S3 and S4's designs and final projects demonstrate how they appropriate some software affordances to make their own family tree representation, which showcases what is criterial for each of them in terms of representation, and also the software features they have mastered, or how they overcame—to some extent—problems with certain features.

For instance, they came to understand aspects of the complicated relation between artifact design and use. Their attempts to incorporate writing and image into the built-in template showed the restrictions users can find in terms of the order in which they take steps: the incorporation of image before written texts complicated things for students, since the organization and layout of the page change in unexpected ways. This allowed students to reflect on the fact that the orchestration of modal resources into the online page or slide is complicated as it is to some extent restricted by design or software default features. To overcome this, students resorted to different strategies when making their final projects: S3 selected a blank unformatted slide—instead of the built-in template—whereas S4 erased all the pre-established features of the default built-in template before using it. However, none of them explored other built-in templates to evaluate whether they would be useful for their representation.

As for their design and final projects, both used particular modal resources to represent their family, showing agency and transforming the original family tree sign while at the same time keeping the conceptual processes it entails. For instance, while S3 used verbal language to show family kinship and hierarchy, S4 represented this through composition. Also, their final projects evince what they considered criterial to be represented. For instance, for S4 it was criterial to only "show new information" and so she decided to exclude herself from the visual representation since her classmates and Vera "already knew her". She only included herself through writing to indicate her relationship with other family members (e.g. *my mother*, *my father*, etc.). For S3 it was criterial to establish the difference between blood and by-law members of the family, so she decided to show this through placing lines in different parts of the tree.

Each student showed a different understanding of the final signs and of meanings: while S4 addressed each image and its corresponding written text as a complete and meaningful unit and focused on arranging

7   Learners as Sign-makers: Technology, Learning and Assessment

each (but not on connecting them to provide explicit textual cohesion); S3 addressed global meanings by using the slideshow functionality to provide cohesion within and across the slides.

All of this leads us to the signs of learning they were able to make, or in other words, the transformation and appropriation they made of the available signs. They demonstrated learning in several ways: through adopting either a subjective or objective orientation to representation, through using compositional resources (e.g. different types of connecting lines) to represent different types of members of the family, and through using modal resources and software affordances in different ways.

Instead of using software affordances to represent an aspect of their social world in a particular way or provide textual cohesion, sometimes a student used an affordance to sing-post learning. For instance, while S4 used salience (font type, color, size, text framing) to equally distribute the graphic space for each member of the family represented, S3 used salience (font type, size and boldness) as a meta-sign of learning. Interestingly, this also shows S4's agency at a larger scale, attempting to shape what signs the shaping agent (Vera) will need to attend to as learning in assessing her multimodal sign use and to define the audience of her sign. While S4's choices constructed her classmates as the audience, S3's focused on the teacher as audience. S4's attempt, however, was not very successful in terms of Vera's assessment of it because it signposts power relations with regards to the task (Vera as the judge and the student as a sign-maker "by request").

Finally, it is also relevant to note that another aspect that impacted students' learning was the tasks themselves. The teacher's framing of the learning situation impacted what they used and what they were able to do to successfully complete the task and produce a complex sign that was recognized as learning. This implied, for some tasks, focusing more on non-verbal resources (e.g. when exploring software affordances) and to relegate the target language. On the contrary, students got to use the target language in other tasks: when designing the final project (written language) and when presenting it before the whole class (oral language). The final section of this chapter will address this in more detail.

The Enactment of *My Neighborhood* Classroom Unit

My neighborhood (unit 5) was the final unit of classroom work. As it took place by the end of the year, it required more work and the making of more complex final tasks by students. In fact, this unit required students to make a 3D map of the school street. Vera told students the map needed to *stick to what they saw in the street* as far as possible and to include things they typically take for granted in the street. As for EFL (linguistic) goals of the whole unit, Vera expected to introduce students to vocabulary for giving directions (for instance, preposition of place), naming stores and the existential *there is/are* for describing places.

Throughout several lessons, students were given a paper map to describe and locate places, as well as to give directions. The textbook also offered a prototypical map with names (of streets, rivers, places, etc.). In interacting with the 2D maps on the textbook, students were given set of language exercises (in this case, existential *there is/there are*) and a set of cloze reading exercises for them to fill out. Students were thus required to demonstrate ability to *read* the map and, at the same time, to choose appropriate language or vocabulary items. The medium available to them (i.e. paper) enabled students to perform certain activities and interact with the map in particular ways. For instance, they had access to the whole map at the same time (no progressive flow of information), they could include their own annotations, draw symbols on it and they could choose their own reading paths as they attempted to answer the questions to demonstrate linguistic skills in EFL.

As for digital literacy goals, Vera expected students to learn how to design a 3D map, which would require different skills from those of reading/designing paper maps. Additionally, she also expected them to learn more about their own neighborhood. Unlike the family tree project, Vera did not plan for students to orally present their 3D maps before their classmates (due to time constraints). Instead, she would evaluate their work by looking at it herself—together with each student—in informal conversations during class breaks.

To do this final project activity, she prepared for three main events. First, she found a software tool for drawing 3D maps (*Sketch up*) since the laptops did not have any such software. Second, she contacted an expert in urban design studies (Luis) who would offer a hands-on presentation to guide students' exploration of the tool. Third, she took students on a tour around the school street to document what it looked like in order for them to draw their 3D map. Unlike the *My family* final project, for which students were assessed by their ability to "be creative" or "transform" a previously made sign (the family tree), this task required students to stick as far as possible to *reality*, to what they documented in the school street, but at the same time to transform it. Unlike final project 1, the 3D map in principle did not require students to use the target language. However, it did require students to use it on two occasions: when attending a session on how to use the software and when presenting the final project to Vera. I will return to both events later in the analysis.

Changing Artifact Status, or Overcoming XO Laptop Limitations

During an interview with the teacher, Vera told me she had searched the web for several 3D map-maker software tools and she had explored some of those at home (with her personal laptop). Unlike the *Open Office* software and other Plan Ceibal tools in the XO laptops, these map makers require a membership and the school would not pay for it, so she decided to select some which offered free trial periods. Once she found *Sketch up*, she contacted an expert on 3D maps and urban studies and they agreed on his presentation for the students.

Extract 7.7 Interview with Vera (10/27/2015)

G: And so, what is the aim of this project?
V: I want them to learn to do more things in groups. Making decisions and dividing tasks between two or three students. To have the responsibility to work with others. They learn language, of course, but they also learn other things, right?
G: And why this particular final project?
V: Because it is related to the topic of the unit. Also because it is a good opportunity for the students to go outside of the school and learn more about this neighborhood.

(continued)

Extract 7.7 (continued)

> G: What do you think they need to learn about the neighborhood?
> V: I want them to look at the neighborhood in a different way. Like… like experts. Yes? I want them to pay attention to details….to learn to pay attention to details and then use those details to make their maps. I think it's useful. It is also hard because I don't know much about the programs… that is why Luis is coming to teach them.
> G: Oh that's nice.
> V: Yes, we planned everything. The only problem is the XO laptops.
> G: What do you mean?
> V: We'll have to use the computer [desktops] room because the software can't be used with the Ceibalitas [XO laptops].
> G: Oh, so you're not using the laptops?
> V: Yes, we are. But in a different… they will use them to record and take pictures, but the map they will need to make the map with the computers [desktops].
> G: Oh, I see.
> V: Yes. It happened many times. This happens sometimes. You want to use something but when you try it doesn't work with the Ceibalitas [XO laptops].

As the Extract 7.7 illustrates, Vera needed to make new arrangements for technology artifact use, since the software was not supported by the XO laptops. Thus, she decided to distribute labor between desktops (at the computer lab room) and XO laptops (see Image 7.6). The former would be used for the actual making of the 3D maps while the latter would be used for documenting the tour around the school street. This XO laptop limitation[6] made students go to the computer lab room, which only happened a few times throughout the academic year.[7]

Exploring Software Affordances

The hands-on session with the expert lasted 40 minutes and was delivered mostly in English.[8] First, Vera had concerns whether students would be able to follow the session if it was delivered completely in English, they seemed to understand well (as their final projects show). The session allowed students and Vera to come together with other

7 Learners as Sign-makers: Technology, Learning and Assessment

Image 7.6 Student using both XO laptop and desktop (Unit 5, Day 11)

social actors—experts—and to discuss and share expertise (Starkey 2012), bridging the gap between the classroom environment and other environments and the social actors who act on it. Throughout the lesson, students worked in pairs or trios to explore how to use several features of 3D map making and its implications for design. The exploration was guided by the expert, who first showed students each feature and then asked students to practice themselves. Luis showed students how to use *Google maps* to find their school street and insert it into the *Sketch up* screen. Next, he explained one of the most important features: how to make the flat image of the map become 3D. Unlike the exploration of XO affordances in unit 1, this time Vera did not regulate students-artifact interaction. Instead, she made rounds to sit with them and explore the program with them (and occasionally took notes to further explore it at home).

In this section, I will analyze data from S5, S6 and S4, who worked together in exploring the *Sketch up* software. Then, I will analyze S5's final map to discuss signs of learning. I chose this group because S5 was the student who designed a 3D map that was quite different from the other students, as shall be discussed later.

Extract 7.8 S4, S5 and S6 interacting with the *Sketch up* software (Unit 5, Day 7)

Time	Participant/s action (gesture, hand, body, gaze)	Verbal interaction	Artifact action
0:38	L points to map on the screen L points to school building (flat image) and to its surroundings	L: So, for example, I'm gonna to do your school and all the buildings surrounding which is basically what you guys are going to do	Arrow points to (flat) school building Arrow circles around the school building
1:01	L points to square	L: So, for example I select the pencil. Ok? And I click and drag, just following the lines I see in the picture. See? I get this square and when I see this green line, whenever I get to an endpoint it's gonna go green.	Arrow points to pencil icon A blue color filled square appears right below the flat school building
1:07	L points to blue-filled square	L: And then automatically when I close it, it fills. See? If I don't close it, it doesn't close, so it means I cannot work with it. S5: Ok	
1:17		L: So now I just click on the square and lift it to make it as high as I want. Ok? How many stories does the school building have? S6: Two L: Ok, so this high is ok.	Arrow on rectangle Rectangle becomes 3D and gets taller and then smaller

This short extract suffices to illustrate how the session went in general terms. Most of the talk and demonstration was done by Luis, but students occasionally asked him questions on software affordances and instructions. Each group of students worked with him, and then on their own to explore these features.

As illustrated in the previous extract—and in other interactions within the lesson—in interacting with this software tools, students started to become aware of several elements they would need to con-

7 Learners as Sign-makers: Technology, Learning and Assessment

sider when designing their own 3D map of the school street so that it would be "as realistic as possible", as Vera had requested. These are the aspects that all groups got to see during the expert demonstration and which Vera also asked them to practice for the making of their own 3D map.

- How to make 3D objects (for instance, buildings) and to map them onto *Google map*
- How to change width, height and distance between elements
- How to insert built-in objects, for instance, trees and cars.
- How to insert text (to draw shop signs, among others)
- How to insert drawing
- How to rotate view
- How to get inside and outside of buildings
- How to move across the map in different directions
- How to manipulate color, size, and so on.

In the next sections, I will explore these students' walk around the school street and how they used the XO laptops to document "details". Then, I will focus on how S5 made use of some of the features they explored in the session with Luis to make his 3D map with the desktop computers.

Walking the School Street

As mentioned earlier, this final project required further division of labor: desktops were used for making the 3D map while XO laptops were used for documenting (audio-recordings, video-recordings and pictures).

The class after Luis' session on *Sketch up*, Vera took students on a walking tour down the school street. Students were grouped the same way they had been grouped for the hands-on session and they were asked to take one XO laptop per group to document their tour (audio recording, video-recording, photographing, etc.) They were also given a sheet of paper so that they could easily draw what they saw, as they documented with the XO laptops. This offered students at least two sources of data: their drawings and notes on the sheet of paper and their pictures and recordings on the XO laptop.

S4, S5 and S6 walked together and documented several aspects of the school block. However, their joint observation and documentation process resulted in very different 3D maps. Like most students, S4 and S6's map focused on details at eye-level (signs, windows, cars, etc.) while S5's map was the only one that focused on details as seen from above (bird's view). I will return to this later in the analysis

3D Mapping: Visual Modality, Details and Perspective

In terms of affordances and limitations, one of the main differences between a 2D map and a 3D one is the adoption of a particular viewpoint. Traditionally, 2D maps adopt a bird's-eye view (or a fixed satellite-like view), which cannot be altered and which presents elements as seen from above. Traditional maps are culturally shaped this way, although potentially any other (fixed) view can also be adopted in a 2D map. In contrast, 3D maps tend to allow users to change view/perspective (up and down) apart from zooming and so on since the map can be navigated interactively. Also, they allow users to change from cartography to photography, change spatial scales, among other affordances (*vid* November et al. 2010).

For students in Vera's class, these differences between 2D and 3D maps required them to entertain many elements during their tour (what they see eye-level, but also what could be seen from other angles and perspectives) and this was certainly different from the 2D map of their textbook and the one they documented on paper while walking the school street. While the final project of unit 5 required students to *stick to the original sign* (i.e. keep the details of the school street in their 3D maps), students' final maps also evince sign transformations which cater for the affor-

7 Learners as Sign-makers: Technology, Learning and Assessment

dances of 3D mapping and the types of transductions they allow. As suggested in the data, S5's map is quite interesting in this respect because it adopts a different perspective from the rest in terms of the *details* included. S5's map shows two interesting phenomena: first, he agentively *copied* the original sign and transformed it; second, he oriented to *details* in particular ways based on his own interest and understanding of the task at hand.

In going over the video-recordings of S5's 3D map design it struck my attention to learn that he spent most of the time working on details which pertained to elements above eye-level view. S5 carefully designed two elements above the roof of the school building and its neighboring buildings: an antenna and a cupola.

Maps are analytical processes which relate different objects in terms of part-whole structures (Kress and van Leeuwen 2006) and so they tend not to prefer details in representation in order to avoid *distracting* the user from what may be actually criterial in a map (finding a particular spot, locating oneself, roughly estimating distance, etc.). For this reason, maps usually have—from a naturalistic perspective—low visual modality (Kress and van Leeuwen 2006; Roderick 2016; van Leeuwen 2004). Given the purposes to which maps are generally put, it makes sense to think that details are eliminated, since they are not needed to express the relation between elements (for instance, to express to scale differences in terms of height, distance, etc.).

S5's 3D map shows what he considered criterial to be represented in his particular map (the details) and what he did not, and in general this coincides to a great extent with the notion of *low modality* assumed in maps. For instance, he did not worry about keeping the exact color of buildings or—as other students did—showing the exact number of floors in a given building (but he did show size differences to a certain extent) or incorporating shop signs. Such decisions implied evaluating what he would "translate" from his records to the actual 3D map. In this process, he decided to pay attention to details above eye-view and in particular to the antenna and to the cupola (Image 7.7).

Image 7.7 S5's representation of cupola

When zooming in one learned that compared to the rest of the 3D map, the antenna, for instance, contains details which go beyond what a person would see with the naked eye and beyond the expected requirements of a map (for instance, S5 even included the sign *DIRECTV* on the antenna). During my interview with him, we discussed this.

Extract 7.9 Interview with S5 (11/6/2015)

G: ¿Qué cosas consideraste al momento de hacer el mapa? (*What things did you bear in mind when making the map?*)
S5: Eh, la distancia… o sea qué edificio estaba al lado de otro. (*Distances… I mean which building was next to which other building*)
G: Ah, y… ¿qué más? (*and what else?*)
S5: Lo grande o chico (*Big and small*)
G: Ah, y ¿cómo lo hiciste eso? (*Oh, and how did you do that?*)
S5: Me fijé en el mapa que dibujamos y en las fotos. No me importaban mucho los pisos, me importaba que el más grande quedara más grande y el chico quedara chico. (*I checked the map we drew and the pictures we took. I didn't care about the number of floors, I cared about making bigger buildings bigger than the smaller ones*)
G: Ok. And what else?
S5: Y estas cosas (*And those things*)… things.
G: What things?
S5: This (points to antenna)
G: Oh the antenna.
S5: And this thing (points to cupola).

(*continued*)

7 Learners as Sign-makers: Technology, Learning and Assessment

Extract 7.9 (continued)

G: And the...cupola.
S5: Yes, esas cosas (*those things*).
G: Wow... you got so many things here... you even wrote something on the antenna...¿hasta escribiste el nombre de la compañía del cable? (laughs) (*you even wrote the name of the cable company?*)
S5: (laughs)
G: So why those details... ¿por qué esos detalles y no otros? (*Why those details and not others?*)
S5: Eh... por...porque la teacher nos dijo que nos fijáramos en cosas que generalmente no nos fijamos de la calle del colegio... entonces me fijé para arriba porque cuando vengo vengo en auto y nunca miro para arriba, siempre miro para los costados (*Because our teacher told us to focus on things we usually don't focus on about the school street.... So I looked up because when I come to school I come by car so I never look up, I always look left and right*)

S5 accounts for his decisions by commenting on what he considered criterial to be represented based on what Vera requested. As in most maps, distance and size of objects was criterial, however, the exact size (i.e. number of buildings) or even the exact color of objects was not considered criterial and therefore the latter were not in his focus. Interestingly, he also found it criterial to represent two elements, which were above eye-view: the antenna and the cupola. Providing details about both (such as the number of beams in the cupola or the name of the cable company for the antenna) was considered criterial by S5 as a way to successfully complete the task: focusing on details they do not focus in everyday life. To signal this meant not only to include details of both elements, but also to maximize modality and incorporate elements the naked eye would not see (such as the name of the cable company). In other words, S5 was aware of what the recontextualization of a map would require in curricular terms: a change in criteriality in, for instance, the degree of detail represented.

For this purpose, S5 drew on his background knowledge and experience (since the design of the antenna is typical of one cable company in Uruguay and not of any other so he could assume what the sign on the antenna read: *DIRECTV* and even remember the logo). While talking to him, S5 also mentioned he focused on those details because he knew in a 3D map there was a chance Vera would zoom in and out to assess his work, and so he needed to be ready to *show some details*. In this respect, he interpersonally constructs Vera not only as the shaping agent of learning, but also as the real audience of his text and plans for the *right amount of details* based on what he assumes her expectations are.

To sum up, S5's choices and his reflection on such choices account for his agency in transforming previous signs (e.g. pictures) into a new sign which foregrounds particular aspects of his tour and which serves Vera's expectations in terms of signs of learning. He is able to decide what details will be eradicated from the representation and which will be maximized as well as why such decisions are made. These decisions also require awareness of a change in medium: unlike a 2D (paper) map, a 3D (digital) map can be zoomed in and out easily and so he needed to incorporate details beyond the naked eye, which required him to switch from low to high naturalistic modality in different sections of the map (based on how he thinks Vera will navigate it) and even to draw on his previous experience to reconstruct what his pictures could not capture (such as the name of the cable company). In this manner, while the two elements (antenna and cupola) on top of the two buildings have somewhat maximized visual modality, elements at eye-level have low modality, as 2D maps generally have (for instance, size differences and distances are not to scale, just to name a few).

From Novice to Expert: Signs Circulating Outside the Classroom

After completing the task, S5 made (at home) his own *YouTube* tutorial for others to learn how to use the *Sketch up* software. In this tutorial, S5 shows his 3D map of the same school street, focusing on an old bakery and showing it from different angles and rotating views. Later, he explains (in written English) that he drew the house based on a picture (and the actual picture of the bakery is shown). Most of the details—such as the name of the bakery—appear at eye-level style, so S5 also demonstrates audience awareness: while Vera's task required him to focus on previously unnoticed details, this new task he engaged in required him to show a more general audience how to use the software and what can be done with it, so the way he approach details also changed (Image 7.8).

7 Learners as Sign-makers: Technology, Learning and Assessment   217

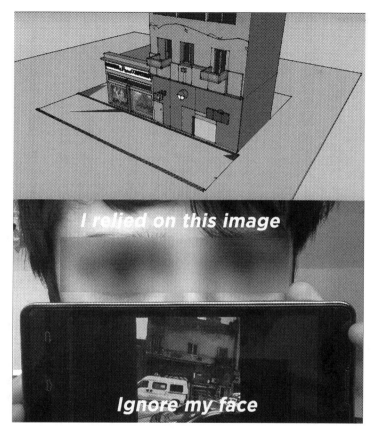

Image 7.8   Stills from S5's *YouTube* tutorial

It is interesting to note that S5 followed the same patterns of the task Vera set and changed roles, becoming the *expert* for other *YouTube* users and sharing his expertise. But he takes this outside of the formal learning scenario of the EFL classroom and shares it with a different audience, some of which also commented on the video. In this respect, the school subject EFL—as Vera expects—has an immediate impact on out-of-school practices (Gee 2007), making S5 transfer his learning experiences to other domains while at the same time he does so in the target language. Vera acknowledged this during one of our interviews.

Extract 7.10 Interview with Vera (11/6/2016)

G: And what about this map [S5's]?
V: Well, he did a great job. He always does a great job. He works really well... and he loves technology.
G: Oh, I see.
V: When I saw his map he talked about the tutorial he made, the *YouTube* thing?
G: Yes, he mentioned that to me too.
V: That is what I want them to learn. See? Que hagan cosas en la clase y que luego las saquen al mundo de afuera (*That they do things in the class and then use them outside*). It is important.
G: So, in what ways do you think he did a good job with the map?
V: Well, he didn't have a lot of details...he had some. But he was creative... I mean, he drew an antenna (laughs). He told me several times he was worried about showing what is on top of the buildings, so he focused on that.
G: Aha.
V: But the most important thing for me is that he made the tutorial.... Who does that? (laughs). That's what's more important for me. He took what he learned to real life.

Vera underscores digital literacy goals over linguistic goals while, at the same time, she highlights S5's use of technology and software used in the EFL classroom outside of the school. This also shows Vera's flexibility in how and what she assesses: while using the software outside of the school was not one of the requirements, she asserts S5 did a very good job and the *YouTube* tutorial he did at home becomes a legitimate sign of learning for her, even when the 3D map of the school street was originally the text over which students would be assessed.

Some Final Remarks about the Enactment of "My Neighborhood" Classroom Unit

The final task for this unit of classroom work required more division of labor and more work for students. It also required them to interact with a more sophisticated software and to sketch a highly multimodal and complex final task (the 3D map).

The type of touring experience students engaged in is relevant for them because it allows them to draw connections between objects, the environment and themselves: "[m]oving between and around locations provides opportunities for learning through making connections by being

7 Learners as Sign-makers: Technology, Learning and Assessment

mobile—simply defined as "touring"" (Sprake 2016, 70). As Sprake suggests, some of the characteristics of this type of activity is that students learn to *micro map*, that is to say, to record details of the environment in order to piece together objects and places in the tour (p. 73). Also, being able to record and document their tour allowed them to draw on several sources of multimodal data (Mills et al. 2014). All of this became evident in S5's tour with S4 and S6 and in the way he used records and documentation to define—according to his own interest and understanding of the task—what objects would be detailed and what objects would not.

The activity also allowed the EFL classroom to re-scale agency and roles in classroom interaction and work. Unlike all the other projects, Vera invited an expert in and offered students the possibility to listen to other voices, perspectives and expertise. Her role, in this respect, was not regulative in terms of students-artifact interaction or in terms of target language use during interaction. Instead, she became another member of the classroom interested in learning how to use the software, while at the same time her presence as the audience of the final map was clear to students, as data from S5's interview suggests: she remained the legitimate judge of their performance, assessing their maps. This made S5 orient to some elements as potential signs of learning for Vera, and for this reason he decided to make a 3D map with different degrees of visual modality (from a naturalistic point of view): while some elements beyond eye-level had maximal modality (such as the antenna and the cupola), elements at eye-level were minimized, as generally happens in 2D maps.

The data also suggest that activities and digital practices that take place outside of the EFL classroom are also considered and assessed by Vera, as the *YouTube* tutorial indicates. This underscores her digital literacy goals for the EFL classroom and, at the same time, reinforces the notion that in her class the target language is mostly used as a means to *learn something else*. This is a clear example of how a student can appropriate new artifacts for new ways of making meanings, even to expand how and when to use verbal resources. Even though it could be argued that Vera's original framing of the task lacks systematicity in when the target language could or would be used (as she herself claimed during an interview with me), S5's tutorial—which incorporates verbal resources—could be taken as an example as for how this task could be reformulated to eventually allow students to expand their resources and use the target language in more varied instances throughout the unit, such as S5 by using writing—among other resources—in his tutorial. This, I shall argue, is one of the most difficult things to balance in a foreign language classroom: how to dwell in an alternative ideology of learning which foregrounds multimodality as communication and learning while still attend to the curricular requirements of a foreign language class which to some extent foregrounds writing and speech among many modes, as mentioned in Chap. 3. For language teachers and for researchers as well, attending to how semiotic modes can be functionalized or specialized for particular purposes in the classroom is fundamental, as is striking a balance between the specificities *of teaching a language* and adopting an alternative ideology of learning which recognizes multimodal work as communication and as evidence of learning. De-centering language and centering multimodality is hard work in general in education, but it is particularly challenging for language education.

Functionalization of Languages in the Design, Making and Assessment of Final Projects

As can be noted from the two units of classroom work analyzed in this chapter, in interacting and working with the XO laptops students engage in several tasks and activities, some of which require reflection on modal resources other than verbal language. Even so, some tasks may not even require the use verbal resources at all while others may not require students to use the target language (and so Spanish is used instead).

It is in this respect that I would like to point to the functionalization of verbal resources in this classroom or, in simpler words, to the use of Spanish and English across each final project design, making and assessment. The two units analyzed—as well as the larger ethnographic data—point to the fact that not all tasks an activities require students to use the target language. Activities pertaining to software exploration and final text design do not require students to use English among themselves—and often times not even with Vera. The lesson by Luis is an exception: since it was delivered in English it required students to listen to instructions and suggestions in English while he demonstrated how to use the soft-

7 Learners as Sign-makers: Technology, Learning and Assessment

ware and students were encouraged to interact with him in the target language.

On the contrary, the final project text required students to use the target language. The exception, again, is the making of the 3D map which, as framed by Vera, did not require any use of the target language. Even though the final task itself did not require the use of English (or any other language), it was indeed required when students presented their work orally, sometimes only to her and other times to the whole class, making meaning-making processes available to other students (Mavers 2007). Vera's assessment of final texts mainly focused on how much students were able to do with the technology artifacts and whether they were able to justify their choices. Even though she expected students to do some of the description and explanation in the target language, assessment *per se* revolved around the use of technology. The fact that she also gives a *traditional test* as required by EFL supervisors (see Chap. 6) also accounts for this division of labor in assessment. However, what is assessed in the paper-based test, as the previous chapter showed, does not pertain to digital literacy but to the vocabulary and the grammar found in the textbook.

It is interesting to look into the final presentations to describe what is it that students are able to demonstrate in the target language, regardless of whether it is actually recognized or legitimated as an event to be assessed in the EFL classroom. Here I do not claim that the target language must be used more or in all tasks. In fact, this would go against my previous characterization of an alternative ideology of learning in the language classroom. However, I do acknowledge that providing students with opportunities to use the target language is a legitimate preoccupation among teachers. However, making sure those opportunities allow for better recognition of how verbal resources interact with other semiotic resources is also a legitimate preoccupation for language education in the twenty-first century.

In the following transcripts of final task presentations, I focus on four aspects: (a) the use of verbal language to add information other than what appears in the slides (in bold), (b) some features of speech during students' presentation (in italics), (c) transformation of verbal resources, for instance changing grammatical structures from the written slides to speech (underlined), and (d) some of the vocabulary, expressions, and so on they use from the unit when answering Vera's on-the-spot questions (double underline). These are not meant to foreground verbal resources as more important than other semiotic resources in communication and learning. On the contrary, these four aspects are explored in order to show that in demonstrating work and learning multimodally, students necessarily demonstrate language use and learning (not in isolation but in orchestration with other semiotic modal resources).

Extract 7.11 S3's oral presentation of her family tree (Unit 5, Day 12)

V: Ok, so ready? You can start then
S3: ok. ¿Qué hago? (*What do I do?*)
V: So, present to us your family.
S3: Ok
S3: (points to image) She is my sister.
V: (stands up and changes seat) Wait a minute!
S3: Teacher! (laughs) Ok?
V: Ok, go.
S3: She is my sister. She is… Eh… eight years old. (points to another image) *and she is short*. She is my sister… her name is XXXX, she is eh… 15 years old. (Points to another image) He is my dad. His name is XXXX *and* he's 42 years old. (Points to another image) She is my mom. Her name is XXXX. She is 20… 34 years old *and* **she's pretty.**
V: So how many people in your family?
S3: Eh?
V: How many people in your family?
S3: Mmm, four or five…five.
V: And do you have a pet?
S3: Yes… three. I have three pets. Two small cats…eh…they are Paloma and (inaudible) and one dog.
V: Ok.
S3: (changes slide) *And* **here this is my family again** (laughs)
V: Ok
S3: This is my (points to image) and these are my sisters again (points to image) (laughs)
V: (points to both S3's slide and the Simpsons' family tree on the board) So, do you see, ¿ves diferencias con el de Los Simpsons? *(Do you see any difference with The Simspsons?)*
S3: Eh?
V: De la manera en que lo hiciste vos y la manera en que está hecho el de Los Simpsons? *(The way you did it and the way the Simpsons' one is done?)*
S3: Yes, This family eh tiene grand… grandparents *(it shows grandparents)*
V: Grandparents? ¿Abuelos? *(Grandparents?)*
S3: Yes, grandparents. El mío no tiene abuelos (*Mine doesn't show grandparents*)

(*continued*)

7 Learners as Sign-makers: Technology, Learning and Assessment

Extract 7.11 (continued)

> V: But the lines are also different, right? En los dos árboles... son distintas ¿Se te corrió una línea? *(In the two family trees [lines] are different. A line just moved?)*
> S3: Ah, this. No, esta la hice así porque es mi hermanastra, la hija de mi padre, pero no de mi madre. *(No, I did it like this because she's my stepsister, she's my father's daughter but not my mother's)*
> V: Can you explain to us?
> S3: Eh, in English?
> V: Yes.
> S3: Well, **my dad and my mom** tuvieron *(had)* my sister and me. And my dad tuvo *(had)* my sister with...eh other woman
> V: Aha, like a stepsister.
> S3: Yes.
> V: So, how do you say stepsister in Spanish?
> S3: "Media hermana", no?
> V: Yes, stepsister. Media hermana. Good. Very good. Very good job! Who's next?

In Extract 7.11, S3 shows appropriation of target language resources to communicate in the classroom. To begin with, she does not just "read" word by word from the slides. On the contrary, she actually omits some of the information shown in the slide and adds other. In this respect, it is important to note that students did not explore the presenter's screen feature on the *Impress*, so they did not have any notes on their screen when they presented. Omissions and additions, then, were not strictly scripted. For instance, when introducing her first sister (slide 2) she adds "and she is short", expanding on the description on the slide. She also uses unscripted speech to mark transitions between slides: when introducing slide three she says "and here is my family again" (see Image 7.5), and when introducing slide two she says "here" to signal the transition from one slide to another, making cohesion between the visuals and her speech explicit. In this respect, S3 shows appropriation of verbal features which pertain to oral presentation skills when using visuals.

She also makes use of *and* as a marker of speech (Halliday 1989), as shown in bold. Additionally, she also uses vocabulary introduced throughout the unit: naming members of the family which are not included in the representation (*grandmother, grandfather*) or naming pets (*dog, cat*). Some of the transformations she makes when orally introducing the written information also implies drawing on vocabulary and grammatical structures from the unit. For instance, she uses possessive pronouns (*His name is XXX* and *Her name is XXX*) to refer to her father and mother, replacing the possessive case (*My father's name is XXX* and *My mother's name is*) used in writing.

Vera's role is also important in this interaction because she asks on-the-spot questions for which students need to use structures and vocabulary from the unit while, at the same time, they need to use their knowledge of their family and the family tree they made. In particular, Vera's question about the design of the family tree (the line to represent her stepsister, see Image 7.5) allows S3 to build up on her vocabulary. When S4 says: *And my dad tuvo (had) my sister with other woman*, Vera signals her understanding by providing the exact word to represent that: *"Aha, like a step-sister"*. More importantly, S3 was also able to briefly introduce and describe her pets even though they were not included in the slides.

S4's final text was assessed by Vera as one of the "poorest". However, there is also evidence of learning in her presentation, as shown in Extract 7.12.

Extract 7.12 S4's oral presentation of her family tree (Unit 5, Day 12)

S4: She's...*this my... this... this...eh this* is my family. She is my mother. She has medium height. She has black hair. Her name is XXX
S4: Eh... her name is XXX. She is my sister. *She is...she...she* is tall. He has has black hair (points to image) Her name is XXX. *He... he...he* is my sister. She is taller than me. She has black hair (points to image) He is my father. He is taller than me. He has black and short hair. *She...she...she* name...his...his name is XXX
V: Aha, very good. Are you sisters older than you or younger?
S4: Older.
V: Both are older?
S4: Yes, they are old older.
V: And your father...he is taller than you, right?
S4: Yes
V: Is he taller than your sisters too?
S4: Yes
V: Is he taller than your mother too?
S4: Eh... yes.
V: So...
S4: ¿Qué? (*What*)
V: So your father is the tall...
S4: the taller.
V: The taller? The tall...
S4: The... No sé (*I don't know*)
V: The tallest
S4: Ah sí, el más grande (*Oh yes, the tallest*)
V: Ok good.

7 Learners as Sign-makers: Technology, Learning and Assessment

If compared with S3, it could be argued that S4's features of speech are mainly hesitations (such as *He...he...he is my sister*) which could construe her oral presentation as less "apt" if compared to S3. Also, she seems to confuse grammatical gender in personal and possessive pronouns, even though she reads from the slide. Contrary to S3, she does not add or omit extra information, but she sticks to reading what is on the screen.

However, S3 is able to answer unexpected questions by Vera, such as those regarding height, which require her to compare heights. She is also able to use the yes/no answer pattern which was introduced in class: *Yes, he is old older*. Finally, even when she might not know the exact word Vera wants her to look for (superlative *tallest* in *So he is the...*), S3 shows understanding of the question (since she answers successfully in Spanish and even translates the word into "el más grande"). As well as in the "stepsister" episode, Vera offers the exact word "tallest" instead of orienting to the student's choice as a blunt *mistake* or as a *language deficit*.

Finally, let us look at S5's final 3D map oral presentation to Vera. Since the actual map did not require the use of writing, I will focus on the vocabulary and structures S5 uses drawing on what was taught in that unit.

Extract 7.13 S5's oral presentation of his 3D map to Vera (Unit 5, Day 12)

V: Ok so show me. Is this the street? (points to street)
S5: Yes, this is the street. This Fleetw...This is Fleetwood. Next to a building. Opposite a...a another building. This is a house (rotates view) House, house, house (keeps rotating view) Edificio (building)... building... building
V: And how do you know the size of the buildings? ¿Cómo la calculaste la medida? (*How did you estimate the size?*)
S5: Según los pisos, más o menos, si eran más pisos lo hacía más alto (*According to the number of floors, if it had more floors then I made it bigger*). More floors are bigger.
V: So which is the biggest one?
S5 (rotates view and points with mouse arrow) This... this is biggest.
V: But you wrote the number of floors when you walked, right?
S5: ¿El número de pisos? (*The number of floors?*) Eh sí, pero no importa el número de pisos, con el tamaño sabes dónde estás (*Yes, but the number of floor is not important, by knowing which is bigger you already know where you are*)
V: Bueno, sí (laughs) tenés razón (*Well, yes, you're right*)
S5: (zooms in) And this is...antenna

(continued)

Extract 7.13 (continued)

V: Oh, which? Where is it?
S5: El el building de al lado (*in the neighboring building*). Building close to school.
V: Oh, I didn't know (laughs)
S5: Yes, and el otro… la cosa esta (And the other…this thing)
V: Ah esta cúspide…cúpula
S5: Eh? Yes. La hice también (I did it too).
V: Good. And why?
S5: Eh?
V: ¿Por qué? (*Why?*)
S5: Ah como si se viera desde arriba, ¿entendés? It is up. Los detalles están arriba (*Oh as if we were looking from above, the details are above*)
V: Ah, ok. Good. Very good. Tienen muchos detalles (*They are very detailed*)

Extract 7.13 shows that the oral presentation of the 3D map is less structured than that of the family tree for two main reasons. First, Vera interacts with the student throughout the whole presentation, asking questions about the design and about their choices. Second, because the very nature of the 3D map does not shape the organization of talk to the same extent an animated presentation does. For instance, the *Impress* presentation is organized around slides, which require a particular temporal unfolding of information, which in turn shapes the unfolding of the oral presentation. On the other hand, the organization of the 3D map does not impose ways of interacting with it during the presentation, so it offers more possibilities while at the same time it can make it harder to organize speech.

Despite these differences, S5 manages to successfully present the information and to coordinate speech with the use of the rotating view and zooming features. He mostly draws on Spanish when explaining his decisions, probably because of the abstract nature of the explanations. For example, when explaining why he focused on details above the eye-level, he says: *"Ah como si se viera desde arriba, entendés? It is up. Los detalles están arriba"*. However, when explaining more concrete aspects, he uses the target language almost exclusively. He draws on vocabulary and grammatical structures from the unit (e.g. adverbs of place) to locate the school building: *"This is Fleetwood. Next to a building. Opposite a…a another building"*.

He is also able to answer on-the-spot questions Vera asks about the map. This requires him to explain and justify his choices, and for these more abstract purposes (which go beyond descriptive language) he may switch between the two languages. For instance, when Vera asks why he drew both the antenna and cupola, he replies "Ah como si se viera desde arriba, entendés? It is up. Los detalles están arriba" (*Oh as if we were looking from above, the details are above*).

He shows understanding of vocabulary that pertains to the unit, such as superlative adjectives: (e.g. *S5: This, this is biggest*); he also shows appropriation of the software affordances and coordination between his speech in the target language and other modal resources. For instance, to illustrate his point he rotates and changes view and then points to the biggest building in his map.

As can be noted, what students are able to do in these oral presentations point to how they draw on different semiotic resources in the target language and in other modes, and also in the orchestrated deployment of verbal resources and other modal resources (such as gestures) to communicate with others. It also points to how they become aware of the artifacts at hand and how they can be used in a particular context (e.g. presenting a slideshow to other students, presenting how a 3D map works to the teacher). Artifact appropriation may vary in terms of how much students can do, but substantial, socially relevant evidence of learning can be found in all three cases under investigation. Regardless of how much target language is used, students demonstrate they can draw on verbal resources, they can orchestrate verbal resources together with other semiotic resources as a particular genre might require, and they can make complex meanings out of such orchestration.

Conclusions

Recognition allows us to attend to what generally passes unnoticed, providing researchers, teachers and other educational stakeholders with good insights into learning. This is key to shift from a traditional ideology of learning toward an alternative one since recognition foregrounds the student as sign-maker and their agency in sign-making, without overlooking the fact that at larger scales other social actors also have agency. This chapter foregrounded students' agency in making meanings with technology in the EFL lesson at the same time that it considered how teacher and artifact agency become articulated with student agency in meaning-making processes.

Students-artifact interaction can be designed as meaningful classroom events for students to gain and demonstrate agency as sign-makers by exploring what particular modal resources can do in terms of representation and communication. Technology artifacts and sign-makers distribute labor in many ways, both in terms of 1:1 but also in terms of a group of students interacting with one artifact. How and for what purposes labor is distributed between humans and artifacts at one scale (for instance, interaction with the artifact or text design) can impact other scales, such as the way in which signs circulate, how the sign audience is shaped or even what the final text is like.

Throughout these processes—and across these scales—technology artifacts become material instruments to carry out an activity rather than the object of the activity itself (Engeström 1991) or the mere medium to complete a classroom task. This is key for policy-making in education since it represents moving forward from "access to technology" (each student having a laptop, for instance) to designing spaces for learning in (inter)action with technology. In turn, this also impacts governing ideologies of learning: division of labor between sign-makers and artifacts requires shifting from the notion that students need to perform a task in isolation and without the "help" of external artifacts (dictionaries, books, notebooks, technology) to demonstrate learning (Engeström 1991) to an understanding that both the environment—or material world—and the sign-maker—or the subject—are both transforming and transformed by interacting, dividing labor and making semiosis.

From a socio-semiotic perspective, the chapter also pointed to how through such interactions learners reflect on ideational, interpersonal and textual meanings. This pertains to the alternative ideology of learning and the foregrounding of communication and learning as multimodal: the school subject (in this case, EFL) is constructed in such a way that the English language becomes *one* of the many legitimate and authorized modes for making meanings in the classroom. In the case

7 Learners as Sign-makers: Technology, Learning and Assessment

under investigation, the division of labor is such that even the use of language(s) in the design and making of each final project seems to entail some functionalization: the target language is used in the oral presentation students need to make to explain/show their final texts to the whole class. On such occasion, the language is used to "practice" rather than for assessment purposes. Through design and exploration of the artifact Spanish becomes the most frequent means of communication among students (and sometimes even between students and Vera). In these tasks, the focus is on digital literacy goals and then the target language becomes secondary. However, the amount of target language used in the classroom is evidently shaped by Vera's framing of tasks. For instance, while the family tree required students to use English in the slides, the 3D map could be made successfully without incorporating English into the final text.

For its part, the analysis of *signs of learning* shed light on the agentive nature of learning, even when there is an external shaping agent (Vera) guiding classroom practices. By interacting with artifacts and with other human participants, students demonstrate appropriation of previous signs and at the same time they learn to appropriate the artifact for various semiotic purposes. They also show how they find ways to go about software limitations, or even their own limitations in exploring meaning-making affordances of tasks.

In moving from a traditional to an alternative ideology of learning, classroom tasks can be designed to interact with technology artifacts so as to overcome some sort of encapsulation of learning (Engeström 1991), or to foster continuity between in-class and out-of-class meaning-making. In our current days, such continuity needs to cater for the fact that students' identities are far more dynamic than before. For instance, while within the classroom walls a sign-maker can be positioned as a learner/student interacting with the software to learn how to make a 3D map, the very same sign-maker becomes an expert and an author/producer around the same topic outside the school, let's say on *YouTube*. This type of mobility of sign-makers' identity is perhaps one of the biggest challenges for current education to serve the communicative purposes of students. It is probably after these types of purposes that education policy fostering the use of technology should go.

Whether by bringing their own life into the classrooms (such as presenting their family) or by going outside to learn about and with the community (by taking a tour around the school street), the school subject is constructed in such a way that modal resources—not only writing and speech—are explored, appreciated and legitimated as ways of communication and learning. The alternative ideology of learning which guides the use of technology artifacts in Vera's classroom—the XO laptop and to a lesser extent the desktops—allows for a particular notion of learning EFL, which implies: (a) making meanings with the language in the context of making meanings with other modal resources and reflecting on how they interact in communication, (b) reflecting on our choices in designing signs and the effect they have on the audience, (c) expanding classroom goals to digital literacy or, in other words, to an alternative notion of literacy in foreign language teaching and learning.

Assessment plays a key role here, while it also represents one of the most complex ideological practices in education. In fact, in the case under investigation assessment clearly shows the co-existence of traditional and alternative ideologies of learning operating at different scales in the classroom and serving the purposes and needs of different audiences. Vera maintains two routes of assessment: traditional paper-based (mechanical) assessment (as requested or expected by EFL supervisors) and alternative ways of assessment for the final projects students designed with XO laptops. The latter entails many ways of assessing students, such as considering the signs they make outside the school (as is the case of S5 and his *YouTube* tutorial). However, all these alternative routes of assessment were, in Vera's own words, less standardized and she knew she eventually needed to come up with more fixed ways to assess students' multimodal doing, even though she felt it was difficult to do so. This phenomenon seems to be indicative of what notions of assessment circulate in traditional ideologies of learning and permeate and dominate school practices. With regards to this—and as posed in the previous chapter—in many ways Vera's practices dwell between traditional and alternative ideologies of learning, as dictated by the historical, educational and political environment in which the EFL lesson is designed and enacted. As stated for other purposes by Collins (2016), we can claim that recognition, it seems, is also a matter of scales, and what is recognized as learning in one scale might not be recognized in another.

To conclude the chapter, the following question could be asked: At a large scale, what does all of this tell us about Plan Ceibal policy? If compared to some general trends in Plan Ceibal *bright spots*, the exploration of the enactment of the EFL lesson shows potential routes for Plan Ceibal en Inglés to shift ideologies of learning as well. While *bright spots* tend to favor technology as a medium to learn EFL (see Chaps. 4 and 5) and foregrounds learning as linguistic achievement only, the exploration of a particular blind spot of the policy (Vera's EFL class) points to one way to move the policy forward and to an alternative way of thinking of Plan Ceibal technology as a goal—together with EFL—instead of as a medium. This is in consonance with the meanings made at the broad Plan Ceibal. I do not intend to say that the policy should be designed after Vera's lesson or to say that her enactment is exemplary. On the contrary, I intend to argue that this enactment can be insightful for the future of Plan Ceibal policy or for other 1:1 education policies. Two key issues for this are (1) the connections between in-school and out-of-school practices (or finding continuity between both environments) and (2) the design of tasks and learning spaces in which technology artifacts are legitimate participants in interaction, communication and learning, distributing labor with sign-makers. Further exploring these issues is necessary for education policies as well as for 1:1 programs, given the ubiquitous role of new technology in school practices and given the demands of twenty-first-century students in our classrooms.

Notes

1. An earlier draft of this chapter was presented at the Multimodality Forum (Centre for Multimodal Research, Institute of Education of the University College London). I am most thankful to the audience for their insights and to the faculty and staff for their support during my research stay.
2. All three are open source software (Open Office). Roughly speaking, *Draw* resembles Window's *Paint*, *Impress* resembles Window's *PowerPoint* and *PiTiVi* resembles Window's *Movie Maker*.
3. Since this final project required students to use "simple" software, Vera felt more comfortable guiding students through the exploration. For more advanced

tools—as shall be seen later—Vera's participation resembles more that of students (i.e. exploring together with them without providing much guidance).
4. Many of the students, for instance, reported to having manipulated the pictures at home so that they would show close ups.
5. In the first case (zooming in/out) the change of size is only apparent to the maker and is not saved in the file while in the second case (shrinking/expanding) it is saved in the file therefore changing the final layout and impacting the audience.
6. At the same time, the mobility of laptops is an affordance in contrast to the desktops.
7. They had actually been at the computer lab room two times before when they have had some practical problems with their classroom. However, they had not used the desktops.
8. Once Vera learned the expert spoke English, she requested him to deliver the session in the target language so that students "would become acquainted with the vocabulary in English".
9. For a socio-semiotic account of the transformations entailed in *copying*, see Mavers (2013).

References

Bezemer, J., & Kress, G. (2016). *Multimodality, Learning and Communication. A Social Semiotic Framework*. London and New York: Routledge.

Collins, J. (2016). Voice, Schooling, Inequality, and Scale. *Anthropology & Education Quarterly, 44*(2), 205–210. https://doi.org/10.1177/2043610615573380

Dicks, B., Flewitt, R., Lancaster, L., & Pahl, K. (2011). Multimodality and Ethnography: Working at the Intersection. *Qualitative Research, 11*(3), 227–237. https://doi.org/10.1177/1468794111400682

Djonov, E., & van Leeuwen, T. (2013). Between the Grid and Composition: Layout in PowerPoint Design and Use. *Semiotica, 197*, 1–34. https://doi.org/10.1515/sem-2013-0078

Engeström, Y. (1991). Non Scolae Sed Vitae Discimus: Toward Overcoming the Encapsulation of School Learning. *Learning and Instruction, 1*(3), 243–259. https://doi.org/10.1016/0959-4752(91)90006-T

Gee, J. P. (2007). *What Video Games have to Teach Us about Learning and Literacy*. New York: Palgrave Macmillan.

Halliday, M. A. K. (1989). *Spoken and Written Language*. Oxford: Oxford University Press.

Kress, G., & Selander, S. (2012). Multimodal Design, Learning and Cultures of Recognition. *Internet and Higher Education, 15*(4), 265–268. https://doi.org/10.1016/j.iheduc.2011.12.003

Kress, G., & van Leeuwen, T. (2006). *Reading Images. The Grammar of Visual Design*. London and New York: Routledge.

Machin, D. (2004). Building the World's Visual Language: The Increasing Global Importance of Image Banks in Corporate Media. *Visual Communication, 3*(3), 316–336. https://doi.org/10.1177/1470357204045785

Mavers, D. (2007). Student Text-making as Semiotic Work. *Journal of Early Child Literacy, 9*(2), 141–155. https://doi.org/10.1177/1468798409105584

Mavers, D. (2013). Semiotic Work in the Apparently Mundane. Completing a Structured Worksheet. In M. Böck & N. Pachler (Eds.), *Multimodality and Social Semiosis: Communication, Meaning-Making and Learning in the Work of Gunther Kress* (pp. 175–181). London and New York: Routledge.

Mills, K. A., Unsworth, L., Bellocchi, A., Park, J.-Y., & Ritchie, S. M. (2014). Children's Multimodal Appraisal of Places: Walking with the Camera. *Australian Journal of Language and Literacy, 37*(3), 171–181.

November, V., Camacho-Hübner, E., & Latour, B. (2010). Entering a Risky Territory: Space in the Age of Digital Navigation. *Environment and Planning D: Society and Space, 28*, 581–599. https://doi.org/10.1068/d10409

Roderick, I. (2016). *Critical Discourse Studies and Technology. A Multimodal Approach to Analysing Technoculture*. London: Bloomsbury.

Silverstein, M., & Urban, G. (1996). The Natural History of Discourse. In M. Silverstein & G. Urban (Eds.), *Natural Histories of Discourse* (pp. 1–17). Chicago: Chicago University Press.

Sprake, J. (2016). Learning-Through-Touring. A Methodology for Mobilising Learners. In J. Traxler & A. Kukulska-Hulme (Eds.), *Mobile Learning. The Next Generation* (pp. 67–80). New York and London: Routledge.

Starkey, L. (2012). *Teaching and Learning in the Digital Age*. London and New York: Routledge.

Urban, G. (2006). Metasemiosis and Metapragmatics. In K. Brown (Ed.), *Encyclopedia of Language and Linguistics* (pp. 88–91). Oxford: Elsevier Pergamon.

van Leeuwen, T. (2004). Ten Reasons Why Linguists Should Pay Attention to Visual Communication. In P. Levine & R. Scollon (Eds.), *Discourse & Technology. Multimodal Discourse Analysis* (pp. 7–19). Washington, DC: Georgetown University Press.

Zhao, S., Djonov, E., & van Leeuwen, T. (2014). Semiotic Technology and Practice: A Multimodal Social Semiotic Approach to PowerPoint. *Text & Talk, 34*(3), 349–375. https://doi.org/10.1080/10350330.2018.1509815

8

Conclusions

Meanings are made *in* and *across* scales, making particular trajectories as they travel through complex environments. This book sought out to explore this phenomenon by looking at how meanings are made across education policy scales and—in particular—how policy key terms such as *technology* and *EFL* come to mean different things, or rather to index particular meanings as different scales of design, implementation and enactment are considered. As was demonstrated throughout the book, meaning-making does not only impact circulating and dominant discourses about policy and its key terms, but also the environment in which learning takes place. Learning can be recognized in different ways and to different extents, and students can demonstrate learning in particular manners depending on how meanings circulate across such scales and how sign-makers are positioned by others and how they position themselves.

Policy blind spots are crucial in the study of meaning trajectories in education policy. They do not face many top-down constraints; they are not subjected to strict policy regulation; stakeholders may not have particular expectations for them, all of which, in general terms, points to the opening of spaces for situated agency in policy enactment. As shown by

Fleetwood School and Vera's classroom enactment of Plan Ceibal in Uruguay, the situated agency we can account for in a blind spot pertains to teachers' and students' sense-making of the policy and the designed space for demonstrating and recognizing learning beyond official expectations and regulations. Needless to say, this does not mean that blind spots do not face other problems and restrictions.

A socio-semiotic and ethnographic account of Plan Ceibal 1:1 policy design, implementation and enactment in Uruguay evinces the complexity of meaning-making across scales when policy key terms such as technology and EFL are considered. These terms index very different meanings in and across scales, comprising the socio-political, ideological, cultural, educational and linguistic. The Plan Ceibal XO laptop, for instance, can index political meanings of democratization and universalization, pointing to the agenda of the left-wing ideology in Uruguay and setting it apart from previous right-wing policy-making. However, in other scales the laptop can index a lower socio-economic status and its iconic design and artifact materiality can lose its positive affect, as happens in some private schools that opt out of Plan Ceibal. When intersected with other policy key terms such as EFL, technology can lose its discursive prominence as the main goal of Plan Ceibal to the point that it can be seen as "problematic", or it can be relegated to a "means" to achieve a higher goal (universalizing and democratizing EFL). In contexts in which technology and EFL had already spread before the policy was set up, such as Fleetwood School, technology can index an unequal distribution of resources and assets, but in an unexpected way. Students can position themselves and others as monolinguals by assuming laptops are to be used by those students who have more free time at school because they do not have—and cannot—take international EFL exams. Since EFL practice is paper-based, the use of laptops seems to index "lacking EFL proficiency". Almost paradoxically, it is in this complex scalar ecology that key terms make the policy achieve political and cultural cohesion, by reproducing a broader dispute over the meaning of social reality via the debate over technology and its meanings.

The scalar nature of meaning and meaning-making does not become less complex when a particular classroom is considered. Technology and EFL as policy key terms also trigger particular meanings in and across scales. Classroom interaction and work, situated agency, the semiotic sediment of the classroom and the curriculum artifacts that make the classroom temporally and spatially cohesive, interact in many ways, shaping pedagogy and curriculum. Curriculum artifacts such as the laptop and the textbook are particularly permeable to this. Regardless of the differences in their design and on the degree to which design can shape interaction, teachers and students interact with artifacts to make sense *of* the classroom and to make sense *in* the classroom, (re)producing particular ideologies of learning and encapsulating such ideologies in artifacts. This has implications for the division of semiotic labor in the classroom.

As for these ideologies, they have curricular and pedagogical dimensions. For instance, the traditional ideology of learning foregrounds oral and written resources as the only legitimate modes of communication to be assessed or *recognized* in the classroom and the only authorized modes for demonstrating learning. Other semiotic resources are of course present, but they are perceived as ornamental in (verbal) communication. The media—such as a paper-based test or a digital screen, are vessels for demonstrating learning linguistically—and for demonstrating learning individually, or in isolation. In the particular case under investigation this also coincides with a traditional view of learning as acquisition, assuming the student accumulates pre-existing and fixed knowledge, which needs to be reproduced in classroom tasks and assessment tests. The alternative ideology of learning foregrounds communication as a multimodal phenomenon by, among other things, de-centering language. Concomitantly, it assumes learning to be the joint transformation of signs. From this angle, the focus of assessment is not so much whether learning takes place or not (since learning is, by definition, entailed in communication), but whether and how we can capture learning by designing spaces for students to make meanings in socially meaningful situations. In this respect, the sign-maker's interest and criteriality in sign transformation account for how they themselves construe a particular task as meaningful and how they go about it.

Needless to say, these ideologies of learning do not exist in isolation but instead co-habit the environment of classrooms, schools and policy-making. However, shifting toward an alternative ideology seems key to better recognizing students' semiotic work, without which their local future cannot be designed in equitable and fair terms. The degree to which this transition is actually taking place obviously depends on the site considered. In the case of Vera's classroom at Fleetwood School, such transition is characterized by (i) the division of labor between the EFL printed textbook and the XO laptop; (ii) the encapsulation—through classroom interaction and work—of a particular ideology by each artifact (e.g. the textbook comes to encapsulate a traditional ideology while the XO laptop comes to encapsulate an alternative ideology); (iii) Vera's awareness of two audiences (students/EFL supervisors and parents) with different expectations and requirement for the EFL lesson; (iv) instability in terms of the tools for recognition used in the classroom (I will return to this point later). These four points pertain to different scales at which the policy is designed, implemented and enacted.

One of the benefits of drawing on an alternative ideology of learning is that it allows teachers to provide—and legitimate—more resources for students to communicate, learn and demonstrate learning. The recognition of several modes in the classroom—at the same time—brings about another positive aspect: what from a traditional ideology could be perceived as a "deficiency" in students' resources in one mode can be understood as a question of design, distribution of semiotic labor among modes and evaluation of the available resources by the sign-maker. For instance, if a word such as "stepsister" is not available to a student, they can still convey this by changing the line connecting a father and his daughter in the family tree representation. This may pass unnoticed in most classrooms and might even seem irrelevant. However, in terms of recognition this is important because it changes our focus from assessing how heavily a student can draw on one specific mode for communication to how much students can communicate through their available resources across modes and media, challenging us to provide learning opportunities for them to demonstrate their agency in meaning-making. In fact, in the twenty-first century it would not be feasible to think that a student will draw on only one semiotic mode for representing experience and communicating (and that this mode will be either writing or speech). On the contrary, it would make more sense to think that students need to evaluate the environment, the affordances and limitations offered and their rhetorical goals so as for their interest and criteriality to lead sign transformation. In terms of classroom pedagogy and curriculum, this implies shifting from *how to demonstrate knowledge* to *how to design a sign to represent and communicate what one intends to* as well as shifting from *choosing the oral and written forms of language that comply with highly valued forms* to *being able to evaluate what modes and media can be employed and how they should be orchestrated for representation and communication*. As can be noted, this shift might require a more radical change from us—teachers, practitioners, researchers, policy-makers—than it might require from students, who already are—by definition—agents of their meaning-making processes.

Of course students' agency does not background the role of teachers' agency in designing spaces for learning. Vera's agency becomes instantiated in several classroom practices and this is needed for pedagogy and curriculum as well. For instance, Vera seeks to find ways to assess students' work beyond the traditional views in EFL and beyond the expectations of EFL and school supervisors, even beyond Plan Ceibal's assessment criteria. She also plays a fundamental role in assisting students in their interaction with the technology artifacts—or in allowing other experts to assist students—and in designing spaces for students to make their own meaning-making processes available to others, reflecting on what transformations took place and why they did so.

In more general terms, it should be noted that how teachers can design these spaces for students to learn and demonstrate learning depends on their interaction with other aspects of the ecology of the classroom and the school, such as technology artifacts. To claim that laptops and students interact and are participants in communication is to say that making meanings with the laptop requires, for human participants, different types of *positioning, expertise* and *uses*. For instance, in Vera's classroom, while most times the XO laptop is the legitimate artifact for making meanings within the final project tasks, for the making of the 3D map compatibility issues with the software caused the laptops to be used to register and document the tour around the school block while the desktop was used to make the actual map. This evinces an affordance and a limitation of such artifact: it will not run certain software, but, at the same time, its design makes it portable and mobile (unlike desktops). Vera's regulative role also changes depending on the software at hand: while she guided exploration of the *Impress* software, more technical software as the *Sketch up* required her to bring other social actors to the classroom (such as an expert on urban design). She opted to collaborate and learn together with students to explore this program.

As for the overall account of learning with technology in the classroom, in broad terms Bezemer and Kress (2016) remind us that learning happens—and is entailed—in communication. To this we could add that learning happens in/as communication regardless of the extent to which those involved in it orient to it as legitimate learning. Some substantial questions to ask, then, are *what counts as learning* or *what does not count as learning* in the classroom, or even *how do/can students interact with technology to better demonstrate learning in the classroom*. In today's complex educational landscape, traditional and alternative ideologies of learning co-exist through many pedagogical and curricular practices and objects: curriculum artifacts, assessments, classroom tasks, and so on. The transition from a traditional to an alternative ideology accounts for the fact that what is legitimated or *recognized* as learning varies, depending on what task students are engaged in and what artifact is being used. In Vera's classroom, EFL goals pertain to vocabulary and grammar, mainly through practice and drilling. Digital literacy goals, however, pertain to how students position themselves as sign-makers and this differentiates this blind spot from bright spots of the policy. In Vera's classroom students need to design and also share complex (multimodal) signs they make with the laptop, as well as to explain their choices. Final projects (such as the family tree or the 3D map) allow students to transform previous signs into new signs which respond to—and come to index—their own interests and criteriality as sign-makers and which evince their appropriation of particular aspects of the environment for sign-making. More importantly, these final projects allow for transformation to be *recognized*. (Recognition, however, has certain limitations, as shall be discussed later). In the final projects analyzed in Chap. 7, students were able to demonstrate how they appropriated available signs to represent experience and communicate with others. Whether by changing the traditional family tree structure to represent "non-traditional" family kinship or by detailing elements of a map which are typically not attended to by the naked eye of a passer-by (such as an antenna and a cupola on top of a building), learners have the chance to overtly demonstrate and discuss their signs of learning. More importantly, they are able to account for such signs of learning by sharing and presenting their projects, sometimes to the whole class and sometimes only to the teacher. Such tasks allow them to integrate resources from different modes to produce complex multimodal signs/texts.

As can be inferred from the abovementioned discussion, the construction of the school subject EFL in Vera's classroom is quite complex, responding to a transition in ideologies of learning in which still traditional and alternative practices operate in the classroom. This instability, however, allows Vera to explore different ways in which Plan Ceibal policy can be enacted by allowing students to interact with the XO laptops in different ways and for different purposes.

Recognizing Recognition, or What a Teacher and Her Students Tell Us About It

The analysis of how Vera's classroom is constructed through the complex interaction of policy scales and by the use of policy curriculum artifacts such as the XO laptop and the printed textbook provides a good insight into what learning as meaning-making is about and how we can better recognize it. This has implications for theory-making and research as well as pedagogical implications for teaching and for understanding the scope and focus of education policy in the twenty-first century.

As a leading principle of pedagogy and curriculum, recognition attempts to expand what counts as evidence of learning (Bezemer and Kress 2016; Kress 2013; Kress and Selander 2012), what tools for recognition are used to identify, value and assess signs of learning, and how teacher and students' identities are (re)constructed in such process. Needless to say, the present book cannot—and does not attempt to—account for all of this. However, findings can help us reflect on recognition as a principle of pedagogy and curriculum. The fact that the school subject under investigation is EFL seems to be particularly relevant. Traditionally, verbal language (writing and speech) has been assumed to be the legitimate mode for learning and communication in the classroom. The language classroom, in this respect, has been in a privileged position. As such, it can be seen as both a space to reproduce or contest such ideology of learning. It can be a space in which ideologies about the role of language in communication are further reinforced or it can be constructed as a space for deploying several resources and for providing students with opportunities to demonstrate learning as meaning-making in socially meaningful situations. For this to happen, emphasis needs to be laid on the choices a sign-maker makes to represent experience to others and to communicate what they want to their audience. In Vera's classroom this was made available by creating spaces in which students had the opportunity to voice their meaning-making processes and to explore and explain their own choices. This, in turn, allowed the teacher to better recognize students' semiotic work and to position them as legitimate sign-makers who transform signs (and not as users of a pre-existing system of fixed signs).

Both the theoretical discussion and findings on learning and recognition in this classroom allow us to reflect on the following question: *What does the study tell us about recognition?* Vera's framing of the XO laptop, her focus on project-based instruction for students to explore and use affordances and students' signs of learning show us the potential of policy as a site to foster change in ideologies of language and communication. The classroom as a complex sign can be constructed in such a way that classroom work, tasks and interaction underscore the multiplicity of modes we draw on and attempts to recognize such modes in assessment.

Secondly, her class tells us about the stage of implementation of technology in Uruguayan education—as well as in other parts of the world—in which artifacts expanded more rapidly than did alternative ideologies of learning and communication. This is evinced by her dual assessment and audiences: she assesses EFL goals by focusing on language drilling and so on as expected by EFL supervisors, but she also assesses digital literacy goals (designing, making and explaining signs) as she considers this is what students actually need for their future. The fact that Vera feels insecure as for how to assess digital literacy goals also evinces this stage of implementation and makes it explicit that tools for recognition are indeed needed (Kress 2013). However, this relative—and expectable—instability in assessment also shows us paths to designing such tools. S5's *YouTube* video using the *Sketch up* shows us potential ways in which assessment could attempt to bridge the school and other out-of-school spaces. As part of his out-of-school practices, S5 decided to make a video showing how he used the software to build a shop he saw in his tour around the block with a view to helping prospective users of the software. In this manner, he recontextualized what he learned in the EFL class by positioning himself as an expert now and as a shaping agent for other people's learning. After uploading his tutorial on *YouTube*, he actually got comments from other users, interacted with them and discussed the best ways to use the software and for what purposes to use it. Users included other students, as well as people he did not necessarily know in advance. This tells us about the need to bridge classroom and home practices in assessment, but also about how assessments can be thought of as signs that circulate and become recontextualized across practices inside and outside of the school. It also tells us about how the task can be framed so that representation and communication in socially meaningful situations become underscored. Ultimately, it tells us about the agentive role students may play in assessment and in understanding what learning is for, as well as the dynamic nature of identities inside and outside of the classroom, for which individuals can be re-scaled as novices or experts in a moment to moment basis.

Policy and Pedagogical Implications

Working toward (a pedagogy of) recognition will help us better understand the close partnership that ought to exist between research, policy and pedagogy. One of Plan Ceibal's main goals in following the 1:1 model is to better prepare students for the twenty-first century by making access to technology more democratic and universal. For such purposes, students' ability to interact with technology for sign-making purposes and to be able to communicate through various modal resources and media seems fundamental.

In the introduction section, I outlined issues of feasibility, scalability and sustainability in policy implementation and enactment (Donato and Tucker 2010; Tucker 2010; Tucker and d'Anglejan 1971). These issues, in fact, also pertain to the politics of recognition in education. In other words, the success of high-stake policies has traditionally been measured with standardized scores that capture the essence of traditional ideologies of learning and which measure learning as accumulation. A lot of what is gained from interacting with the technology, transforming signs and communicating with others is obscured. To illustrate my point, let us consider the following. From the perspective of a traditional ideology of learning, Vera's students and the average Plan Ceibal en Inglés student achieve roughly the same "degree of proficiency" in the target language (A1 level, or break-through beginner), according to the CEFRL (*online*). This is what both Vera's final written test scores and what official statistics provided by Ceibal en Inglés show,[1] as indicated in Chap. 4. From our perspective, however, the question is not what students are able to demonstrate in controlled and semi-controlled practice scenarios (filling out blanks, multiple choice, etc.) or what they can demonstrate in EFL only. On the contrary, the question is: *what are these tests able to recognize of students' actual learning?* Vera's class shows that it is complicated to design tools that are able to capture much of what goes on in students' learning. However, Vera's awareness of her own limitations in this respect also demonstrates an ideological transition taking place. In broader terms, it is also fair to say that *bright* and *blind spots* face different restrictions: since schools in public education are the main interest of the policy, they need assessment standardized scores to "demonstrate" how much the policy works and to justify their budget. Private schools as Fleetwood, however, are not State-funded and therefore they do not have to present official statistics about students' performance.

Finally, it should be noted that current education policy discourse (such as the 1:1 model) foregrounds the need to universalize and democratize access to various resources, such as technology and EFL, among others, as is the case under investigation. While assuring this is important for designing the local future, this study also points to the complexity of policy as meaning-making. Recontextualization of policy discourse and key terms implies gains and losses in meanings, some of which can trigger unexpected or even re-elaborated forms of inequality. These can be more or less visible to policy and policy-makers, depending on the extent to which the site is a blind or a bright spot. For instance, while Plan Ceibal discourse can clearly draw on a traditional unequal distribution of resources based on the historical differences between the more and less privileged socio-economic classes and between private and public education, it cannot capture the fact that key terms such as technology and EFL become recontextualized and trigger other positionings which can in turn reproduce inequality in a different manner. A Fleetwood student, for instance, can be positioned as "monolingual" by having access to the XO while another student can be thought to be "bilingual" by having traditional paper-based test as curricular practice to take an international exam. While at one scale using the laptop can mean to insert a student in the twenty-first century and to equip them with opportunities, at another scale it can mean—by default—that the student uses the laptop because they do not have full access to a highly valuable foreign language in the community (EFL) and therefore the student does not participate in certain school practices such as taking international exams. This asymmetric positioning—which probably existed before but is now instantiated in a specific manner with the introduction of technology in local education—is particularly relevant since overcoming it is required for full and equal recognition.

To study the situatedness and scalar nature of meaning-making and learning is necessary in a growingly complex world in which meaning-making resources, modes and media are fast changing and even unstable, affecting the environments in which semiosis takes place and at the same time being affected by such environments. In a similar vein, it is also important to study how and to what extent meaning-making and learning are recognized in formal learning settings and to explore what scalar analysis has to offer to the study of learning and meaning-making in policy and—broadly speaking—in education. Given the ubiquitous role of new technology in education and what it seems to demand or impose in the new century, detailed investigations of how learners interact, make meanings and learn with such technology can be one of the many routes to further exploring recognition. Exploring how teachers can accompany this process by designing appropriate spaces for learning with technology is also fundamental for research and also for pedagogy. Expanding our notion of recognition has the potential to impact teaching and learning practices by fostering alternative ideologies of learning which foreground the learners as agentive sign-makers who act and interact in complex environments and who shape and transform available signs by exerting their situated agency.

Note

1. A description of the adaptive test and the items assessed by Ceibal en Inglés is available at: http://www.ceibal.edu.uy/Documents/Presentaci%C3%B3n%20Prueba%20Adaptativa%20Ingl%C3%A9s.pdf (Last accessed: 02/12/2017). On the other hand, students' final scores in the paper-based test were reported by the school head.

References

Bezemer, J., & Kress, G. (2016). *Multimodality, Learning and Communication. A Social Semiotic Framework.* London and New York: Routledge.

Donato, R., & Tucker, G. R. (2010). *A Tale of Two Schools. Developing Sustainable Early Foreign Language Programs.* Bristol and Buffalo, NY and Toronto: Multilingual Matters.

Kress, G. (2013). Recognizing Learning. A Perspective from a Social Semiotic Theory of Multimodality. In I. de Saint-Georges & J. J. Weber (Eds.), *Multilingualism and Multimodality. Current Challenges for Educational Studies* (pp. 120–140). Rotterdam: Sense.

Kress, G., & Selander, S. (2012). Multimodal Design, Learning and Cultures of Recognition. *Internet and Higher Education, 15*(4), 265–268. https://doi.org/10.1016/j.iheduc.2011.12.003

Tucker, G. R. (2010). Some Thoughts Concerning Innovative Language Education Programmes. *Journal of Multilingual and Multicultural*

Development, 17(2/4), 315–320. https://doi.org/10.1080/01434639608666285

Tucker, G. R., & d'Anglejan, A. (1971). Some Thoughts Concerning Bilingual Education Programs. *The Modern Language Journal, 55*(8), 491–493. https://doi.org/10.1111/j.1540-4781.1971.tb04611.x

Appendix: Description of All Five Units of Classroom Work (As Documented by the Researcher)

Unit 1: My Family[1]

Day 1. Curriculum artifact used: textbook
Family tree, definition and explanation
Family members' vocabulary exercise
Revision of adjectives of attribution (physical appearance, colors, etc.)
Description of family from the textbook
Day 2. Curriculum artifacts used: textbook, XO Laptop, pictures on the whiteboard
Description of famous families 1: The Simpsons
Writing about your own family
Choosing a famous family and describing it
Oral description of each family and guessing game
Day 3. Curriculum artifacts used: textbook, XO laptop
The Simpsons family (continued)
Crosswords with family members' vocabulary
Word search with family members' vocabulary
Oral questions to describe your own family
Describing other families

Day 4. Curriculum artifacts used: handout, pictures on the whiteboard
Description of famous families 2: The Incredibles and Harry Potter.
Comparison with the Simpsons family
Writing about family members (revision of vocabulary to describe appearance and to describe abilities)
Explanation of unit Project
Day 5. Curriculum artifacts used: XO laptop, handout
Final project work 1: exploring laptop's software to design a text introducing your family (open office software: Impress, Draw, PiTiVi)
Day 6. Curriculum artifact used: XO laptop
Final project work 2: students bring texts, images, etc. they want to use for their final project and design the text using the software at hand
Day 7. Curriculum artifact used: XO laptop
Final project work 3 (continued)
Basic vocabulary for using/talking about the software they are learning to use
Day 8. Curriculum artifacts used: XO laptop, handout
Basic vocabulary for using/talking about the software they are learning to use
Day 9. Curriculum artifacts used: school laptop, data projector
Final project presentation (oral presentation of their texts introducing their family with the software they have decided to use to present their family).

Unit 2: My Favorite Band

Day 1. Curriculum artifacts used: Textbook, pictures on the whiteboard
Learning vocabulary about music: instruments and types of music
Day 2. Curriculum artifacts used: textbook, handout
Describing music and musicians you like and don't like: love/like/hate + ing verbs.
Revision of vocabulary from previous lesson
Day 3. Curriculum artifacts used: XO laptop
Describing bands I listen to. How to write a paragraph showing my likes/dislikes. Use of like, hate, love, etc. Searching the web to find out more about a band or musician I like

Appendix: Description of All Five Units of Classroom Work (As... 251

Day 4. Curriculum artifact used: XO laptop

Learning to interview: how to interview to get information. Designing an interview to know more about your classmate's likes and dislikes in music. Do and WH- questions

Day 5. Curriculum artifact used: handout

Revision of previous vocabulary to describe an artist: Miley Cyrus. Using vocabulary to describe physical appearance and personality. Positive and negative adjectives to describe people and personality. "Guessing the personality" oral game

Day 6. Curriculum artifacts used: XO laptop, pictures on the board

Learning to name instruments and to recognize them by the sounds they make. Matching instruments to sounds and to famous musicians who play those instruments.

Day 7. Curriculum artifact used: XO laptop

Final project work 1: "My favorite band" Searching online to find information about a band they like (they work on how to get information and where to get it from and on how to document the information they got)

Day 8. Curriculum artifact used: XO laptop

Final project work 2 (continued). They start writing a description of their favorite band and using pictures and images in their description. They have to use Impress software to create slides to give clues to other students about the band they chose

Day 9. Curriculum artifact used: XO laptop

Final project work 3: game. They play a guessing game by showing their slides to other students. Each slide should describe the band, personality and physical appearance of each member and the instrument they play

Unit 3: My Routine

Day 1. Curriculum artifacts used: textbook

My favorite's band routine: Students talk about the imagined routine of their favorite's band members. Learning to talk about routines (basic vocabulary).

Day 2. Curriculum artifacts used: textbook, pictures on the board
Talking about everyday routines: present simple. Action verbs. Talking about the time of the day. Week days and weekends.
Day 3. Curriculum artifact used: pictures on the board
Revision: writing a description. My favorite band and their routines. Using action verbs in the description.
Day 4. Curriculum artifact used: pictures on the board
Oral activity: reading descriptions out loud. Students ask oral questions to each other about their bands. Students ask her questions about it
Teacher describes her favorite band.
Day 5. Curriculum artifact used: XO laptop
What is a comic? Final project work 1: Learning to use the software "Playcomic". Students get in pairs and explore the software. Reporting on what they learned to do with the software.
Day 6. Curriculum artifacts used: XO laptop, desktop computers at the lab room
"The Simpsons" routine. Video about Homer's "mood swing" (changing his routine and sleep affected his mood). Learning to "read" gestures and body language to learn about people's personality.
Day 7. Curriculum artifacts used: XO laptop, pictures on the board
Talking about Homer's routine. Using adjectives to describe his physical appearance and personality. Describing what they saw in the video and how image and sound changed their views of Homer's mood.
Day 8. Curriculum artifact used: pictures on the board
Describing your family's routine. Using adjectives and action verbs to describe their routines. Asking DO and WH- questions to learn about other family's routines.
Day 9. Curriculum artifact used: XO laptop
Final project work 2: describing my house using the "Playcomic software". Oral questions from the teacher to each student to describe their house and routine.
Day 10. Curriculum artifacts used: XO laptop, handout
Final project work 3: planning my "comic routine". Students have to plan how they will do the comic of their own routine using the software. Drawing what the comic may look like. Exploring what I can

and what I can't do with the program. Teacher asks "can" and "can't" questions to students about the software and their ability to use it

Day 11. Curriculum artifact used: XO laptop
Final project 4: Designing my routine comic. Students use the software to design their own comic about their routines.

Day 12. Curriculum artifact used: XO laptop
Final project 5: Oral presentations of their comic. Students explain their routines

Unit 4: My Personality

Day 1. Curriculum artifact used: textbook
Revision of adjectives. Adjective position in English. Adjectives to describe things and people

Day 2. Curriculum artifact used: textbook
Describing characters from the book. Talking about their physical appearance and their personality. Adjectives to describe personality traits. Positive and negative adjectives.

Day 3. Curriculum artifacts used: laptop, handout
How do other people see me? Designing questions for an interview to ask other people about me. Practicing descriptions. Has/has got.

Day 4. Curriculum artifact used: textbook
Oral report: each student tells the other what they have learned from the interviews they conducted. Differences and similarities between their own views of themselves and how other people see them. Asking questions to other students using have/has got.

Day 5. Curriculum artifact used: XO laptop
Final project work 1: Noting down important words from the interview (adjectives) and translating those words into English with online dictionaries. Categorizing words into positive, neutral and negative.

Day 6. Curriculum artifact used: XO laptop
Final project work 2 (continued). Students continue to look up words in the dictionary and categorize to describe their own personality. Categorizing interviewees into: family, friends, acquaintances, school mates, etc. Students bring pictures of those people into the classroom.

Day 7. Curriculum artifacts used: XO laptop

Final project work 3: Learning to use PiTiVi to make a presentation about your personality. Students form pairs and explore the software. They design how they will organize the video, what pictures they will include and what adjectives they will write for each picture.

Day 8. Curriculum artifacts used: school laptop, data projector

Final project work 4: Oral presentations. Students show their final work to others, explaining who the people are, what they think of them, why and what each adjective means.

Unit 5: My Neighborhood

Day 1. Curriculum artifacts used: textbook, pictures on the board

Naming places and stores in a neighborhood. Basic vocabulary. Prepositions of place.

Day 2. Curriculum artifacts used: textbook, handout, pictures on the board

Prepositions of place. Revision of basic vocabulary for naming places and store in a neighborhood. There is/There are to describe places

Day 3. Curriculum artifact used: pictures on the board

Questions about your own neighborhood. What places are there? Is there/Are there?

Revision of prepositions of place.

Day 4. Curriculum artifacts used: XO laptop, textbook, handout

Naming products. What product belongs to what store? Where do you buy things?

"Where is…" game in groups.

Using maps to locate places in a neighborhood

Guessing game in pairs (guessing information about each map). Using Google maps and a paper map

Day 5. Curriculum artifacts used: handout, data projector, pictures on the board

Revising the name of places and stores in a neighborhood. Group questions about their own neighborhood, their house and their families.

Appendix: Description of All Five Units of Classroom Work (As... 255

Day 6. Curriculum artifact used: handout

Final project work 1: Teacher makes group for students to work together on the final assignment.

Revision of prepositions of place and stores.

Day 7. Curriculum artifact used: desktop at the computer lab room, handout

Final project work 2: Guest speaker shows students how to use the Sketch-up software for making 3D maps and cities. Explanation of what an urban study is.

Day 8. Curriculum artifact used: desktop at the computer lab room

Final project work 3: Learning the basic vocabulary to use the software. Map and city building practice.

Day 9. Curriculum artifact used: desktops at the computer lab room

Final project work 4: Each student explains orally what they have learned to do with the software and what they still haven't figured out about it. One student who downloaded the software at home explains more about it.

Day 10. Curriculum artifacts used: XO laptop, handout

Final project work 5: A tour around the block. Students go out in groups, together with the teacher and me, to document their block with a view to drawing a 3D map about it. Taking pictures, making recordings and interviewing people to know more about the neighborhood and the block.

Day 11. Curriculum artifacts used: XO laptop, desktops at the computer lab room

Final project work 6: Students work on the desktops and XO laptops to go over the data they collected and to use it to build the 3D block. Students plan their oral presentations.

Day 12. Curriculum artifacts used: XO laptop, desktops at the computer lab room

Final project 7: Students present their maps orally (to Vera), showing the tour of the block. Some of these presentations take place during the class break.

Note

1. I keep the name of the units Vera used in the classroom with students and on the teacher book (which do not always correspond with the name of the unit in the textbook).

Index[1]

A

Additional language, *see* Language
Additional language studies, *see* Language
Administración Nacional de Educación Pública, 9, 89
Affordances
  modal, 123
  of software, 178, 186, 203, 205, 208–211, 227
Agency
  distributed, 177, 185
  situated, 5, 7, 25, 47, 65, 68, 72, 120, 138, 139, 170, 171, 177, 235–237, 246
  student's, 12, 57, 69, 139, 144, 195, 228, 239
  teacher's, 12, 129, 133n7, 138, 148, 168, 239

Agent
  collective, 67
  individual, 67
  institutional, 67
ANEP, *see* Administración Nacional de Educación Pública
Artifact
  cultural, 29, 32–33
  curriculum, 12, 47, 48, 56, 66, 68, 83, 92, 137–171, 177, 237, 240, 241, 249–255
  design, 171, 189, 203, 204
  interaction, 68, 140, 141, 145, 177
  laptop as, 15n9, 139–142, 170
  manipulation of, 165
  material, 236
  mental, 65
  semiotic, 65

[1] Note: Page numbers followed by 'n' refer to notes.

Index

Artifact (*cont.*)
　status, 207–208
　technology, 5, 10, 11, 46, 47, 66, 69, 72, 84, 91, 92, 108, 110, 117, 120–123, 125, 127, 129, 141, 142, 148, 178, 208, 221, 228–231, 239
　textbook as, 158, 170
　use, 68, 108, 146, 150, 163, 165, 168, 171, 189, 203, 208
Assessment
　practices, 58, 178, 243
　traditional, 230

B

Bilingual
　stream, 35, 99, 100, 124–129, 143, 172n5 (*see also* Regular stream)
　student, 128 (*see also* Monolingual student)
British Council in Uruguay, 93–95, 115, 118

C

Choice
　lexico-grammatical, 114, 116, 148, 167
　semiotic, 55
Classroom
　audience, 138, 144–146, 170, 171, 217
　as an ecology, 64, 65, 68, 92, 110, 120, 121, 239
　environment, 66, 83, 131, 138, 141, 142, 145, 149, 170, 171, 178, 209
　interaction and work, 124, 141, 168, 170, 219, 237, 238
　as multimodal sign, 64, 178, 179, 240
　teacher (*see also* Teacher, remote)
Cognition
　distributed, 50
　situated, 50
Collaboration
　exploration in, 169
　human-artifact, 50
Competence
　communicative, 71, 73n4
　multimodal, 71
　strategic, 73n4
Computer, 1, 8, 45, 55, 88, 94, 100, 114, 132, 133n5, 149, 159, 208, 211, 232n7, 252, 255
　desktop, 1, 34, 89, 100, 111, 132, 208, 209, 211, 230, 232n6, 232n7, 239, 252, 255
Criticality, 62–63, 69, 179, 190–203, 215, 237, 238, 240
Critique
　generative, 4
　negative, 4
CT, *see* Teacher, classroom
Culture, 43, 51, 53, 55, 62, 65, 66, 87, 172n4
　monomodal literacy culture (*see* Literacy)
Curriculum
　English as a Foreign Language curriculum (*see* English as a Foreign Language)
　implications for, 168, 169
　National EFL curriculum, 131
　official, 83, 85, 129, 170

D

Data collection
  density of, 29
  sources of, 28
Democratization, *see* Discourse
Design
  of artifact (*see* Artifact)
  of (local) future, 237, 245
Dialectics, 43, 66
Digital divide, 2, 88, 89
Discourse, 169
  of access, 8, 132
  analysis, 20, 44
  of democratization, 132
  policy discourse (*see* Policy)
  regulatory, 138, 150, 157

E

Ecology
  of the classroom (*see* Classroom)
  validity, 30
Education
  policy, 2, 3, 6–8, 10, 12, 13, 20, 22, 24, 41, 47, 70, 72, 83, 89, 91, 116, 137, 229, 231, 235, 241, 244
  primary, 1, 8, 87–89, 92, 94, 110, 115, 125
  private, 8, 9, 14n5, 14n6, 85, 86, 89, 95–96, 114–116, 119, 120, 133n5
  public, 8, 14n5, 35, 85–87, 89, 92, 93, 96, 97, 108–110, 113–115, 117, 119, 125, 129, 141, 142, 244, 245
  secondary, 2, 35, 86, 87, 94, 99
Educational authorities, 34, 86, 93
Educational commodity
  language as, 2, 116, 125
  technology as, 2, 4
Educational media, 3
EFL, *see* English as a Foreign Language
Encapsulation
  of ideology in artifacts, 238
  of learning in education, 229
Engagement, 29, 34, 53, 55, 56, 62, 123, 159, 178–179, 186, 187
  shaping, 123, 186, 187
English as a foreign language
  bilingual stream, 99, 124, 127–129, 143, 172n5
  curriculum, 9, 12, 59, 60, 96, 129, 131, 170, 181
  instruction, 141
  program, 2, 8, 89, 92, 95, 119
  regular stream, 99, 124, 125, 129, 131, 143
  teacher, 1, 2, 9, 33, 35, 59, 89, 92, 100, 110, 115, 147, 172n5
  test, 94, 97, 99, 102n4, 119, 120, 129, 146, 170, 221
  textbook, 12, 101, 138, 142–144, 147, 169, 172n3, 172n5, 177, 187
Entextualization, 24
Ethnography
  focused, 29
  and multimodality (*see* Multimodality)

H

Heterochrony, 21, 26

Identity
  of sign-maker, 229
  of students, 153, 156
  of teacher, 95, 153
Ideology
  of language, 242
  of learning, 3, 11, 13, 42, 48–52,
    56–58, 60, 61, 63, 70, 72, 83,
    119, 121, 124, 130, 138, 140,
    141, 144, 168–170, 172n7,
    177–179, 182, 220, 221,
    227–231, 237, 238, 240–242,
    244, 246
  left-wing, 13n3, 34, 120, 236
  right-wing, 13n3
  traditional ideology of
    bilingualism, 125
Index, 3, 12, 21, 25, 61, 101, 106,
    168, 235, 236, 240
  of lower socio-economic status,
    236
Interest, 23, 33, 35, 45, 49, 54, 55,
    62–63, 68, 69, 83, 100, 118,
    130, 172n7, 179, 189, 213,
    219, 237, 238, 240, 244
  of the sign-maker, 45
Intertextuality, 24

Key terms
  English as a Foreign Language as
    key term in policy, 2
  in policy, 3, 7, 130, 137, 235,
    236
  technology as key term in policy,
    130, 235, 245

Language
  additional language, 14n6, 29, 70,
    71, 73n4
  additional language studies,
    70–72, 140
  classroom, 68, 70, 158, 220, 221,
    242
  education, 6, 10, 70–72, 84, 220,
    221
  as educational commodity (*see*
    Educational commodity)
  foreign language teaching, 11,
    66, 85, 87, 102n3, 116, 140,
    230
  functionalization of, 220–227,
    229
  policy, 5, 6, 8, 10, 13n3, 22, 29,
    73, 84, 86, 88, 170
Laptop, 2, 8, 31, 59, 88, 90,
    106–113, 137–171, 177, 178,
    182–190, 207–208, 236, 249
  XO laptop (*see* Plan Ceibal, XO
    laptop)
Learner
  agency, 41, 47, 49–51, 67–69,
    139, 140, 177, 190–203
  criticality, 62–63, 190–203
  interest, 49, 62–63
  recognizing the, 50, 57, 178–179
  as sign-maker, 41, 54, 62–63, 83,
    177–231, 246
Learning
  as acquisition, 49, 57, 237
  agentive nature of, 179, 229
  alternative ideology of, 49–57,
    60–62, 169, 170, 177, 178,
    220, 221, 228–230, 237, 238

alternative view of, 49 (*see also* Alternative ideology of learning)
appropriate, 140, 246
authorized, 83, 139, 142, 237
and communication, 3, 5, 42, 49, 53, 70–72, 177, 220, 222, 228, 230, 231, 240, 242
environment, 7, 54, 55, 63, 141, 149, 178
evidence of, 53, 55, 186, 195, 220, 224, 227, 241
as expansion, 51, 53, 54
language-based theories of, 51
legitimate, 3, 52, 58, 64, 122, 138, 140, 170, 172n7, 178, 179, 197, 218, 238, 240, 242
other-initiated (*see* Route B of learning)
recognizing, 5, 12, 57, 62, 101, 178, 205, 220, 235, 236, 240, 241, 244, 245
route A of, 55, 56
route B of, 55, 56, 179
self-initiated (*see* Route A of learning)
as a semiotic process, 50
sign of learning, 197, 202, 218
traditional ideology of, 48, 49, 51, 52, 57, 58, 70, 71, 119, 121, 130, 168–170, 172n7, 177, 179, 182, 227, 230, 237, 238, 244
traditional view of, 140, 237 (*see also* Traditional ideology of learning)
as transformation, 50–58, 72
in the 21st century, 1–13

Lesson
English as a Foreign Language, 1, 2, 9, 12, 34, 35, 92, 95, 99–101, 119, 121–124, 127, 129, 131, 144, 148, 165, 167, 170, 177, 228, 230, 231, 238
remote, 121
Literacy
digital, 10, 15n9, 121, 129, 131, 143, 144, 147, 159, 169, 187, 206, 218, 219, 221, 230, 240, 242, 243
as linguistic achievement, 47
monomodal literacy culture, 140

M

Map
2D map, 160, 206, 212, 216, 219
3D map, 145, 206–216, 218, 219, 221, 225–227, 229, 239, 240, 255
Meaning-making
situated (nature of), 28, 29, 41, 106
socially meaningful opportunities for, 7, 56, 143, 237, 242, 243
with technology, 41, 42, 189, 236
Meta-function, 43
ideational, 43
interpersonal, 150
organizational, 43
textual, 43
Metaphor
of acquisition, 49
of development, 51
of expansion, 53
of learning, 49

262 Index

Meta-sign, *see* Sign
Ministry of Education and Culture, 8, 88
Modality
  high, 216
  low, 213, 216
  pedagogic, 149
  visual, 212–216, 219
Modes
  ensemble of, 60
  functionalization of, 45
  kinesthetic, 153
  oral, 12, 70
  orchestration of, 71
  speech, 28, 71, 238, 242
  verbal, 70, 153, 190 (*see also* Speech mode)
  writing, 28, 71, 238, 242
  written, 12, 70 (*see also* Writing mode)
Monolingual student, 124, 125, 128, 236, 245
  See also Bilingual student
Multimodality
  multimodality and technology, 9, 41, 42, 46–48
  partnership between multimodal social semiotics and ethnography, 5
Multimodal social semiotics, 5, 9, 13, 20, 28–29
  See also Multimodality

N

National English as a Foreign Language curriculum, *see* Curriculum

Negotiation sequence, 150, 151, 153, 157, 163
New London Group, the, 4
Noticing, 55

O

Orientation
  objective (*see* Representation)
  subjective (*see* Representation)

P

Pedagogy, 7, 49, 66, 69, 144, 147, 168, 169, 179, 237–239, 241, 243, 246
Plan Ceibal
  Ceibalitas (*see* Plan Ceibal, XO laptop)
  en Inglés, 8, 9, 32, 33, 35, 73, 89, 92–97, 101n2, 106, 108, 109, 111, 115–125, 130, 133n3, 231, 244, 246n1
  Executive Summary, 113, 114
  policy, 10–12, 20, 22, 30, 83–101, 106–108, 114, 115, 141, 168, 231, 241
  TV advertisement, 108
  XO laptop, 34, 88, 95, 96, 100, 101, 107–115, 121–123, 129, 130, 137, 141, 142, 148, 207, 236
Policy
  blind spot, 7, 11, 34, 96–100, 118, 119, 124–131, 231, 235, 236, 245
  bright spot, 6, 11, 97, 117–124, 129–131, 231, 240, 245

Index

design, 6, 11, 26, 27, 91, 105, 113, 130, 132, 171, 236
discourse, 7, 8, 96, 112–117, 244, 245
education policy, 2, 6–8, 12, 13, 20, 22, 24, 41, 116, 137, 229, 235, 241, 244
enactment, 3, 5, 10, 120, 124, 142, 235
foreign language, 5, 6, 8, 84, 86, 88
implementation, 6, 10, 26, 119, 138, 244
recontextualization, 5, 7, 24, 26, 105, 137, 245
regulation, 58, 235
social, 4, 111
transformation, 25, 26

Recognition
  a culture of, 58, 179
  a generosity of, 58, 179
  of learning, 56–62
  of semiotic work, 56, 61, 70, 72, 221
  tools for, 58, 63, 238, 243
Recontextualization
  of meaning, 24, 113, 177, 190
  of policy (*see* Policy)
Register
  instructional register, 148
  regulative register, 148
Regular stream, 99, 124, 125, 127–129, 131, 143
  See also Bilingual stream
Repertoire, 51, 55

Representation
  classificational process, 200
  of conceptual process, 193, 202
  family tree, 202, 203, 238
  graphic, 181
  map, 160
  objective orientation to, 205
  subjective orientation to, 205
Resemiotization, 25
Reservoir, 51, 55
Resources
  availability of, 179
  computer screen, 45
  modal, 42, 45–47, 60, 62, 63, 70, 71, 156, 177, 187–189, 191, 192, 204, 205, 220, 222, 227, 228, 230, 244
  modal orchestration, 45, 46, 71, 204, 222
  multiplicity of, 177
  non-verbal, 60, 72, 73–74n4, 149, 186, 205
  of printed page, 45
  use of, 25, 74n4, 83, 121
  verbal, 47, 51, 54, 59, 60, 73n4, 180, 181, 219–221, 227
RT, *see* Teacher, remote

Scalar
  analysis, 20, 22, 41, 106, 245
  nature of meaning, 20, 236, 245
Scale
  heterogeneous, 107
  hierarchy of, 21, 22
  in and across, 19, 235, 236
  meaning across, 3, 19–35

Sediment
  cultural, 171
  semiotic, 64, 169, 177, 237
Semiosis, 12, 24, 42, 44, 71, 97, 105, 137, 140, 149, 190, 197, 228, 245
Semiotic
  distribution of semiotic labor, 12, 101, 238
  chain, 56
  labor, 12, 50, 53, 56, 60, 61, 101, 168, 237
  work (see Semiotic labor)
Shaping agent, 55–57, 69, 123, 179, 189, 195, 197, 205, 216, 229, 243
Sign
  appropriation of, 203, 205, 229
  complex, 42, 61, 64, 193, 242
  of engagement, 55, 56, 62, 123, 178
  of learning (see Learning)
  meta-sign, 195, 205
  multimodal, 64, 178, 179, 195, 205, 240, 241
  transformation, 55, 62, 212, 237, 238
  transforming available, 12, 139
Signifier
  of bilingualism, 128, 132
  of innovation, 127
  of progress, 141
  of successful learning, 148
  See also Index
Sign-making
  ideological purposes of, 54
  students/learners and, 178
Sociolinguistics, 21
Social practice, 4, 19, 26, 28, 43, 46, 52–54, 64, 65, 71, 108, 113, 190

Social relations, 43, 64
Software, 31, 59, 95, 121, 143, 159, 178–180, 182, 183, 186, 187, 189–191, 193, 195–197, 201, 203–211, 216, 218–221, 227, 229, 231n2, 231n3, 239, 240, 243, 250–255
Space
  of the classroom, 165, 166, 168, 169, 177
  design of space for learning (see Design)
  of learning, 138, 139, 148, 168, 177, 178, 228, 231, 239, 246
  of the students, 167, 169
  of the teacher, 167, 169
Spanish, 2, 8, 15n8, 32, 88, 92, 93, 110, 113, 115, 124, 125, 190, 220, 225, 226, 229
Speech function, 150, 151, 163
Sydney School, the, 51, 52, 149
Systemic Functional Linguistics, 50, 51

Tablet, 2, 8, 13n1, 34, 89, 91, 107, 108
Target language, 9, 60, 74n4, 101n2, 117, 123, 132, 177, 179, 186, 187, 190, 205, 207, 217, 219–221, 223, 226, 227, 229, 232n8, 244
Teacher
  classroom, 2, 9, 93, 95, 115, 119, 121–123, 133n5, 141 (see also Teacher, remote)
  demonstration, 166
  English as a foreign language teacher (see English as a Foreign Language)

Index

regulatory discourse (*see* Discourse)
remote, 93, 95, 110, 116, 118, 119, 121–123, 129, 133n3, 133n5 (*see also* Teacher, classroom)
Technology
    access to, 3–5, 8, 84, 88, 89, 97, 112, 115, 117, 228, 243
    artifact (*see* Artifact)
    as educational commodity (*see* Educational commodity)
    digital, 144, 172n7
    new, 3–6, 9, 14n3, 35, 41, 42, 45, 46, 48, 69, 83, 89, 100, 114, 117, 124, 129, 148, 169, 172n6, 231, 245
    utopian and dystopian views, 2
    video-conference screen, 2, 9, 93, 94, 108, 117, 119, 121–123, 141, 142
    wi-fi, 8, 88, 95
Test, 131, 221
    English as a Foreign language test (*see* English as a Foreign Language)
    final, 146
    paper-based, 123, 221, 237, 245, 246n1
    standardized, 58, 131
    See also Assessment
Textbook
    English as a foreign language textbook (*see* English as a foreign language)
    printed, 1, 66, 117, 138, 140, 142, 168, 171, 238, 241
TNLP, *see* New London Group

Transduction, 25, 191, 213
Transitivity analysis, 153

Universalization, *see* Discourse
Uruguay
    government, 2, 8, 13n3, 88–90, 110, 111
    literacy rate, 84
    population, 84, 85, 91
    statistics, 87

Video-conference screen, 2, 9, 93, 94, 108, 117, 119, 121–123, 141, 142

Work
    classroom, 6, 30, 85, 119, 122, 123, 143, 144, 159, 167, 178, 179, 206, 218, 220, 242, 249–255
    ideological, 49
    interaction, 124, 141, 168, 170, 219, 237, 238
    multimodal, 42, 147, 220
    semiotic, 3, 12, 13, 49, 56–59, 61, 65, 66, 70, 72, 83, 84, 178, 179, 237, 242

YouTube, 216–219, 229, 230, 243